395 GOLF LESSONS

by
GARY PLAYER

DIGEST BOOKS, INC., NORTHFIELD, ILLINOIS

- *Instruction by* **Gary Player**

- *Script by* **Iain Reid**

- *Drawings by* **Gary Keane** *and* **Paul Trevillion**

- *From photographs by* **Sydney Harris** *and* **Norman Potter**

- *Cover photographs by* **Bill Morrissey, Lester Nehamkin** *and* **Frank Gardner**

- *Editorial supervision by* **Earl Puckett**

- *Publisher:* **Sheldon L. Factor**

Published by Digest Books, Inc., 540 Frontage Rd., Northfield, Ill. 60093

ISBN 0-695-80334-4 Library of Congress Catalog Card #78-186997

TABLE OF CONTENTS

SECTION SIXTEEN— Common Faults and Cures

Gary Player's 10 Commandments Of Golf

1 THE GOLF SWING MUST BE RHYTHMICAL

Rhythm is important for all golf shots —woods, irons, wedge shots and putts.

2 PAY CAREFUL ATTENTION TO YOUR ADDRESS POSITION

A good golf swing is difficult if not impossible to make from a poor address position.

3 MAKE A COMPLETE BACKSWING

Swing the club away from the ball low, straight and in a wide arc—with a complete (90°) shoulder turn.

4 THE DOWNSWING MUST BE INITIATED BY PROPER LEG ACTION AND FOOTWORK

This insures a late hit position with the hands and eliminates hitting from the top.

5 KEEP YOUR HEAD STEADY THROUGHOUT THE SWING

A moving head is the major cause of missed golf shots.

6 EXTEND FULLY THRU THE BALL TO A HIGH FINISH

Concentrate on follow-through once downswing begins.

7 FEAR NOT THE SAND

Sand shots must be made with confidence and ease. You must not force the club in the sand.

8 PLAY WITH CONFIDENCE

There is no place in golf for negative thoughts. Be positive—take dead aim and trust your swing.

9 KNOW THE RULES OF GOLF

The rules carry rights and privileges as well as prohibitions.

10 OBSERVE THE ETIQUETTE OF GOLF

Be especially aware of Slow Play —Fast, Steady Play *is important.*

INTRODUCTION

by Gary Player

I WOULD LIKE to make it plain from the start that this is a book of practical golf instruction, aimed, first and foremost, at the weekend golfer. Consequently, great care has been taken to keep all my advice and explanations simple and straightforward.

That is not to say that there is nothing here for the advanced golfer. On the contrary, I think that the low-handicap player will find much that is useful to him in this book but, I repeat, it is the *weekend golfer* I am particularly anxious to help in these strips.

Someone may ask, how do I define a weekend golfer? Well, I would say that Iain and Tom, my pupils in this series, are fairly typical examples of the breed.

Like all weekenders, they are out and out optimists. Every time they take out a three-wood they expect to hit the heart of the green! Well, as I keep telling them; they aren't *supposed* to be able to do that with their handicaps.

Then, in keeping with weekenders throughout the world, they slice far more often than they hook, they hit from the top, they hit off the back foot, they panic in sand traps and they always, repeat always, underclub!

But, in the true tradition of the weekend golfer they never give up hope, even when I kid them a bit—like the time Iain asked me what he should do to stop himself shanking. I told him the only thing to do in his case was to take a rest from golf for a fortnight, then give it up completely! But he didn't give it up and I'm pleased to report that his game is definitely improving.

Yes, I would say that Iain and Tom are typical of the millions of weekenders who form the backbone of golf. Without them the game would fall apart at the seams.

Gratefully, then, I dedicate this book to the *weekend golfer*.

SECTION ONE

Swing Fundamentals

A flat-bottomed circle

LOTS OF PEOPLE SAY THAT THE GOLF SWING SHOULD BE A PERFECT CIRCLE. THAT, IN MY VIEW, IS A VERY BAD GOLF SWING
THE FIRST PART OF THE SWING SHOULD BE FLAT
AND THE CIRCLE SHOULD FLATTEN OUT AGAIN AS YOU HIT THROUGH THE BALL
THEREFORE, THE CORRECT GOLF SWING IS A CIRCLE WITH A FLAT BOTTOM

The grip for small hands

GRIP THE CLUB IN THE FINGERS OF THE RIGHT HAND
BOTH "V'S" MUST POINT TO YOUR RIGHT SHOULDER
I USE THE ORTHODOX VARDON GRIP WITH THE LITTLE FINGER OF MY RIGHT HAND OVERLAPPING MY LEFT INDEX FINGER
BUT PEOPLE WITH SMALL HANDS SHOULD MAKE A SLIGHT VARIATION AND INTERLOCK THESE TWO FINGERS... AS DO SUCH FAMOUS PLAYERS AS GENE SARAZEN AND JACK NICKLAUS

Grip the club properly...with both hands

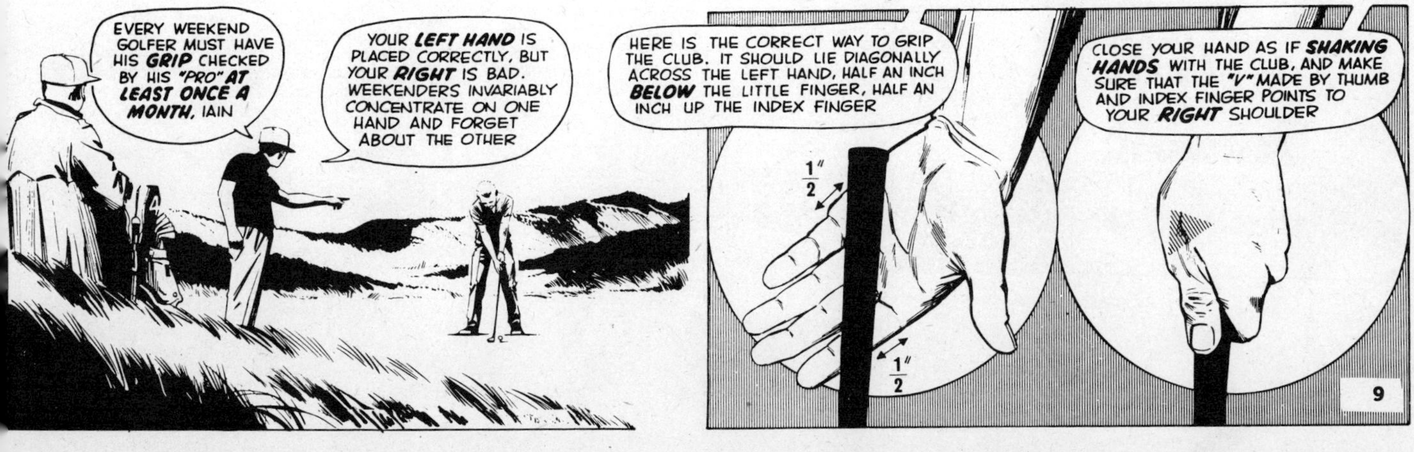
EVERY WEEKEND GOLFER MUST HAVE HIS GRIP CHECKED BY HIS "PRO" AT LEAST ONCE A MONTH, IAIN
YOUR LEFT HAND IS PLACED CORRECTLY, BUT YOUR RIGHT IS BAD. WEEKENDERS INVARIABLY CONCENTRATE ON ONE HAND AND FORGET ABOUT THE OTHER
HERE IS THE CORRECT WAY TO GRIP THE CLUB. IT SHOULD LIE DIAGONALLY ACROSS THE LEFT HAND, HALF AN INCH BELOW THE LITTLE FINGER, HALF AN INCH UP THE INDEX FINGER
1/2"
1/2"
CLOSE YOUR HAND AS IF SHAKING HANDS WITH THE CLUB, AND MAKE SURE THAT THE "V" MADE BY THUMB AND INDEX FINGER POINTS TO YOUR RIGHT SHOULDER

Two hands are better than one

PEOPLE ARE ALWAYS ASKING ME WHETHER THEY SHOULD HIT THE BALL WITH THE LEFT HAND OR WITH THE RIGHT. WELL, HERE YOU CAN SEE I AM HITTING IT WITH THE LEFT...
... AND HERE I AM HITTING IT WITH THE RIGHT HAND. THIS ILLUSTRATES HOW SILLY THE WHOLE THING IS. YOU PUT BOTH HANDS ON THE CLUB, SO WHY NOT HIT THE BALL WITH BOTH HANDS? TWO MUST BE STRONGER THAN ONE!
BUT, GARY, ISN'T THERE ANYTHING IN THE THEORY THAT THE LEFT HAND OUGHT TO DOMINATE?
I DON'T THINK SO, IAIN. I THINK YOU SHOULD GRIP THE CLUB COMPACTLY AND MAKE BOTH OF YOUR HANDS INTO ONE HAND. DON'T TRY TO MAKE ONE OF YOUR HANDS INTO BOTH!

The life-line tip

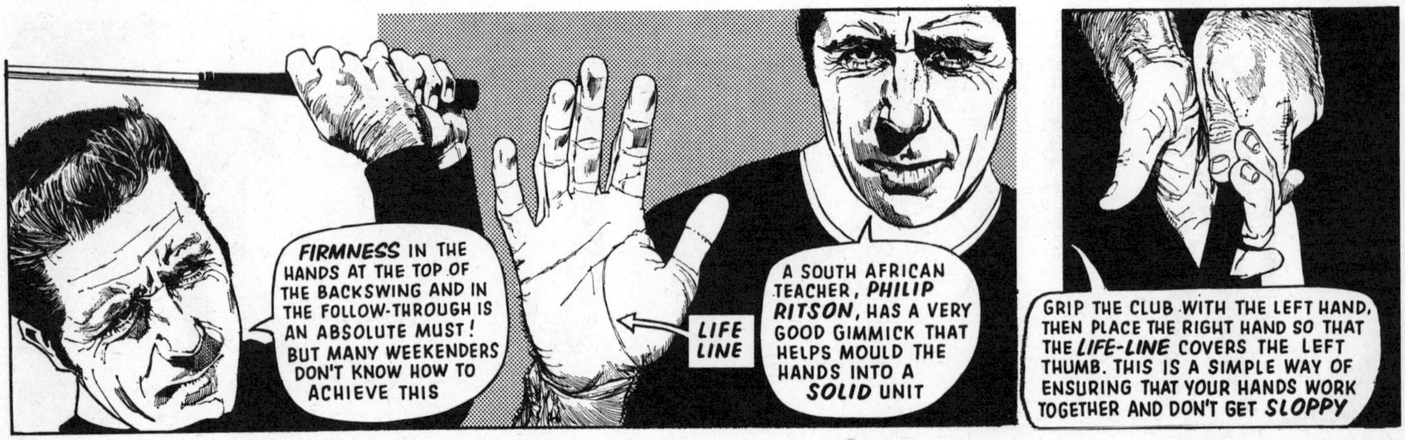

FIRMNESS IN THE HANDS AT THE TOP OF THE BACKSWING AND IN THE FOLLOW-THROUGH IS AN ABSOLUTE MUST! BUT MANY WEEKENDERS DON'T KNOW HOW TO ACHIEVE THIS
LIFE LINE
A SOUTH AFRICAN TEACHER, PHILIP RITSON, HAS A VERY GOOD GIMMICK THAT HELPS MOULD THE HANDS INTO A SOLID UNIT
GRIP THE CLUB WITH THE LEFT HAND, THEN PLACE THE RIGHT HAND SO THAT THE LIFE-LINE COVERS THE LEFT THUMB. THIS IS A SIMPLE WAY OF ENSURING THAT YOUR HANDS WORK TOGETHER AND DON'T GET SLOPPY

The correct grip

GRIP NUMBER ONE SHOWS TOO MANY KNUCKLES. THAT IS A HOOKER'S GRIP.
TOO STRONG
GRIP NUMBER TWO SHOWS NO KNUCKLES. THAT IS A SLICER'S GRIP.
TOO WEAK
IF YOU HAVE DIFFICULTY GRIPPING THE CLUB CORRECTLY JUST BRING YOUR HANDS TOGETHER LIKE THIS.
NOW, WITHOUT TURNING YOUR HANDS, SLIDE THEM DOWN OVER THE CLUB AND GRIP IT.

The "piccolo" grip

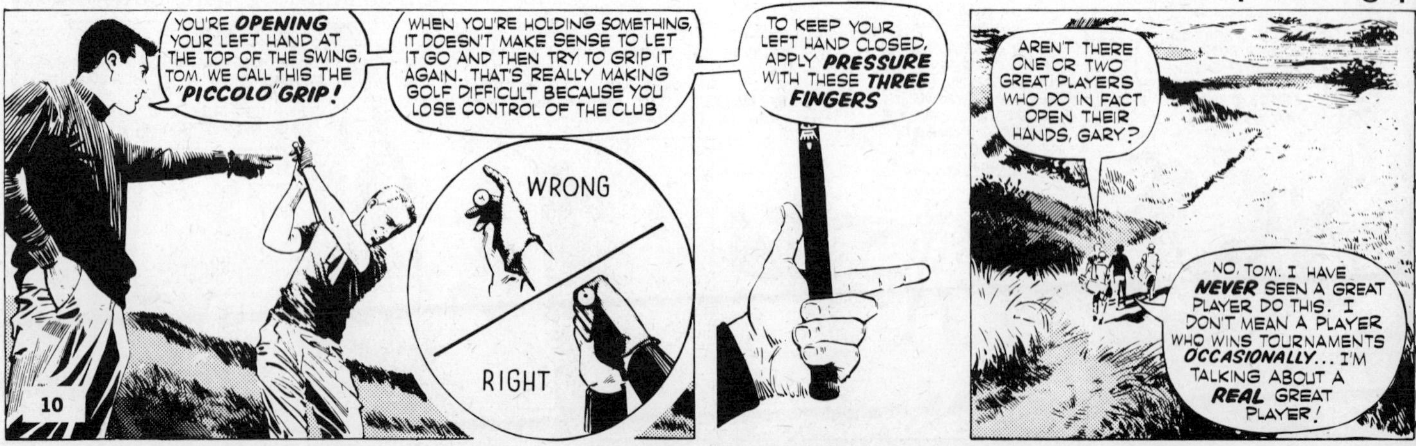

YOU'RE OPENING YOUR LEFT HAND AT THE TOP OF THE SWING, TOM. WE CALL THIS THE "PICCOLO" GRIP!
WHEN YOU'RE HOLDING SOMETHING, IT DOESN'T MAKE SENSE TO LET IT GO AND THEN TRY TO GRIP IT AGAIN. THAT'S REALLY MAKING GOLF DIFFICULT BECAUSE YOU LOSE CONTROL OF THE CLUB
WRONG
RIGHT
TO KEEP YOUR LEFT HAND CLOSED, APPLY PRESSURE WITH THESE THREE FINGERS
AREN'T THERE ONE OR TWO GREAT PLAYERS WHO DO IN FACT OPEN THEIR HANDS, GARY?
NO, TOM. I HAVE NEVER SEEN A GREAT PLAYER DO THIS. I DON'T MEAN A PLAYER WHO WINS TOURNAMENTS OCCASIONALLY... I'M TALKING ABOUT A REAL GREAT PLAYER!

The coin test

IAIN, I AM GOING TO PROVE THAT YOU ARE OPENING YOUR LEFT HAND AT THE TOP OF THE BACKSWING. PLACE THIS SIXPENCE UNDER THE PAD OF YOUR LEFT HAND THEN HAVE A SWING
SEE! THE COIN DROPS OUT!
THE LEFT HAND MUST STAY CLOSED THROUGHOUT THE ENTIRE SWING!
WHEN I TAKE MY RIGHT HAND OFF THE CLUB AT THE END OF THE FOLLOW-THROUGH, YOU CAN SEE THAT THE COIN IS STILL THERE!

How do you do!

IF ONLY YOU KNEW THE FEEL OF THE CORRECT GRIP, IAIN, YOU COULD NEVER GRIP THE CLUB SO BADLY!
WHAT SHOULD IT FEEL LIKE, GARY?
RIGHT HAND TOO MUCH ON TOP OF SHAFT
WELL, IAIN, YOU SHOULD FEEL AS IF YOU ARE SHAKING HANDS WITH THE CLUB. JUST PUT YOUR LEFT HAND STRAIGHT OUT AND GRIP IT
SIMILARLY, WITH THE RIGHT HAND. WHEN YOU SHAKE HANDS WITH A PERSON YOU DON'T TWIST YOUR HAND TO THE RIGHT OR THE LEFT—YOU HOLD IT STRAIGHT. THE SAME SHOULD APPLY WHEN GRIPPING A GOLF CLUB

Pinch the club

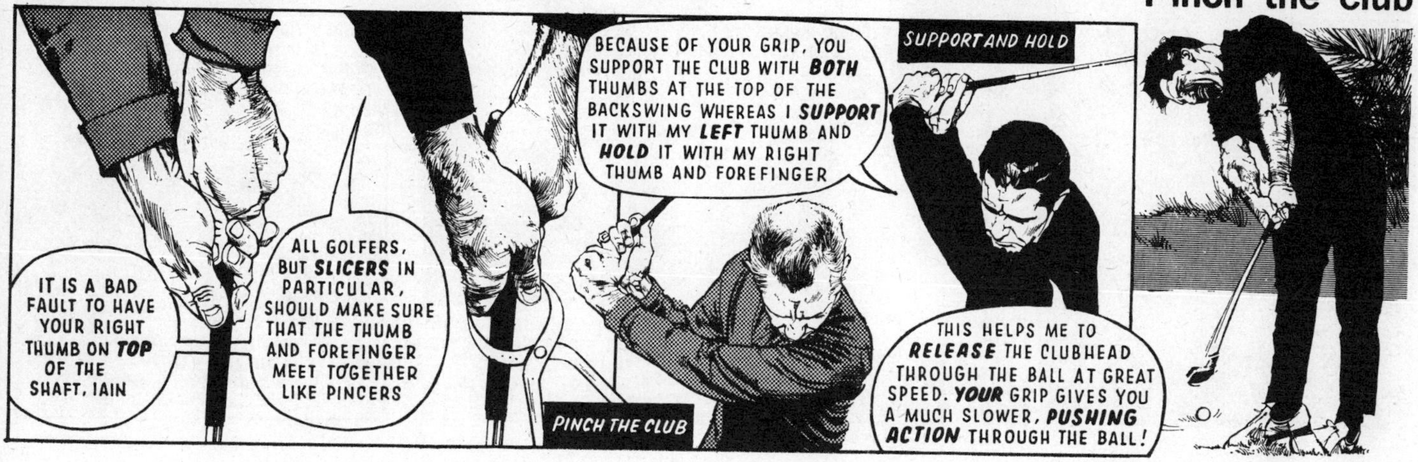
IT IS A BAD FAULT TO HAVE YOUR RIGHT THUMB ON TOP OF THE SHAFT, IAIN
ALL GOLFERS, BUT SLICERS IN PARTICULAR, SHOULD MAKE SURE THAT THE THUMB AND FOREFINGER MEET TOGETHER LIKE PINCERS
PINCH THE CLUB
BECAUSE OF YOUR GRIP, YOU SUPPORT THE CLUB WITH BOTH THUMBS AT THE TOP OF THE BACKSWING WHEREAS I SUPPORT IT WITH MY LEFT THUMB AND HOLD IT WITH MY RIGHT THUMB AND FOREFINGER
SUPPORT AND HOLD
THIS HELPS ME TO RELEASE THE CLUBHEAD THROUGH THE BALL AT GREAT SPEED. YOUR GRIP GIVES YOU A MUCH SLOWER, PUSHING ACTION THROUGH THE BALL!

Test your grip

YOUR CLUB IS HITTING YOUR RIGHT SHOULDER ON THE BACKSWING, IAIN! THIS IS BECAUSE YOU HAVE NO GRIP AT ALL WITH YOUR RIGHT THUMB AND INDEX FINGER
ALL THE GREAT GOLFERS HAVE FIRMNESS IN THESE TWO FINGERS AT THE TOP. HOGAN IS A GOOD EXAMPLE OF THIS
TO TEST YOUR GRIP, GET TO THE TOP OF THE SWING, THEN SEE IF YOU CAN HOLD THE CLUB SECURELY IN POSITION WITH ONLY THE THUMB AND INDEX FINGER

A bonded grip

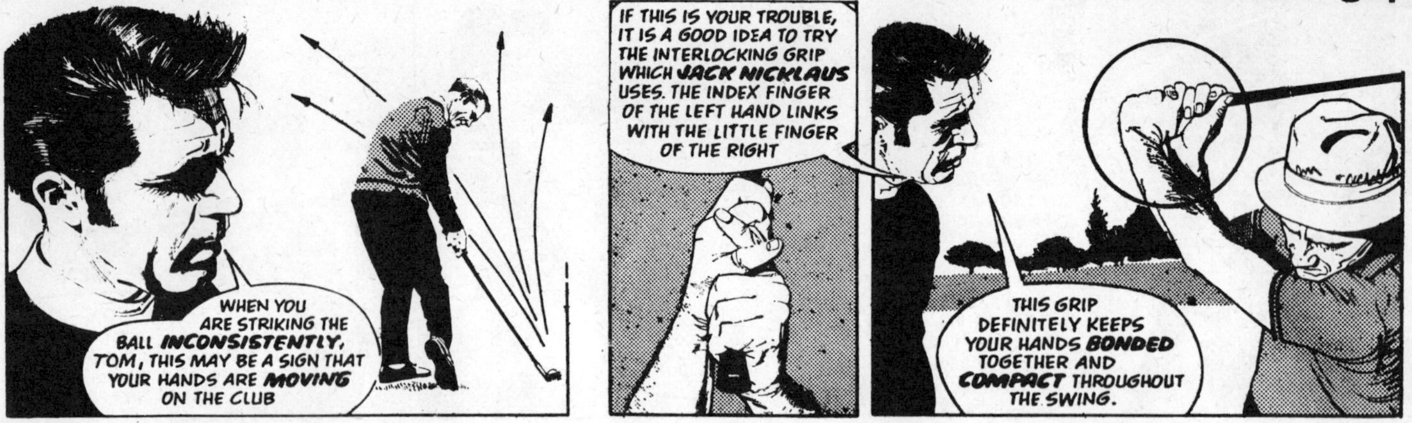

WHEN YOU ARE STRIKING THE BALL INCONSISTENTLY, TOM, THIS MAY BE A SIGN THAT YOUR HANDS ARE MOVING ON THE CLUB
IF THIS IS YOUR TROUBLE, IT IS A GOOD IDEA TO TRY THE INTERLOCKING GRIP WHICH JACK NICKLAUS USES. THE INDEX FINGER OF THE LEFT HAND LINKS WITH THE LITTLE FINGER OF THE RIGHT
THIS GRIP DEFINITELY KEEPS YOUR HANDS BONDED TOGETHER AND COMPACT THROUGHOUT THE SWING.

Keep those fingers moving

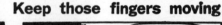

I'VE NOTICED THAT YOU NEVER COMPLETE YOUR RIGHT HAND GRIP UNTIL JUST BEFORE YOU TAKE THE CLUB BACK, GARY! YOU SEEM ALMOST TO BE PLAYING A TUNE WITH YOUR FINGERS!
THAT'S RIGHT, IAIN. I MOVE MY FINGERS IN ORDER TO "FEEL" THE CLUB. THIS ALSO PREVENTS ME FROM GRIPPING TOO TIGHTLY WITH MY RIGHT HAND AND ENSURES THAT I GRIP THE CLUB IN THE FINGERS OF THAT HAND, NOT THE PALM!
MANY GOLFERS LOOK AS IF THEY ARE TRYING TO STRANGLE THE CLUB! THIS FINGER MOVEMENT WOULD REMOVE THE TENSION FROM THEIR RIGHT ARMS AND GIVE THEM THAT LITTLE BIT OF RELAXATION THAT IS SO IMPORTANT BEFORE STARTING THE BACKSWING
IT MIGHT ALSO BE A SOLUTION TO THOSE PEOPLE WHO FIND BOTH THE "WAGGLE" AND THE "FORWARD PRESS" TOO DIFFICULT FOR THEM

Grip tip

NO WONDER YOU'RE SLICING THE BALL, TOM. YOUR LEFT HAND GRIP IS TOO WEAK. YOU NEED TO MOVE YOUR THUMB MORE TO YOUR RIGHT
TO HELP YOU REMEMBER, GET YOUR PRO TO PUT ON GRIPS THAT HAVE A LINE RUNNING DOWN THE MIDDLE . . .
BUT ASK HIM TO TURN THE GRIPS SLIGHTLY SO THAT THE LINE IS RIGHT OF CENTRE
NORMAL
FOR SLICERS
NOW, EVERY TIME YOU GRIP THE CLUB, PLACE YOUR THUMB ON THE LINE AND YOU WILL HAVE A STRONGER GRIP
HOOKERS SHOULD HAVE THE LINE LEFT OF CENTRE

Proper alignment

THE MORE EXPERIENCE I HAVE OF GOLF, IAIN, THE MORE I FIND OUT THAT GETTING LINED UP CORRECTLY IS ONE OF THE MOST IMPORTANT THINGS
LOOK! YOU ARE FACING WELL TO THE RIGHT OF THE TARGET!
BECAUSE OF THIS, YOU WILL TAKE BACK THE CLUB WELL INSIDE THE TARGET LINE. SO, IN ORDER TO HIT THE BALL STRAIGHT AT THE FLAG, YOU WILL HAVE TO INTRODUCE A LOOP INTO YOUR SWING
THIS MAKES GOLF TWICE AS DIFFICULT! YOU'VE GOT TO BE A GENIUS TO HIT THE BALL STRAIGHT WITH A LOOP SWING!
NOTICE HOW THE LINES ACROSS MY SHOULDERS AND TOES BOTH POINT DIRECTLY AT THE FLAG. NOW I CAN TAKE THE CLUB STRAIGHT BACK AND BRING IT STRAIGHT FORWARD ON THE TARGET LINE, WITHOUT LOOPING

Not too near, not too far

IAIN, YOU'RE STANDING MILES TOO FAR AWAY FROM THE BALL! THIS WILL GIVE YOU A VERY FLAT SWING, AND YOU'LL HAVE DIFFICULTY KEEPING YOUR BALANCE
NOW YOU'VE GONE TO THE OTHER EXTREME! YOU'RE STANDING SO CLOSE YOU'RE PRACTICALLY GUARANTEED TO SLICE EVERY SHOT!

CLUB PARALLEL TO CHEST

The right elbow method

IAIN, YOU ARE STANDING MUCH TOO FAR FROM THE BALL!
HOW CAN I KNOW WHEN I AM THE RIGHT DISTANCE FROM IT, GARY?
THERE IS AN EASY WAY OF DETERMINING THIS, IAIN! SIMPLY ENSURE THAT YOUR RIGHT ELBOW IS TUCKED INTO YOUR SIDE! THEN YOU WILL KNOW YOU ARE THE CORRECT DISTANCE FROM THE BALL EVERY TIME!
THIS ELBOW METHOD OF MEASURING OFF APPLIES TO EVERY CLUB IN THE BAG—FROM YOUR PUTTER TO YOUR DRIVER!
ELBOW TUCKED IN
DRIVER
WEDGE

Think of three things

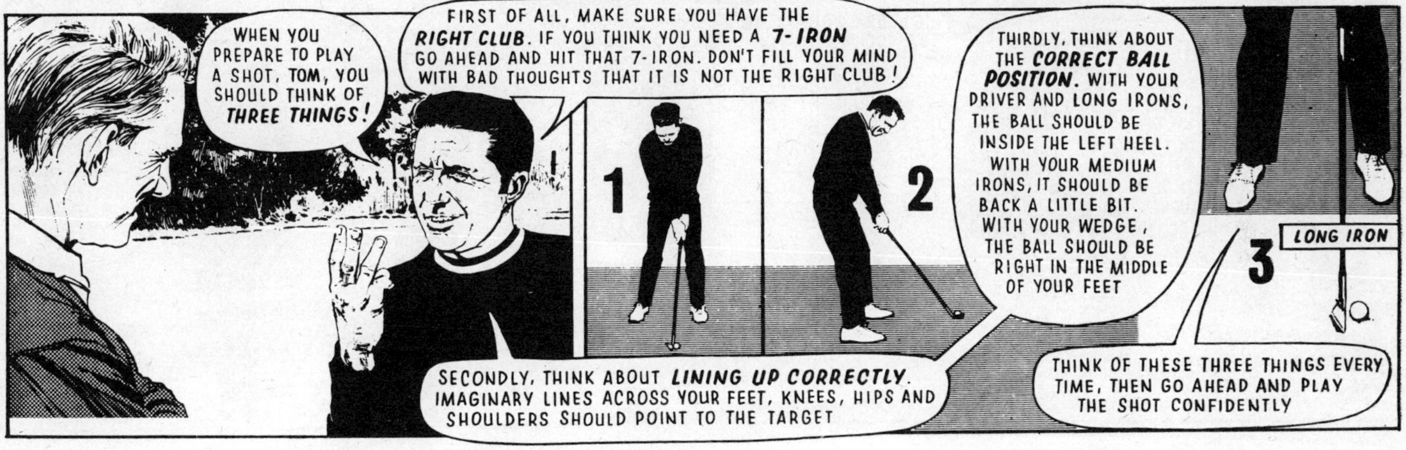

WHEN YOU PREPARE TO PLAY A SHOT, TOM, YOU SHOULD THINK OF THREE THINGS!
FIRST OF ALL, MAKE SURE YOU HAVE THE RIGHT CLUB. IF YOU THINK YOU NEED A 7-IRON GO AHEAD AND HIT THAT 7-IRON. DON'T FILL YOUR MIND WITH BAD THOUGHTS THAT IT IS NOT THE RIGHT CLUB!
1
2
SECONDLY, THINK ABOUT LINING UP CORRECTLY. IMAGINARY LINES ACROSS YOUR FEET, KNEES, HIPS AND SHOULDERS SHOULD POINT TO THE TARGET
THIRDLY, THINK ABOUT THE CORRECT BALL POSITION. WITH YOUR DRIVER AND LONG IRONS, THE BALL SHOULD BE INSIDE THE LEFT HEEL. WITH YOUR MEDIUM IRONS, IT SHOULD BE BACK A LITTLE BIT. WITH YOUR WEDGE, THE BALL SHOULD BE RIGHT IN THE MIDDLE OF YOUR FEET
LONG IRON
3
THINK OF THESE THREE THINGS EVERY TIME, THEN GO AHEAD AND PLAY THE SHOT CONFIDENTLY

How to watch the ball

WHEN I ADDRESS THE BALL, GARY, SHOULD I BE LOOKING AT ANY SPECIFIC PART OF IT?
YOU CERTAINLY SHOULD, IAIN, BUT MOST AVERAGE PLAYERS ONLY HALF FOCUS ON THE BALL WITHOUT WATCHING ANYTHING IN PARTICULAR
IRON SHOTS SHOULD BE HIT DOWN AND THROUGH, SO KEEP YOUR EYE ON THE TOP OF THE BALL AND TRY TO HIT DOWN ON THAT SPOT
BUT, WITH A DRIVER, THE BALL SHOULD BE HIT ON THE UPSWING SO YOU MUST WATCH THE BACK OF THE BALL
A VERY GOOD TIP IS TO PLACE THE BALL ON THE TEE SO THAT THE NAME ON THE BALL IS AT THE BACK. THEN KEEP YOUR EYE FIXED ON THE NAME THROUGHOUT THE BACKSWING

How to walk

The importance of good alignment

The knee bend

That tied-up feeling

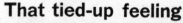

Relax your right side

YOU ARE STANDING TO THE BALL VERY POORLY, IAIN. YOUR RIGHT SIDE IS AS STIFF AS A BOARD!
ANYONE WHO WANTS TO PLAY GOOD GOLF, MUST LEARN TO RELAX THE RIGHT SIDE
A RELAXED RIGHT SIDE ENABLES YOU TO GET A GOOD, FREE TURN AND MAKES THE SWING MUCH MORE FLUID. IT ALSO ENCOURAGES YOU TO COME UNDER THE BALL AND HELPS YOU RELEASE THROUGH THE BALL
YOU CAN RELAX YOUR RIGHT SIDE SIMPLY BY DROPPING THE RIGHT SHOULDER TWO INCHES, TUCKING YOUR RIGHT ELBOW INTO YOUR SIDE AND MOVING YOUR RIGHT KNEE IN TWO INCHES. NOW YOU LOOK LIKE A GOLFER

Check your stance

IAIN, YOUR STANCE IS SO WIDE. THERE'S NO POSSIBLE WAY YOU CAN GET PROPER WEIGHT TRANSFERENCE OR A GOOD LEG ACTION IN YOUR SWING
MY STANCE IS THE WIDTH OF MY SHOULDERS. AND MY KNEES ARE BENT. THIS RELAXES MY WHOLE BODY
WHEN YOUR FEET ARE TOO FAR APART, IT'S VERY DIFFICULT TO GET YOUR WEIGHT ON TO YOUR LEFT SIDE ON THE DOWNSWING
SHOULD YOU ACHIEVE THIS, YOU WILL PROBABLY FIND YOUR RIGHT LEG IS AS STRAIGHT AS A RAMROD. AND THAT'S BAD!
WHAT HAPPENS TO YOUR STANCE WHEN YOU'RE USING A DRIVER, GARY?
WELL, NATURALLY, IT'S WIDER THAN WITH A PITCHING WEDGE! BUT I DON'T THINK THE STANCE SHOULD EVER BE WIDER THAN YOUR SHOULDERS!

Where the power should be

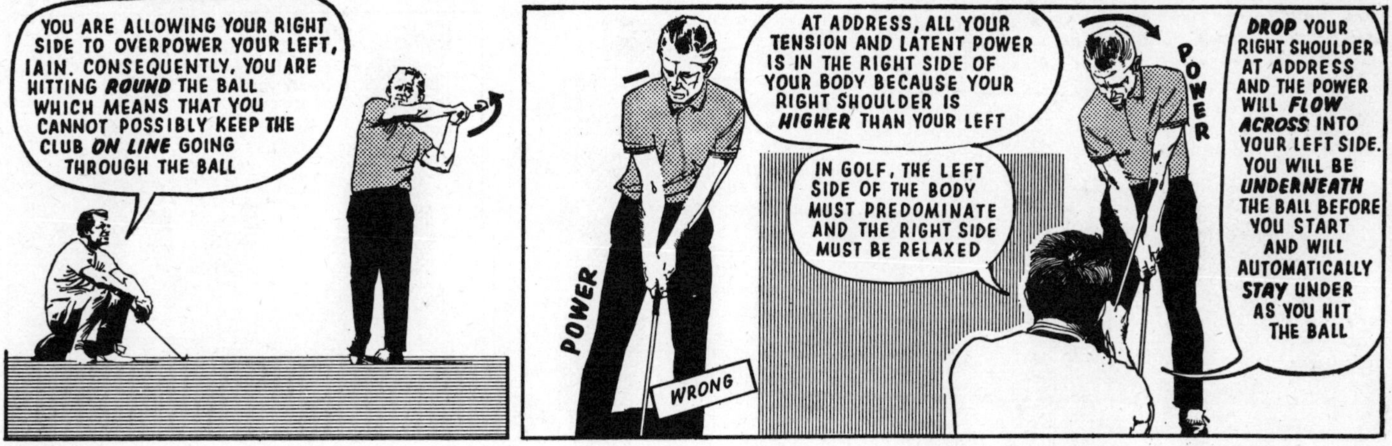

YOU ARE ALLOWING YOUR RIGHT SIDE TO OVERPOWER YOUR LEFT, IAIN. CONSEQUENTLY, YOU ARE HITTING ROUND THE BALL WHICH MEANS THAT YOU CANNOT POSSIBLY KEEP THE CLUB ON LINE GOING THROUGH THE BALL
POWER
WRONG
AT ADDRESS, ALL YOUR TENSION AND LATENT POWER IS IN THE RIGHT SIDE OF YOUR BODY BECAUSE YOUR RIGHT SHOULDER IS HIGHER THAN YOUR LEFT
IN GOLF, THE LEFT SIDE OF THE BODY MUST PREDOMINATE AND THE RIGHT SIDE MUST BE RELAXED
POWER
DROP YOUR RIGHT SHOULDER AT ADDRESS AND THE POWER WILL FLOW ACROSS INTO YOUR LEFT SIDE. YOU WILL BE UNDERNEATH THE BALL BEFORE YOU START AND WILL AUTOMATICALLY STAY UNDER AS YOU HIT THE BALL

Take your shoe off

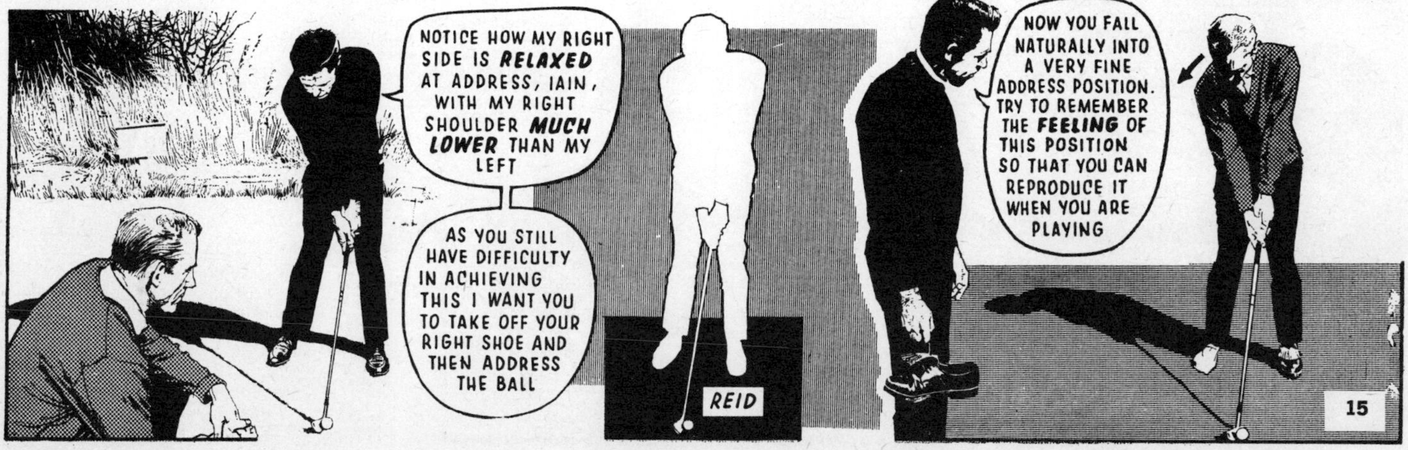

NOTICE HOW MY RIGHT SIDE IS RELAXED AT ADDRESS, IAIN, WITH MY RIGHT SHOULDER MUCH LOWER THAN MY LEFT
AS YOU STILL HAVE DIFFICULTY IN ACHIEVING THIS I WANT YOU TO TAKE OFF YOUR RIGHT SHOE AND THEN ADDRESS THE BALL
REID
NOW YOU FALL NATURALLY INTO A VERY FINE ADDRESS POSITION. TRY TO REMEMBER THE FEELING OF THIS POSITION SO THAT YOU CAN REPRODUCE IT WHEN YOU ARE PLAYING

Sitting on a seat stick

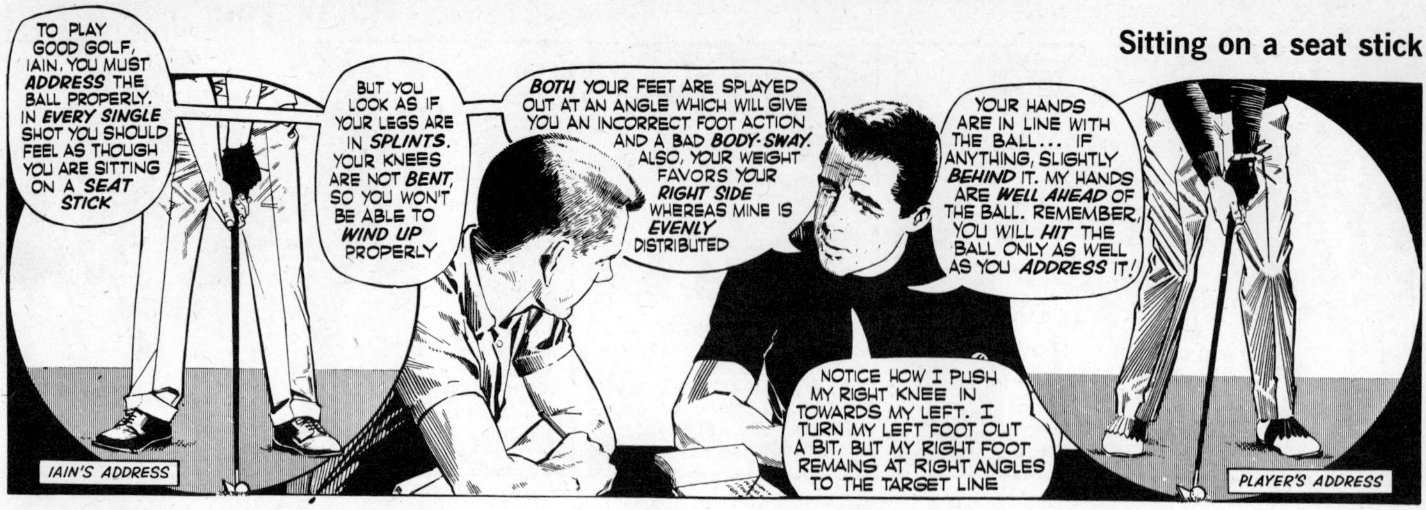

TO PLAY GOOD GOLF, IAIN, YOU MUST ADDRESS THE BALL PROPERLY. IN EVERY SINGLE SHOT YOU SHOULD FEEL AS THOUGH YOU ARE SITTING ON A SEAT STICK
BUT YOU LOOK AS IF YOUR LEGS ARE IN SPLINTS. YOUR KNEES ARE NOT BENT, SO YOU WON'T BE ABLE TO WIND UP PROPERLY
BOTH YOUR FEET ARE SPLAYED OUT AT AN ANGLE WHICH WILL GIVE YOU AN INCORRECT FOOT ACTION AND A BAD BODY-SWAY. ALSO, YOUR WEIGHT FAVORS YOUR RIGHT SIDE WHEREAS MINE IS EVENLY DISTRIBUTED
YOUR HANDS ARE IN LINE WITH THE BALL... IF ANYTHING, SLIGHTLY BEHIND IT. MY HANDS ARE WELL AHEAD OF THE BALL. REMEMBER, YOU WILL HIT THE BALL ONLY AS WELL AS YOU ADDRESS IT!
NOTICE HOW I PUSH MY RIGHT KNEE IN TOWARDS MY LEFT. I TURN MY LEFT FOOT OUT A BIT, BUT MY RIGHT FOOT REMAINS AT RIGHT ANGLES TO THE TARGET LINE
IAIN'S ADDRESS
PLAYER'S ADDRESS

Knees in!

GARY, I SEE LOTS OF WEEKEND GOLFERS ADDRESS THE BALL WITH THEIR KNEES POINTING OUT LIKE THIS—IS THAT A VERY BAD FAULT?
TOO TRUE IT IS, IAIN! JUST GO TO THE TOP OF YOUR BACKSWING AND FEEL HOW RESTRICTED YOU ARE
SOUTH AFRICAN GOLFER COBIE LEGRANGE HAD THIS FAULT EARLY IN HIS CAREER. BUT, AS SOON AS HE DEVELOPED THE CORRECT KNEE ACTION, HIS GAME IMPROVED
THE KNEES MUST BE INCLINED INWARDS AT ADDRESS SO THAT THEY ARE PREPARED OR EDUCATED FOR THEIR ROLE IN THE GOLF SWING
THAT IS, THE LEFT KNEE GOES ACROSS THE BALL ON THE BACKSWING AND THE RIGHT KNEE GOES ACROSS ON THE FOLLOW-THROUGH
NOW, SIMPLY BY HAVING THE KNEES IN THE CORRECT POSITION AT ADDRESS, YOUR BACKSWING IS AT LEAST TWO FEET LONGER

Sixty—forty!

YOU ARE COMING OVER AND AROUND THE BALL WITH YOUR DRIVER, IAIN
THIS IS BECAUSE YOU HAVE TOO MUCH WEIGHT ON YOUR LEFT FOOT AT ADDRESS
THIS MAKES YOU BREAK YOUR WRISTS FAR TOO QUICKLY ON THE BACKSWING. NOW IT IS IMPOSSIBLE TO COME UNDER THE BALL
WITH MY DRIVER, I HAVE 60 PER CENT OF MY WEIGHT ON MY RIGHT FOOT AT ADDRESS
60
40
THIS HELPS ME TO TRANSFER MY WEIGHT ON TO MY RIGHT SIDE WHICH ENABLES ME TO COME UNDER THE BALL

The importance of square hips

WHAT A MIXTURE, IAIN! YOUR SHOULDERS ARE SQUARE, YOUR HIPS ARE OPEN AND YOUR FEET ARE CLOSED!
I FIND IT VERY DIFFICULT TO GET ALL THREE LINED UP WITH THE HOLE, GARY
SQUARE
OPEN
CLOSED
I WOULD SAY THAT MOST WEEKENDERS GET THEIR FEET REASONABLY WELL LINED UP. BUT THEY ALL SEEM TO HAVE TROUBLE LINING UP THEIR HIPS—AND IT IS THE HIPS THAT REALLY DETERMINE THE DIRECTION OF THE SHOT
IN MY OPINION, THE HIPS SHOULD BE THE MAIN CHECKPOINT WHEN LINING UP. ALL GOLFERS SHOULD CONCENTRATE ON GETTING THEM SQUARE BECAUSE, IF THE HIPS ARE SQUARE, THE SHOULDERS AND THE FEET WILL BE SQUARE TOO
SQUARE
GET HIPS SQUARE
SQUARE

Positioning the ball

Where to position the ball

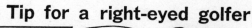

Tip for a right-eyed golfer

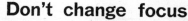

Don't change focus

The eye test

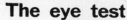

Stick out your chest

Two stroke-savers

How to waggle

The waggle

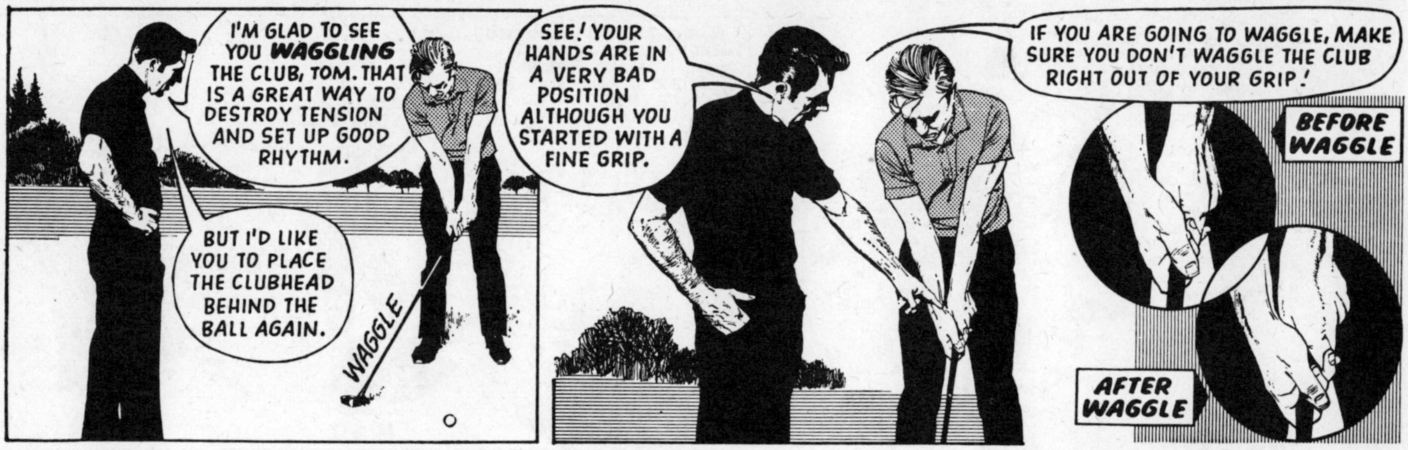

I'M GLAD TO SEE YOU WAGGLING THE CLUB, TOM. THAT IS A GREAT WAY TO DESTROY TENSION AND SET UP GOOD RHYTHM.
BUT I'D LIKE YOU TO PLACE THE CLUBHEAD BEHIND THE BALL AGAIN.
WAGGLE
SEE! YOUR HANDS ARE IN A VERY BAD POSITION ALTHOUGH YOU STARTED WITH A FINE GRIP.
IF YOU ARE GOING TO WAGGLE, MAKE SURE YOU DON'T WAGGLE THE CLUB RIGHT OUT OF YOUR GRIP!
BEFORE WAGGLE
AFTER WAGGLE

Three ways to release tension

YOU ARE MUCH TOO TENSE AT ADDRESS, IAIN, AND IT IS VITAL TO RELEASE THIS TENSION BEFORE STARTING YOUR SWING. LET ME SHOW YOU THREE WAYS OF DOING THIS . . .
1
HAND PRESS
IT IS IMPORTANT TO START YOUR BACKSWING FROM A MOVING POSITION, NOT A DEAD ONE, SO PRESS YOUR HANDS FORWARD, THEN IMMEDIATELY START YOUR BACKSWING . . .
OR, BE LIKE ARNOLD PALMER AND SAM SNEAD AND GIVE A LITTLE "WAGGLE". THIS RELEASES A LOT OF TENSION. BUT BE CERTAIN THAT YOU "WAGGLE" THE CLUB ON THE SAME PATH IT IS GOING TO TAKE ON THE BACKSWING. THAT IS IMPORTANT
2
WAGGLE
I PERSONALLY LIKE TO START MY SWING BY PUSHING MY RIGHT KNEE IN A BIT, BECAUSE, AT IMPACT, I WANT THIS KNEE TO COME RIGHT INTO THE BALL. THIS KNEE PRESS ALSO LOCKS ME, AND PREVENTS ME FROM SWAYING
3
KNEE PRESS

The biggest load of nonsense ever

GARY, I'VE READ THAT THE RIGHT ELBOW SHOULD REMAIN SO CLOSE TO YOUR SIDE THAT A HANDKERCHIEF PLACED UNDER THE ARM WOULD STAY THERE THROUGHOUT THE SWING
I'VE READ THAT TOO, TOM. AND IT'S THE BIGGEST LOAD OF NONSENSE THAT'S EVER BEEN WRITTEN. IT GIVES YOU A CRAMPED BACKSWING WITH A NARROW ARC
ELBOW MUST POINT DOWN
IT WAS ALL RIGHT IN THE OLD DAYS WHEN THEY WERE ONLY THINKING OF HITTING 250 YARDS, BUT TODAY POWER IS IMPORTANT... SO THERE MUST BE A GAP BETWEEN SIDE AND ELBOW!
THE IMPORTANT THING IS TO BE CONSCIOUS OF BRINGING THE RIGHT ELBOW BACK INTO THE SIDE ON THE DOWNSWING... BACK TO WHERE IT WAS AT ADDRESS

Play the Y's way

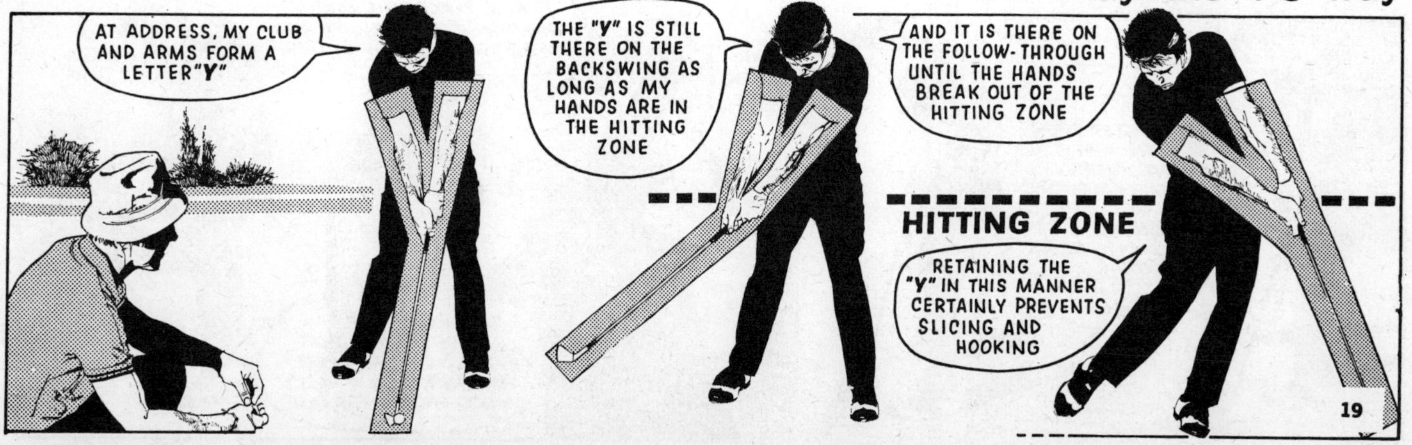

AT ADDRESS, MY CLUB AND ARMS FORM A LETTER "Y"
THE "Y" IS STILL THERE ON THE BACKSWING AS LONG AS MY HANDS ARE IN THE HITTING ZONE
AND IT IS THERE ON THE FOLLOW-THROUGH UNTIL THE HANDS BREAK OUT OF THE HITTING ZONE
HITTING ZONE
RETAINING THE "Y" IN THIS MANNER CERTAINLY PREVENTS SLICING AND HOOKING

One good turn deserves another

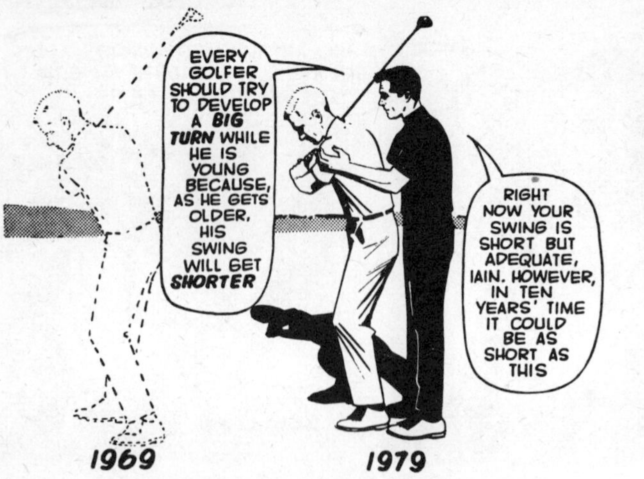

Check your shoulder turn

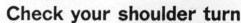

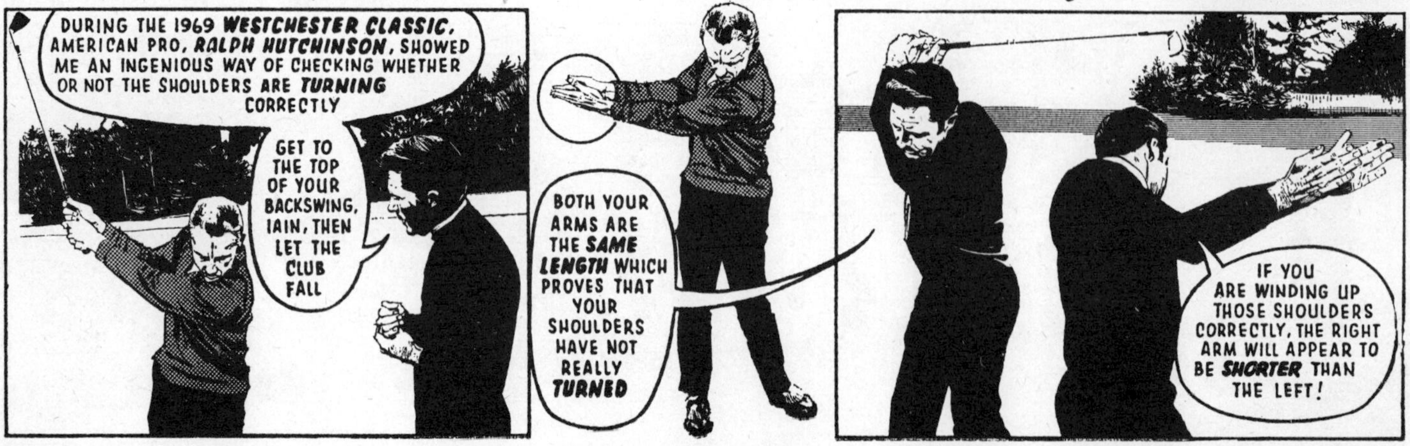

Complete the backswing

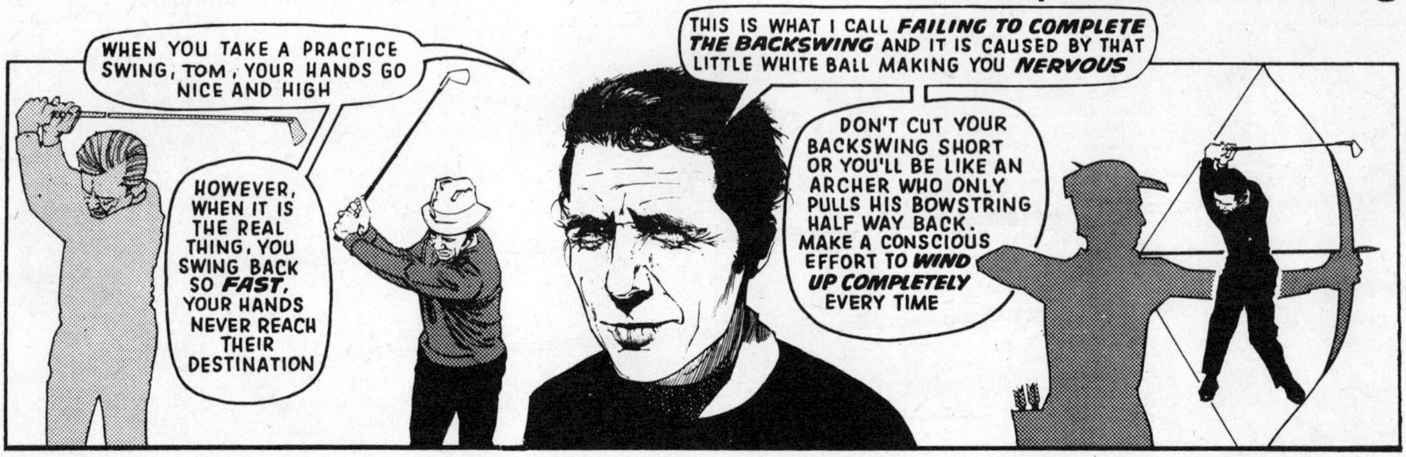

Square to square junk!

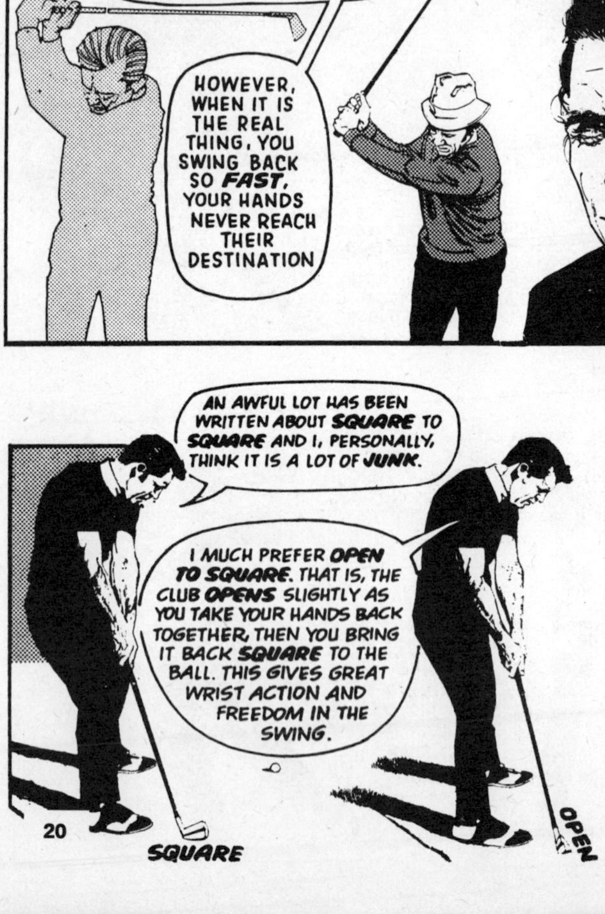

The big secret

THAT IS THE FINEST SWING I HAVE EVER SEEN YOU DO, IAIN
YOU HAVE A BEAUTIFUL, LONG, HIGH FOLLOW-THROUGH AND YOU HAVE HIT RIGHT THROUGH THE BALL
THIS ALL STEMMED FROM THE FACT THAT YOU STARTED THE BACKSWING CORRECTLY. YOU TOOK THE CLUB BACK IN ONE PIECE WITH NO EARLY BREAKING OF THE WRISTS
THE BIG SECRET
THIS GAVE YOU A WIDE BACKSWING ARC, HELPED YOU TO START DOWN ON THE INSIDE WITH A DELAYED HIT AND TREMENDOUS CLUBHEAD SPEED THROUGH THE BALL
I WILL NEVER TIRE OF STRESSING HOW IMPORTANT IT IS TO START THE SWING CORRECTLY

How to take the club back low

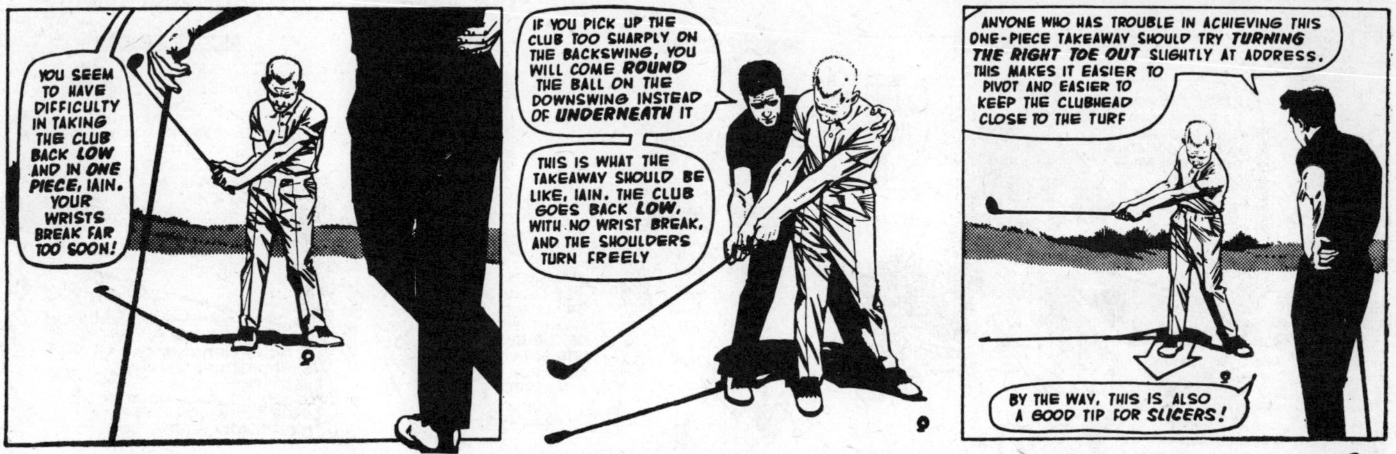

YOU SEEM TO HAVE DIFFICULTY IN TAKING THE CLUB BACK LOW AND IN ONE PIECE, IAIN. YOUR WRISTS BREAK FAR TOO SOON!
IF YOU PICK UP THE CLUB TOO SHARPLY ON THE BACKSWING, YOU WILL COME ROUND THE BALL ON THE DOWNSWING INSTEAD OF UNDERNEATH IT
THIS IS WHAT THE TAKEAWAY SHOULD BE LIKE, IAIN. THE CLUB GOES BACK LOW, WITH NO WRIST BREAK, AND THE SHOULDERS TURN FREELY
ANYONE WHO HAS TROUBLE IN ACHIEVING THIS ONE-PIECE TAKEAWAY SHOULD TRY TURNING THE RIGHT TOE OUT SLIGHTLY AT ADDRESS. THIS MAKES IT EASIER TO PIVOT AND EASIER TO KEEP THE CLUBHEAD CLOSE TO THE TURF
BY THE WAY, THIS IS ALSO A GOOD TIP FOR SLICERS!

Tall men, take heed!

TALL PEOPLE CAN BE AT A DISADVANTAGE IN GOLF, TOM...
IF THEY TAKE A FULL BACKSWING, THERE IS MORE ROOM FOR THEM TO GO WRONG THAN IF YOU OR I TAKE A FULL SWING — SIMPLY BECAUSE THEIR ARC IS BIGGER!
I OFTEN FIND THAT WHEN A TALL MAN HAS A LONG, SLOPPY BACKSWING, HIS CLUBHEAD SPEED PETERS OUT, AND HE GETS NO FOLLOW-THROUGH
THREE-QUARTER BACKSWING
I BELIEVE THAT A TALL MAN SHOULD RESTRICT HIMSELF TO A MORE EASILY-CONTROLLED THREE-QUARTER BACKSWING— WHICH WILL STILL BE EQUIVALENT TO THE FULL SWING OF A NORMAL MAN!

A tip for the heavyweight!

VICTOR HAS A VERY RESTRICTED TURN ON HIS BACKSWING, GARY
THAT'S BECAUSE HE IS A HEFTY FELLOW, IAIN. ALSO HE DOESN'T PLAY A LOT. IF HE ALTERS THE POSITION OF HIS LEFT FOOT HE WILL GET A MUCH BIGGER TURN
TOP PLAYER
HEAVY MAN
MOST OF THE BEST GOLFERS TODAY HAVE THEIR RIGHT FOOT SQUARE TO THE LINE AND THEIR LEFT FOOT POINTED OUT A BIT...
BUT A HEAVILY BUILT MAN MUST NOT TURN OUT HIS LEFT TOE. HE MUST KEEP IT ABSOLUTELY SQUARE
BY DOING THIS, VICTOR PUTS AT LEAST 6-8 INCHES ON THE LENGTH OF HIS BACKSWING WHICH, BELIEVE ME, WILL GREATLY INCREASE THE SPEED AT WHICH HIS CLUBHEAD WILL HIT THROUGH THE BALL

Checking the swing plane

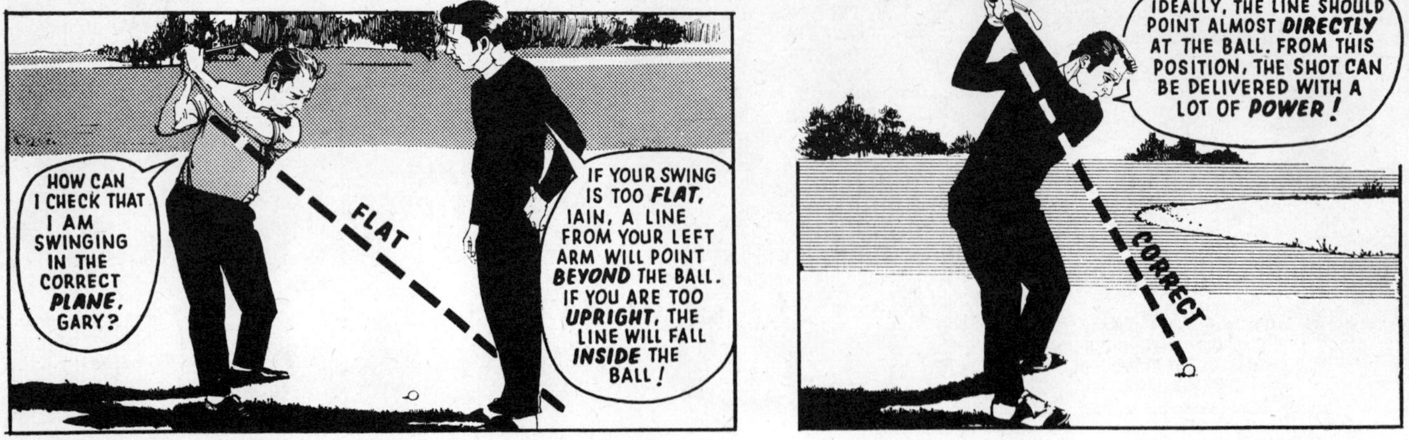
HOW CAN I CHECK THAT I AM SWINGING IN THE CORRECT PLANE, GARY?
IF YOUR SWING IS TOO FLAT, IAIN, A LINE FROM YOUR LEFT ARM WILL POINT BEYOND THE BALL. IF YOU ARE TOO UPRIGHT, THE LINE WILL FALL INSIDE THE BALL!
FLAT
IDEALLY, THE LINE SHOULD POINT ALMOST DIRECTLY AT THE BALL. FROM THIS POSITION, THE SHOT CAN BE DELIVERED WITH A LOT OF POWER!
CORRECT

Four ways to start your downswing . . .

METHOD ONE
TODAY, I'M GOING TO SHOW YOU FOUR DIFFERENT WAYS OF STARTING THE DOWNSWING, IAIN...
FIRST, BY TURNING THE LEFT HIP AWAY AND GETTING YOUR WEIGHT ONTO YOUR LEFT SIDE
METHOD TWO
SECOND, BY BRINGING THE RIGHT KNEE IN TOWARDS THE LEFT KNEE
METHOD THREE
THIRD, BY PULLING THE CLUB DOWN FROM THE TOP OF THE SWING WITH BOTH HANDS, AS IF PULLING A BELL-ROPE
METHOD FOUR
AND, FOURTH, BY MOVING THE RIGHT SHOULDER UNDERNEATH THE CHIN
TRY EACH OF THESE METHODS OF STARTING THE DOWNSWING, IAIN. THEY ARE ALL GOOD... BUT YOU MUST FIND OUT WHICH ONE SUITS YOU BEST!

The late hit

I KNOW I SHOULD HIT LATE, GARY, BUT I STILL CAN'T GET THE FEELING OF IT!
RIGHT, IAIN, GET TO THE TOP OF THE SWING AND HOLD IT...
NOW, WITH YOUR CLUBHEAD HOOKED ONTO MY CLUB, PULL DOWN WITH YOUR HANDS. NOW YOU CAN FEEL HOW THE CLUB STAYS BEHIND THE HANDS. THIS BRINGS YOU DOWN ON THE INSIDE AND GIVES YOU A LOT OF CLUBHEAD SPEED
ANYONE WHO DOESN'T HAVE A FRIEND CAN PRACTISE THIS IN THE BACK GARDEN WITH A CLOTHES-LINE

The importance of good leg action

IAIN, I KEEP PREACHING THE NEED FOR GOOD LEG ACTION BUT I SOMETIMES WONDER IF YOU REALLY APPRECIATE THE IMPORTANCE OF WHAT I AM SAYING
IN ORDER TO GET THE MESSAGE THROUGH TO YOU, I WOULD LIKE YOU TO HIT A DOZEN 6-IRON SHOTS REMAINING ABSOLUTELY FLAT-FOOTED
IT FEELS TERRIBLE, GARY...
THAT'S RIGHT, IAIN! YOUR FOLLOW-THROUGH STOPS SHORT, AND THE SHOT HAS NO "CRACK" IN IT!
GARY! I'M CONVINCED!
NOW, FEEL THE DIFFERENCE WHEN YOU USE YOUR LEGS! YOUR WEIGHT TRANSFERS TO YOUR RIGHT FOOT ON THE BACKSWING THEN FORWARD ON TO YOUR LEFT FOOT ON THE DOWNSWING — AND LOOK AT THE BIG INCREASE IN YOUR FOLLOW-THROUGH!

The importance of the right arm

ONE OF THE MOST IMPORTANT THINGS WHEN HITTING A GOLF BALL IS TO HAVE GOOD EXTENSION ON THE FOLLOW THROUGH. THIS COMES FROM HITTING THE BALL LATE!
MY RIGHT ARM IS AS STRAIGHT AS A RAMROD AND IN LINE WITH THE CLUB. THAT'S WHAT WE CALL EXTENSION
BY KEEPING MY RIGHT ARM STRAIGHT, I AM MORE OR LESS FORCING THE BALL TO GO TO THE HOLE. YOUR RIGHT ARM IS BENT BECAUSE YOU HIT EARLY. THE BALL COULD GO ANYWHERE!
STRAIGHT RIGHT ARM GIVES ACCURATE SHOTS
GOOD EXTENSION NOT ONLY GIVES ACCURACY... IT ADDS TREMENDOUS POWER TO THE SHOT
BENT RIGHT ARM GIVES INACCURATE SHOTS
YOU MUST MAKE A CONSCIOUS EFFORT TO KEEP YOUR RIGHT ARM STRAIGHT WHEN HITTING THE BALL, AND ON THE FOLLOW-THROUGH

If you are stout or if you are old...

GARY, THIS GENTLEMAN IS WONDERING IF YOU HAVE ANY ADVICE FOR STOUT GOLFERS?
I CERTAINLY DO, IAIN. STOUT PEOPLE, AND THOSE WHO ARE GETTING ON IN YEARS, ARE NOT CAPABLE OF USING THEIR BODIES IN THE SWING AS THEY ARE NOT SUPPLE ENOUGH. THEY SHOULD BECOME "HAND" GOLFERS!
USING YOUR HANDS ONLY, TAKE BACK THE CLUB IN ONE PIECE AND YOU WILL GET A REASONABLY WIDE ARC WITH VERY LITTLE BODY MOVEMENT
THIS WILL GET YOU NICELY TO THE TOP OF THE SWING WITH A FULL WRIST COCK. NOW START YOUR DOWNSWING BY PULLING DOWN WITH THE LEFT HAND
TAKE CLUB BACK IN ONE PIECE
PULL THE LEFT HAND RIGHT THROUGH THE BALL ... I DON'T SAY HIT! PULL THROUGH AND THIS WILL MAKE YOU USE YOUR BODY AS MUCH AS IS PHYSICALLY POSSIBLE
WHEN A STOUT MAN TRIES TO BE A "BODY SWINGER" HE SWAYS AND FLOPS ALL OVER THE PLACE. BUT ONCE HE BECOMES A "HAND PLAYER", HE CAN HIT THE BALL MUCH BETTER AND STRAIGHTER

SECTION TWO

The Tee Shot

The important first hole

IN MY OPINION, NOT NEARLY ENOUGH HAS BEEN WRITTEN ABOUT THE IMPORTANCE OF THE FIRST HOLE IN A ROUND OF GOLF.
YOU, TOM, TEND TO HURRY ONTO THE TEE, GRAB YOUR DRIVER AND GET THE SHOT OVER WITH!
CONSEQUENTLY, YOU RUSH YOUR SWING, LIFT YOUR HEAD AND QUIT ON THE BALL.
I ALWAYS WALK ON SLOWLY, HAVING FIRST HIT MY QUOTA OF PRACTICE BALLS. I SWING SLOWLY, KEEP MY HEAD DOWN AND FOLLOW-THROUGH COMPLETELY.
NOW I AM IN A POSITION TO BIRDIE THE HOLE AND YOU WILL PROBABLY GO ONE OVER. IT CERTAINLY MAKES A BIG DIFFERENCE IF YOU LOSE TWO STROKES TO A MAN AT THE FIRST HOLE!

Wide open fairways

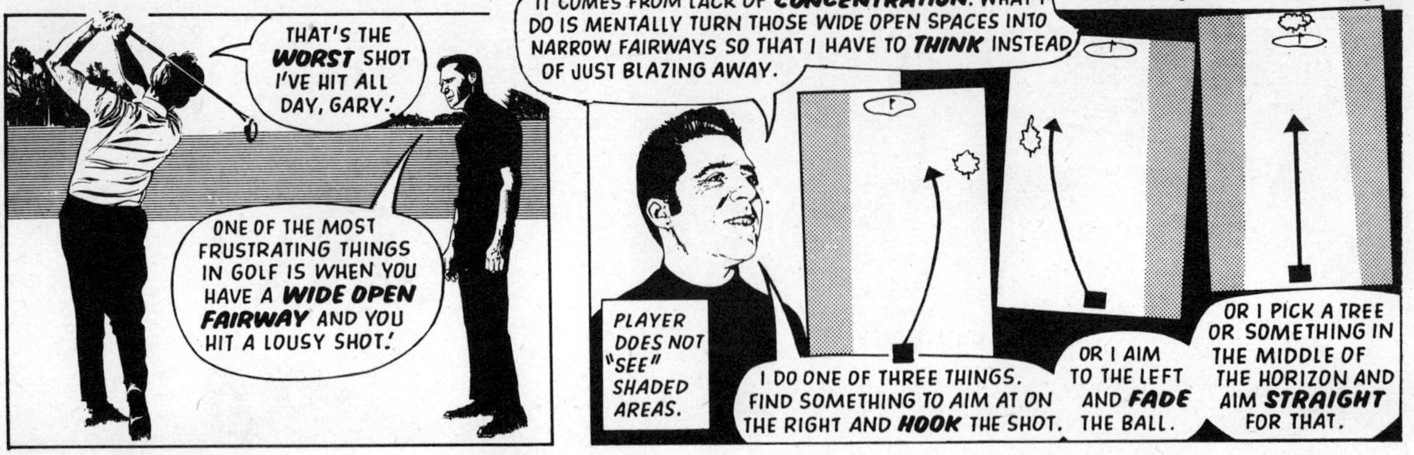

THAT'S THE WORST SHOT I'VE HIT ALL DAY, GARY.'
ONE OF THE MOST FRUSTRATING THINGS IN GOLF IS WHEN YOU HAVE A WIDE OPEN FAIRWAY AND YOU HIT A LOUSY SHOT.'
IT COMES FROM LACK OF CONCENTRATION. WHAT I DO IS MENTALLY TURN THOSE WIDE OPEN SPACES INTO NARROW FAIRWAYS SO THAT I HAVE TO THINK INSTEAD OF JUST BLAZING AWAY.
PLAYER DOES NOT "SEE" SHADED AREAS.
I DO ONE OF THREE THINGS. FIND SOMETHING TO AIM AT ON THE RIGHT AND HOOK THE SHOT.
OR I AIM TO THE LEFT AND FADE THE BALL.
OR I PICK A TREE OR SOMETHING IN THE MIDDLE OF THE HORIZON AND AIM STRAIGHT FOR THAT.

On narrow fairways . . .

THIS IS THE NARROWEST FAIRWAY ON THE COURSE, GARY. I NEARLY ALWAYS END UP IN THE TREES
THAT IS A VERY NEGATIVE APPROACH, IAIN !
ON A NARROW FAIRWAY LIKE THIS, WHAT YOU NEED IS SOMETHING TO DIVERT YOUR MIND FROM THE TROUBLE ON BOTH SIDES — SOMETHING TO GIVE YOU A POSITIVE OUTLOOK !
I PICK OUT ONE TREE ON THE HORIZON AND AIM FOR THAT. BY CONCENTRATING ON A TARGET, IT TAKES MY MIND OFF THE NARROWNESS OF THE FAIRWAY. I HARDLY EVEN NOTICE THE TREES ON EACH SIDE !

Learn to maneuver the ball

WHY DO YOU SPEND SO MUCH TIME DRAWING THE BALL AND FADING IT ON THE PRACTICE TEE, GARY ?
WELL, TOM, MANY GOLFERS HIT THE SAME SHOT ALL THE TIME, BUT I BELIEVE THE BEST GOLFERS ARE THOSE WHO CAN MANEUVER THE BALL
THE ABILITY TO DO SO CAN BE VERY HELPFUL. FOR EXAMPLE, IF THERE IS OUT-OF-BOUNDS ON THE RIGHT, I AIM AT THE TROUBLE SPOT AND HOOK THE BALL AWAY FROM IT. IF THE DANGER IS ON THE LEFT, I AIM LEFT AND FADE THE SHOT
OUT-OF-BOUNDS

The drive

GARY, DO YOU AGREE THAT YOU DRIVE FOR SHOW... PUTT FOR DOUGH?
AS A PRO, TOM, ALL MY SHOTS ARE FOR DOUGH. NEVER UNDERESTIMATE THE IMPORTANCE OF GOOD, ACCURATE DRIVING
IN THE DRIVE, BOTH HANDS SHOULD TAKE BACK THE CLUB TOGETHER, SO THAT HANDS AND CLUB ARE IN LINE WITH EACH OTHER
AT THE TOP OF MY BACKSWING MY LEFT ARM IS STRAIGHT AND MY RIGHT ARM IS BENT
AT IMPACT, MY LEFT ARM IS STRAIGHT, MY RIGHT SHOULDER COMES UP UNDER MY CHIN, AND MY RIGHT KNEE POINTS INTO MY LEFT KNEE

Tee up with care

I'M IN THE TREES, GARY!
IF IT'S ANY COMFORT, IAIN, YOU CAN BLAME THE TEEING GROUND!
YOU SEE, ON THIS HOLE, THE TEE POINTS ONE WAY AND THE FAIRWAY GOES ANOTHER..!
THERE IS ALWAYS A TENDENCY TO AIM THE WAY THE TEE IS POINTING, REGARDLESS OF THE DIRECTION OF THE FAIRWAY! EVEN THE BEST PLAYERS OFTEN GET CAUGHT OUT!
IF YOU LINE UP WITH THE TEE AS YOU DID, YOU ARE ALMOST CERTAIN TO END UP IN THE TREES
WHAT I DO IS I IGNORE THE TEE AND THE MARKERS AND PICK OUT A LANDMARK ON THE HORIZON—AND AIM FOR THAT!

Where to tee up your ball

I AM GOING TO TRY AND FADE THIS ONE INTO THE GREEN, GARY
WELL THEN, YOU'RE STANDING ON THE WRONG SIDE OF THE TEE, IAIN. YOU'RE AIMING DIRECTLY AT THE TREES WHICH MEANS THAT IF YOUR BALL GOES STRAIGHT INSTEAD OF FADING, YOU WILL BE IN TROUBLE!
IF YOU LIKE TO FADE THE BALL, TEE UP ON THE RIGHT! NOW YOU WILL AIM TO THE LEFT AND, EVEN IF YOU HIT THE BALL STRAIGHT, IT WILL STILL STAY ON THE FAIRWAY. IN OTHER WORDS, YOU ARE GIVING YOURSELF A BIGGER MARGIN FOR ERROR
IT'S FOR THIS SAME REASON THAT I TEE UP ON THE LEFT. UNLIKE YOU, I LIKE TO HOOK THE BALL

Watch how you tee up

IAIN, THIS IS A VERY NARROW FAIRWAY. YOU'RE TAKING A BIG CHANCE TEEING UP YOUR BALL SO HIGH!
HOOK
SLICE
IF YOU HOOK OR SLICE, THE BALL WILL ALMOST CERTAINLY CARRY INTO THE TREES!
WHEN THE FAIRWAY IS TIGHT, I TEE THE BALL LOW SO THAT IT WILL NOT STAY IN THE AIR SO LONG. EVEN IF I HOOK OR SLICE, IT WILL HIT THE GROUND FAIRLY QUICKLY AND HAVE A GOOD CHANCE OF STAYING ON THE FAIRWAY
HOOK
SLICE
I HAVE NOTICED THAT WHENEVER ARNOLD PALMER COMES TO A NARROW HOLE, HE HITS THE BALL PARTICULARLY LOW TO MAKE CERTAIN OF KEEPING OUT OF TROUBLE

Give yourself three chances

DON'T AIM DOWN THE MIDDLE, IAIN! THIS FAIRWAY IS ONLY 50 YARDS WIDE AND IT SLOPES STEEPLY FROM RIGHT TO LEFT...
SLOPE
IF YOU HIT A STRAIGHT BALL, IT WILL BOUNCE OFF TO THE LEFT OF THE FAIRWAY AND PERHAPS EVEN REACH THE ROUGH
IF YOU HOOK IT, THE BALL WILL DEFINITELY END UP IN THE ROUGH
YOU HAVE ONLY ONE REAL CHANCE OF STAYING ON THE FAIRWAY AND THAT IS TO FADE THE BALL!
I PREFER TO GIVE MYSELF THREE CHANCES BY AIMING DOWN THE RIGHT!
IF I HIT A STRAIGHT BALL, THE SLOPE WILL CARRY IT TOWARDS THE MIDDLE OF THE FAIRWAY. IF I FADE THE BALL, THE SLOPE WILL KEEP IT FROM RUNNING INTO THE ROUGH. AND, EVEN IF I HOOK IT, I'LL STILL BE ON THE FAIRWAY!

Forget the straight ball!

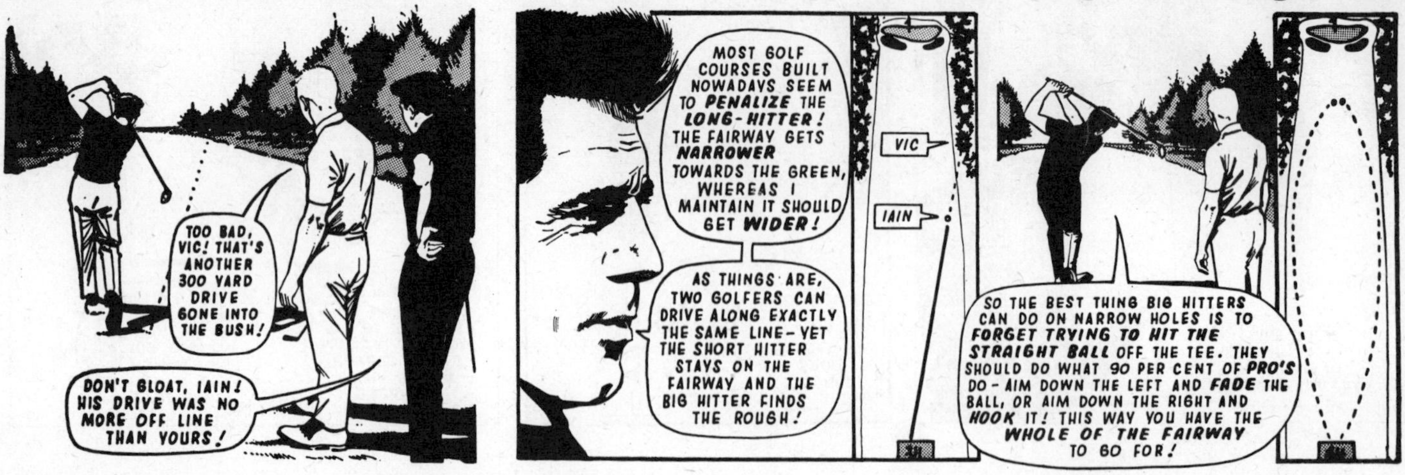

TOO BAD, VIC! THAT'S ANOTHER 300 YARD DRIVE GONE INTO THE BUSH!
DON'T GLOAT, IAIN! HIS DRIVE WAS NO MORE OFF LINE THAN YOURS!
MOST GOLF COURSES BUILT NOWADAYS SEEM TO PENALIZE THE LONG-HITTER! THE FAIRWAY GETS NARROWER TOWARDS THE GREEN, WHEREAS I MAINTAIN IT SHOULD GET WIDER!
AS THINGS ARE, TWO GOLFERS CAN DRIVE ALONG EXACTLY THE SAME LINE-YET THE SHORT HITTER STAYS ON THE FAIRWAY AND THE BIG HITTER FINDS THE ROUGH!
VIC
IAIN
SO THE BEST THING BIG HITTERS CAN DO ON NARROW HOLES IS TO FORGET TRYING TO HIT THE STRAIGHT BALL OFF THE TEE. THEY SHOULD DO WHAT 90 PER CENT OF PRO'S DO-AIM DOWN THE LEFT AND FADE THE BALL, OR AIM DOWN THE RIGHT AND HOOK IT! THIS WAY YOU HAVE THE WHOLE OF THE FAIRWAY TO GO FOR!

When it's wet, hit high

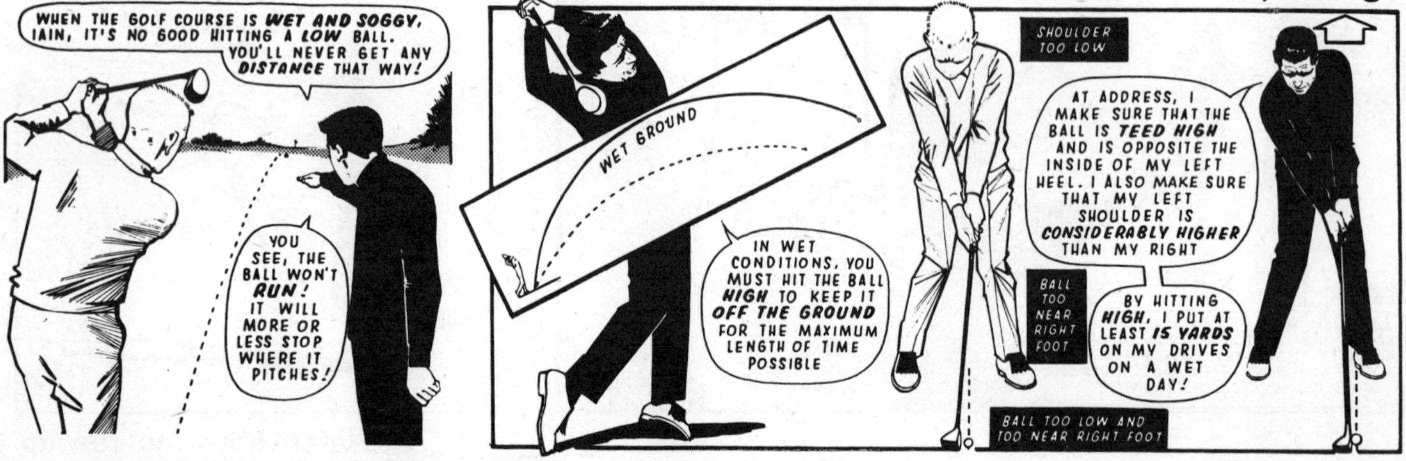

WHEN THE GOLF COURSE IS WET AND SOGGY, IAIN, IT'S NO GOOD HITTING A LOW BALL. YOU'LL NEVER GET ANY DISTANCE THAT WAY!
YOU SEE, THE BALL WON'T RUN! IT WILL MORE OR LESS STOP WHERE IT PITCHES!
WET GROUND
IN WET CONDITIONS, YOU MUST HIT THE BALL HIGH TO KEEP IT OFF THE GROUND FOR THE MAXIMUM LENGTH OF TIME POSSIBLE
SHOULDER TOO LOW
BALL TOO NEAR RIGHT FOOT
BALL TOO LOW AND TOO NEAR RIGHT FOOT
AT ADDRESS, I MAKE SURE THAT THE BALL IS TEED HIGH AND IS OPPOSITE THE INSIDE OF MY LEFT HEEL. I ALSO MAKE SURE THAT MY LEFT SHOULDER IS CONSIDERABLY HIGHER THAN MY RIGHT
BY HITTING HIGH, I PUT AT LEAST 15 YARDS ON MY DRIVES ON A WET DAY!

Play the right ball

IT'S NO GOOD PLAYING WITH MY GOLF BALLS, IAIN. YOU DON'T DEVELOP ENOUGH CLUBHEAD SPEED TO COMPRESS SUCH A BALL AND THEREFORE YOU HIT IT NO DISTANCE AT ALL!
IT'S VERY IMPORTANT TO USE THE BALL THAT SUITS YOUR GAME. FOR EXAMPLE, JACK NICKLAUS USES 100 COMPRESSION- I USE 95. THE AVERAGE WEEKEND GOLFER SHOULD USE NO MORE THAN AN 85 COMPRESSION BALL
HOW CAN A PLAYER KNOW WHICH BALL IS RIGHT FOR HIM, GARY?
HE SHOULD ASK HIS GOLF PROFESSIONAL. HE WILL ADVISE HIM

How to hit an extra 10 yards

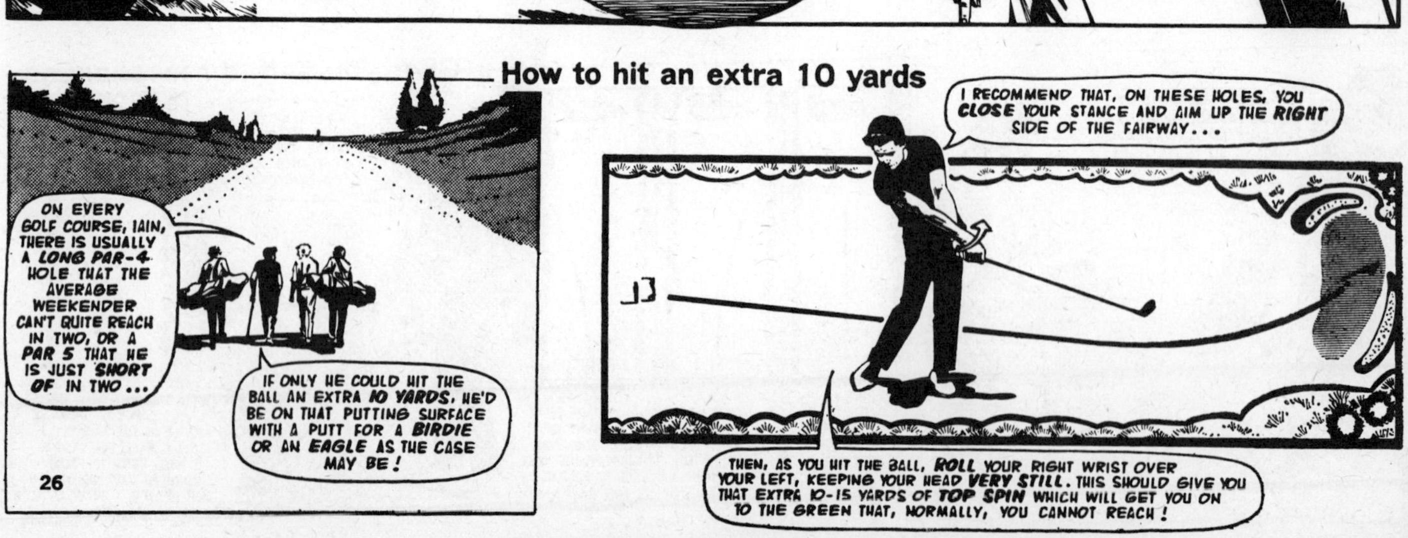

ON EVERY GOLF COURSE, IAIN, THERE IS USUALLY A LONG PAR-4 HOLE THAT THE AVERAGE WEEKENDER CAN'T QUITE REACH IN TWO, OR A PAR 5 THAT HE IS JUST SHORT OF IN TWO...
IF ONLY HE COULD HIT THE BALL AN EXTRA 10 YARDS, HE'D BE ON THAT PUTTING SURFACE WITH A PUTT FOR A BIRDIE OR AN EAGLE AS THE CASE MAY BE!
I RECOMMEND THAT, ON THESE HOLES, YOU CLOSE YOUR STANCE AND AIM UP THE RIGHT SIDE OF THE FAIRWAY...
THEN, AS YOU HIT THE BALL, ROLL YOUR RIGHT WRIST OVER YOUR LEFT, KEEPING YOUR HEAD VERY STILL. THIS SHOULD GIVE YOU THAT EXTRA 10-15 YARDS OF TOP SPIN WHICH WILL GET YOU ON TO THE GREEN THAT, NORMALLY, YOU CANNOT REACH!

SECTION THREE

Fairway Shots

Fairway Woods and Long Irons

The long irons

ON LONG-IRON SHOTS I POSITION THE BALL OPPOSITE MY LEFT FOOT AS THIS HELPS ME GET THE BALL UP IN THE AIR
NOTE MY FULL SHOULDER TURN... A GOOD PIVOT IS ESSENTIAL
KNEES BENT TO DISPEL TENSION
AS I HIT THE BALL, MY WEIGHT IS MOVING ACROSS TO MY LEFT SIDE, MY RIGHT KNEE IS COMING IN, AND MY BELT BUCKLE IS ALREADY POINTING TO THE HOLE
ONE OF THE THINGS TO STRIVE FOR IS A GOOD FINISH SO, WHEN YOU PRACTISE, HOLD YOUR FINISH ...THAT'S VERY IMPORTANT
RIGHT SHOULDER UNDER CHIN
HIGH FOLLOW-THROUGH
WEIGHT ALL ON LEFT SIDE
RIGHT KNEE IN
PERFECT BALANCE
IF, LIKE MOST WEEKENDERS, TOM, YOU'RE TERRIFIED OF NOT GETTING THE BALL UP IN THE AIR WITH YOUR LONG IRONS, TRY IMAGINING YOU HAVE A 9-IRON IN YOUR HANDS, AND PLAY THE SHOT WITH EXACTLY THE SAME SWING AND RHYTHM YOU WOULD USE FOR THAT CLUB
DON'T SCOOP! HIT DOWN AND THROUGH THE BALL!

Long iron trouble

I CAN'T COME UNDER THE BALL WITH MY LONG IRONS, GARY! I ALWAYS RISE UP AT IMPACT!
THAT IS BECAUSE YOU STAND TOO CLOSE TO THE BALL, IAIN. A TALL MAN CAN STAND THAT CLOSE AND STILL HIT UNDER THE BALL, BUT YOU CAN'T BECAUSE YOUR SWING IS NATURALLY FLATTER!
TRY STANDING A COUPLE OF INCHES FURTHER BACK FROM THE BALL WITH YOUR TWO AND THREE IRONS...
THIS WILL GIVE YOUR RIGHT SHOULDER MORE ROOM IN WHICH TO TRAVEL THROUGH UNDERNEATH YOUR CHIN!

A five second tip

CAN YOU GIVE ME A FIVE SECOND TIP TO HELP ME HIT MY LONG IRONS BETTER, GARY?
YES, IAIN. HOLD THE CLUB SHORT. THIS WILL GIVE YOU A NICE, FIRM GRIP, WITH YOUR LEFT HAND ENTIRELY ON THE CLUB FOR GOOD CONTROL
YOU WILL FIND THAT YOUR SWING ARC IS NOW MUCH FIRMER. THE MORE COMPACT THE ARC, THE BETTER THE AVERAGE WEEKENDER WILL PLAY
A LONG, LOOSE SWING LEAVES TOO MUCH ROOM FOR ERROR!

Watch it fly

YOU WILL NEVER GET YOUR FAIRWAY WOOD SHOTS AIRBORNE IF YOU LIFT UP THE CLUBHEAD AT IMPACT. YOU ARE ONLY HITTING HALF A BALL!
WHEN YOU HIT THROUGH THE BALL, IAIN, YOUR CLUB MUST REALLY HUG THE GROUND AND STAY WITH THE BALL!
THE GREATEST TIP I CAN GIVE YOU IS THIS... TRY TO HIT THE BALL ALONG THE GROUND – THEN WATCH IT FLY!

Getting height with the fairway woods

I FIND IT HARD TO GET ANY HEIGHT AT ALL WITH A WOOD OFF THE FAIRWAY, GARY!
THAT'S NOT UNCOMMON, IAIN. GETTING THE BALL UP IN THE AIR IS ONE OF THE CHIEF CONCERNS WHEN PLAYING A FAIRWAY WOOD SHOT. HOWEVER, THERE ARE ONE OR TWO THINGS YOU CAN DO TO HELP YOU GET HEIGHT
FIRST, MAKE SURE YOU GET YOUR RIGHT KNEE INTO THE SHOT, WITH ALL YOUR WEIGHT ON YOUR LEFT SIDE. I KEEP MENTIONING THE RIGHT KNEE, IAIN, BECAUSE IT IS SO VERY IMPORTANT!
DON'T LET YOUR HEAD THRUST FORWARD. KEEP IT ANCHORED BEHIND THE BALL
HIT PAST AND UNDERNEATH YOUR CHIN, NOT ACROSS IT LIKE A BASEBALL PLAYER!
THEN FINISH WITH YOUR HANDS IN A HIGH FOLLOW THROUGH

SECTION FOUR

The Wedge Shot

The wedge shot

WHEN PLAYING A WEDGE SHOT, IAIN, YOU MUST NOT TAKE THE CLUB BACK IN ONE PIECE. YOUR WRISTS HAVE NOT BROKEN AT ALL, AND THIS WILL RESULT IN A SLOPPY SWING
AS I HAVE MENTIONED BEFORE, YOU MUST BREAK YOUR WRISTS VERY SHARPLY ON THE BACKSWING FOR ALL WEDGE SHOTS
MY BACKSWING IS SHORT, AND I SAVE ALL MY POWER AND SNAP FOR WHEN I ACTUALLY STRIKE THE BALL
BY HAVING A LONG BACKSWING AND A LONG FOLLOW-THROUGH LIKE A DRIVER SHOT, YOU'LL GET NO SNAP INTO THE SHOT. THE WEDGE SHOT MUST BE PLAYED CRISPLY
MY FOLLOW-THROUGH IS NOT LONG, YET IT EXTENDS COMPLETELY THROUGH THE BALL. YOUR HEAD MOVED FORWARD, BUT MINE REMAINS BEHIND WHERE THE BALL WAS SITTING
AND, VERY IMPORTANT, MY RIGHT KNEE IS IN, AND MY WEIGHT IS ALL ON MY LEFT SIDE

The wedge to the green

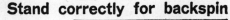

Stand correctly for backspin

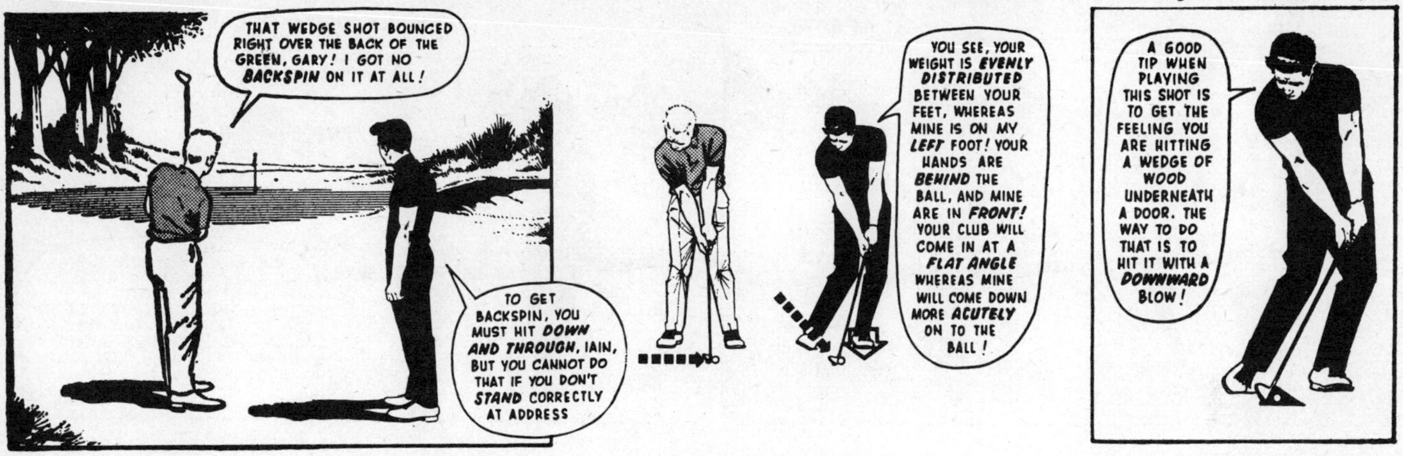

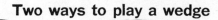

Two ways to play a wedge

Hit it high

Two different approaches

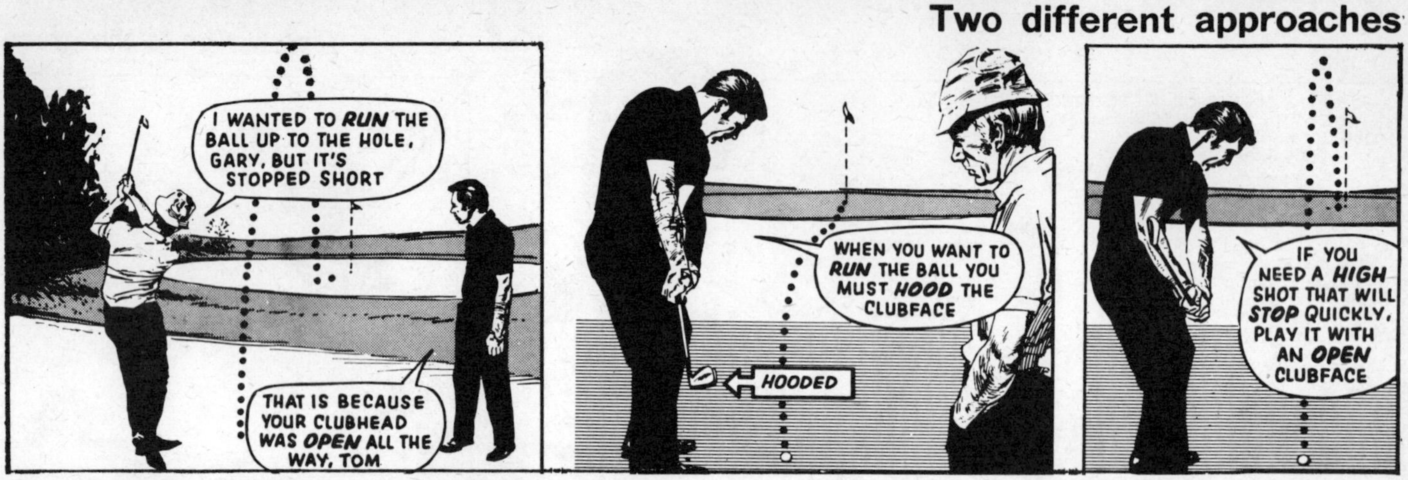
I WANTED TO RUN THE BALL UP TO THE HOLE, GARY, BUT IT'S STOPPED SHORT
THAT IS BECAUSE YOUR CLUBHEAD WAS OPEN ALL THE WAY, TOM
WHEN YOU WANT TO RUN THE BALL YOU MUST HOOD THE CLUBFACE
HOODED
IF YOU NEED A HIGH SHOT THAT WILL STOP QUICKLY, PLAY IT WITH AN OPEN CLUBFACE

Don't roll your wrists

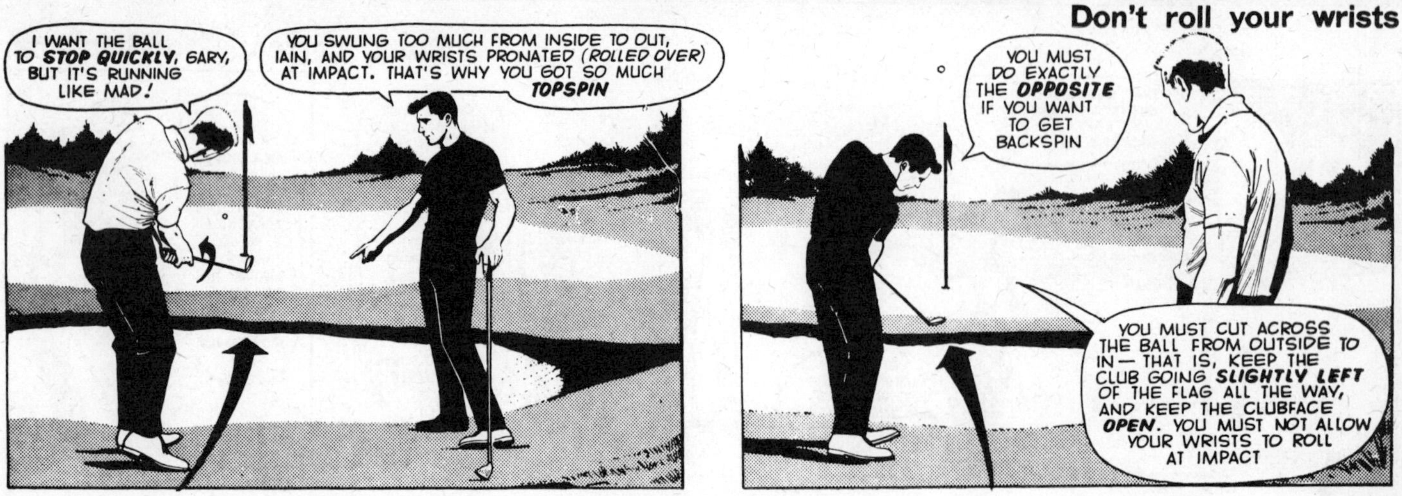
I WANT THE BALL TO STOP QUICKLY, GARY, BUT IT'S RUNNING LIKE MAD!
YOU SWUNG TOO MUCH FROM INSIDE TO OUT, IAIN, AND YOUR WRISTS PRONATED (ROLLED OVER) AT IMPACT. THAT'S WHY YOU GOT SO MUCH TOPSPIN
YOU MUST DO EXACTLY THE OPPOSITE IF YOU WANT TO GET BACKSPIN
YOU MUST CUT ACROSS THE BALL FROM OUTSIDE TO IN — THAT IS, KEEP THE CLUB GOING SLIGHTLY LEFT OF THE FLAG ALL THE WAY, AND KEEP THE CLUBFACE OPEN. YOU MUST NOT ALLOW YOUR WRISTS TO ROLL AT IMPACT

Feathering the ball

HERE, IAIN, YOU'VE GOT TO LOFT THE BALL OVER THE TRAP AND MAKE IT LAND SOFTLY BECAUSE THE FLAG IS AT THE FRONT OF THE GREEN!
BUT YOU WILL NEVER DO IT IF YOU STAND SO CLOSE TO THE BALL! YOUR HANDS HAVE NO FREEDOM OF MOVEMENT!
I STAND A LITTLE BIT FURTHER AWAY FROM THE BALL AND OPEN THE FACE OF THE CLUB. MY STANCE IS ALSO SLIGHTLY OPEN
OPEN CLUBFACE
ON THE BACKSWING, MY CLUB OPENS UP SOME MORE AND I STRIKE THE BALL WITH AN OUT-TO-IN CUTTING ACTION WHICH FEATHERS THE BALL ONTO THE GREEN
IF YOU STAND TOO CLOSE TO THE BALL, IAIN, IT IS HARD TO CUT ACROSS IT BECAUSE YOUR BODY GETS IN THE WAY!

The "flip" shot

THAT'S A VERY FINE ACTION FOR THE NORMAL RUN-UP SHOT TO THE HOLE, IAIN. BUT WITH THAT SAND TRAP TO GET OVER YOU OUGHT TO HAVE PLAYED A "FLIP" SHOT TO GIVE YOU HEIGHT AND BACKSPIN TO STOP YOUR BALL QUICKLY
USING A SAND-IRON, I ADDRESS THE BALL WITH AN OPEN STANCE AND AN OPEN CLUB FACE. IN ALL NORMAL SHOTS THE HANDS SHOULD BE IN FRONT OF THE BALL, BUT HERE, AS I WANT GREAT HEIGHT, MY HANDS ARE IN LINE WITH IT
I BREAK MY WRISTS VERY QUICKLY ON THE BACKSWING...
...AND, ON THE FOLLOW-THROUGH, MY HANDS STAY BACK AND THE CLUBHEAD SWEEPS THROUGH UNDERNEATH THE BALL WHICH GETS IT AIRBORNE VERY QUICKLY
I ONLY USE THE "FLIP" SHOT WHEN THERE IS AN OBSTACLE BETWEEN ME AND THE HOLE. NORMALLY, THE RUN-UP SHOT IS A FAR SAFER STROKE

Don't be short...

LOOK AT THAT, GARY! I NEVER GET THESE SHORT PITCH SHOTS UP TO THE HOLE!
LIKE MOST WEEKENDERS, YOU FORGET THAT THE WEDGE OR SAND WEDGE HAS A TREMENDOUS LOFT WHICH MAKES THE BALL GO VERY HIGH. THIS, NATURALLY, REDUCES THE DISTANCE THE BALL WILL TRAVEL
THE AVERAGE WEEKENDER DOES NOT TAKE ENOUGH BACKSWING WHEN PLAYING THESE SHORT PITCHES. HE'S ALSO INCLINED TO TAKE THE CLUB BACK STIFF-WRISTED
LOFT
SO GIVE YOURSELF A CHANCE OF GETTING THE BALL UP TO THE HOLE BY TAKING A GOOD BACKSWING AND ALLOWING YOUR WRISTS TO BREAK NATURALLY

Aim for the top

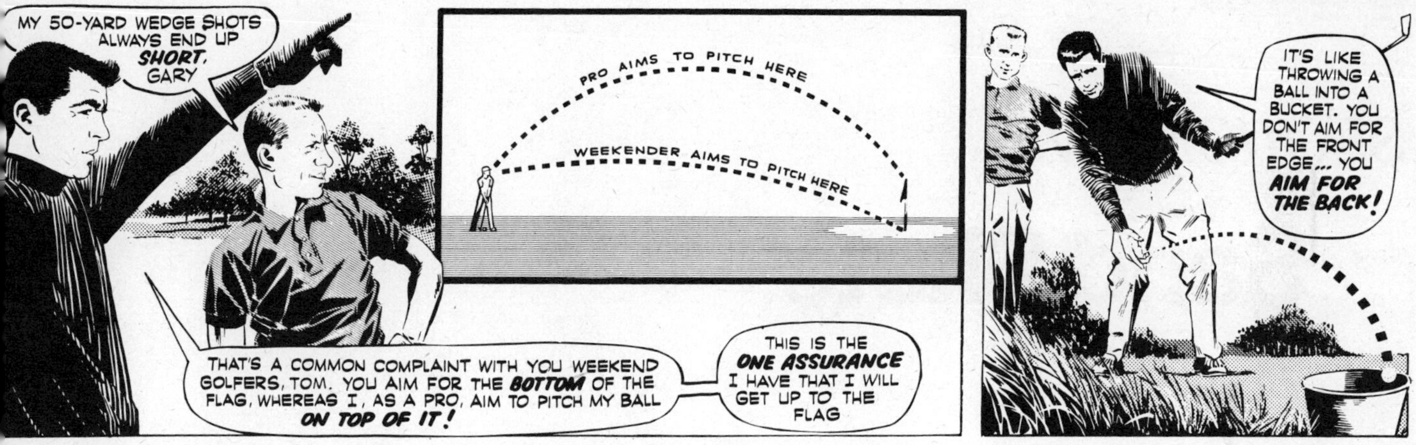
MY 50-YARD WEDGE SHOTS ALWAYS END UP SHORT, GARY
PRO AIMS TO PITCH HERE
WEEKENDER AIMS TO PITCH HERE
THAT'S A COMMON COMPLAINT WITH YOU WEEKEND GOLFERS, TOM. YOU AIM FOR THE BOTTOM OF THE FLAG, WHEREAS I, AS A PRO, AIM TO PITCH MY BALL ON TOP OF IT!
THIS IS THE ONE ASSURANCE I HAVE THAT I WILL GET UP TO THE FLAG
IT'S LIKE THROWING A BALL INTO A BUCKET. YOU DON'T AIM FOR THE FRONT EDGE... YOU AIM FOR THE BACK!

The 30-yard wedge shot

YOU'RE STILL SCOOPING THOSE 30-40 YARD WEDGE SHOTS, IAIN!
FAULT
WEIGHT ON RIGHT FOOT
THE SECRET IS TO KEEP YOUR RIGHT SIDE RELAXED AT ALL TIMES, WITH YOUR WEIGHT ON YOUR LEFT FOOT THROUGHOUT THE SWING
AT ADDRESS, I BEAR DOWN EMPHATICALLY ON MY LEFT HEEL AND LEAN INTO THE SHOT, KEEPING MY HANDS AHEAD OF THE BALL
THE SPIKES OF MY RIGHT SHOE CAN BE CLEARLY SEEN WHICH PROVES THAT MY WEIGHT IS ON MY LEFT SIDE
I HIT DOWN ON THE BALL CRISPLY, AND MY CLUB GOES THROUGH LOW
THIS MAKES THE BALL RUN UP THE CLUBFACE WHICH PRODUCES THE BACKSPIN THAT IS NEEDED
BACKSPIN

To an elevated green

WHEN YOU HAVE TO PLAY A HIGH, SOFT SHOT ONTO AN ELEVATED GREEN, TOM, IT'S NO GOOD HAVING A SHORT BACKSWING, THEN TRYING TO FORCE THE BALL UP INTO THE AIR.
TOO SHORT
YOU MUST HAVE A LONGISH BACKSWING WHICH WILL GIVE YOU MORE RHYTHM AND ENABLE YOU TO GET THE BALL UP IN THE AIR.
THEN MAKE SURE YOU FOLLOW RIGHT THROUGH, AND HERE IS THE SECRET – PLAY THE SHOT WITH THE EASY RHYTHM OF A BUNKER SHOT!

Pitching over a mound

IF I HAD MANAGED TO PITCH MY BALL JUST THIS SIDE OF THE TOP OF THE MOUND, IT WOULD HAVE RUN UP NICELY TO THE HOLE!
BUT YOU'RE NOT GOOD ENOUGH TO PITCH ON TO SUCH A SMALL TARGET, IAIN!
IF YOU ARE SHORT, THE BALL RUNS BACK AT YOU AND, IF YOU PITCH IT ON THE DOWNSLOPE, IT RUNS YARDS PAST THE HOLE
YOU'VE GOT A HOLDING GREEN HERE, SO WHY BE UPSET BY THE MOUND? PLAY THE SHOT AS IF IT DOESN'T EXIST. PITCH YOUR BALL ON TO THE FRONT EDGE OF THE GREEN AND IT WILL STOP IN TIME
KEEP COOL IN THIS KIND OF SITUATION AND THINK! SO MUCH OF GOLF IS PLAYED BETWEEN THE EARS, YOU KNOW!

SECTION FIVE

Sand Shots

Bunker refresher course

THE AVERAGE WEEKENDER IS SO TERRIFIED IN A BUNKER, A LITTLE REFRESHER PROBABLY IS NOT OUT OF PLACE
SHUFFLE YOUR FEET INTO THE SAND TO PREVENT YOUR SLIPPING—AT THE SAME TIME MAKE SURE YOUR STANCE IS OPEN
ADDRESS THE BALL WITH THE CLUBFACE OPEN—THAT IS, FACING RIGHT OF TARGET
TO TARGET
TAKE THE CLUB BACK A LITTLE BIT OUTSIDE THE LINE
OUTSIDE
ENTER THE SAND AN INCH OR SO BEHIND THE BALL AND FOLLOW RIGHT THROUGH. NEVER, NEVER QUIT ON THE BALL!

Throw one—hit one!

YOU MUST NEVER QUIT IN THE SAND, IAIN!
I'VE GOT ABSOLUTELY NO FEELING FOR SAND SHOTS, GARY!

WHEN PRACTISING, IT IS A GOOD IDEA TO THROW A BALL AND THEN TO HIT A BALL
THIS UNDERARM THROWING ACTION IS EXACTLY WHAT IS NEEDED IN A BUNKER
CONTINUE THROWING AND HITTING ALTERNATELY UNTIL YOU HAVE ABSORBED THE FEELING OF PLAYING OUT OF SAND!

THROW THEN HIT

Greenkeeper's nightmare

YOU ARE A GREENKEEPER'S NIGHTMARE THE WAY YOU CHOP ALL THAT SAND OUT OF HIS TRAPS, IAIN!
IN ORDER TO PLAY A GOOD BUNKER SHOT YOU MUST GO THROUGH THE SAND!
YOU CANNOT DO THAT IF YOU ADDRESS THE BALL OPPOSITE YOUR RIGHT FOOT BECAUSE THE CLUB WILL COME DOWN TOO STEEPLY!
REID
PLAYER
ADDRESS THE BALL OFF THE LEFT FOOT AND THE CLUB WILL COME DOWN AT A SHALLOWER ANGLE AND SKIM THROUGH THE SAND.

Bunkers off the green

YOU ARE HOLDING THE CLUB FACE MUCH TOO SQUARE FOR THESE BUNKER SHOTS OFF THE EDGE OF THE GREEN, TOM. ALSO, THE BALL SHOULD NOT BE MIDWAY BETWEEN YOUR FEET
CLOSED FACE

ANOTHER THING I ALWAYS DO WHEN PLAYING BUNKER SHOTS, OR ANY SHOT AROUND THE GREEN, IS TO GRIP THE CLUB A LITTLE SHORT. I FIND THIS GIVES ME MUCH BETTER CLUBHEAD 'FEEL'

Dig in deep

THIS IS INTERESTING, TOM. WE'VE BOTH PLAYED BUNKER SHOTS, AND LOOK AT THE DIFFERENCE IN THE FOOTMARKS WE'VE LEFT IN THE SAND
EH?
YOU CAN SEE I'VE BURIED MY FEET IN THE SAND, WHEREAS YOU'VE JUST TAKEN A NORMAL STANCE
HOW DOES THIS AFFECT THE SHOT, GARY?
WITH YOUR STANCE, YOU WILL INEVITABLY SLIP DURING THE STROKE. IN ALL BUNKERS, YOU SHOULD MAKE CERTAIN YOU'VE GOT A FIRM FOOTING BY BURYING YOUR FEET IN THE SAND. SWIVEL THEM AROUND SO YOU CAN FEEL THE TEXTURE OF THE SOIL... WHETHER IT'S WET, DRY, HARD OR SOFT
BELIEVE ME, TOM, YOUR STANCE WILL MAKE IT IMPOSSIBLE TO HIT CONSISTENTLY GOOD BUNKER SHOTS ...THAT'S WHY I ALWAYS DIG IN DEEP!

Hitting out high

I NEEDED TO HIT THAT ONE HIGH OUT OF THE BUNKER, GARY, BUT IT SCUTTLED OUT LOW INTO THE ROUGH
THAT'S BECAUSE YOU LEANED BACK, WITH ALL YOUR WEIGHT ON YOUR RIGHT LEG, AND TRIED TO 'SCOOP' THE BALL UP INTO THE AIR
GOLF IS FUNNY, TOM. WHEN YOU LEAN BACK AND TRY TO HIT THE BALL HIGH, IT'LL GO LOW...
BUT IF YOU DON'T LEAN BACK AND TRY TO HIT IT DOWN, IT WILL GO HIGH!
WHEN I WANT HEIGHT, MY WEIGHT MOVES TO MY LEFT SIDE, MY RIGHT KNEE COMES IN, MY RIGHT SHOULDER MOVES UNDER MY CHIN...
...AND MY RIGHT ARM SWEEPS ON TO A FULL FOLLOW THROUGH!

Hit it out high

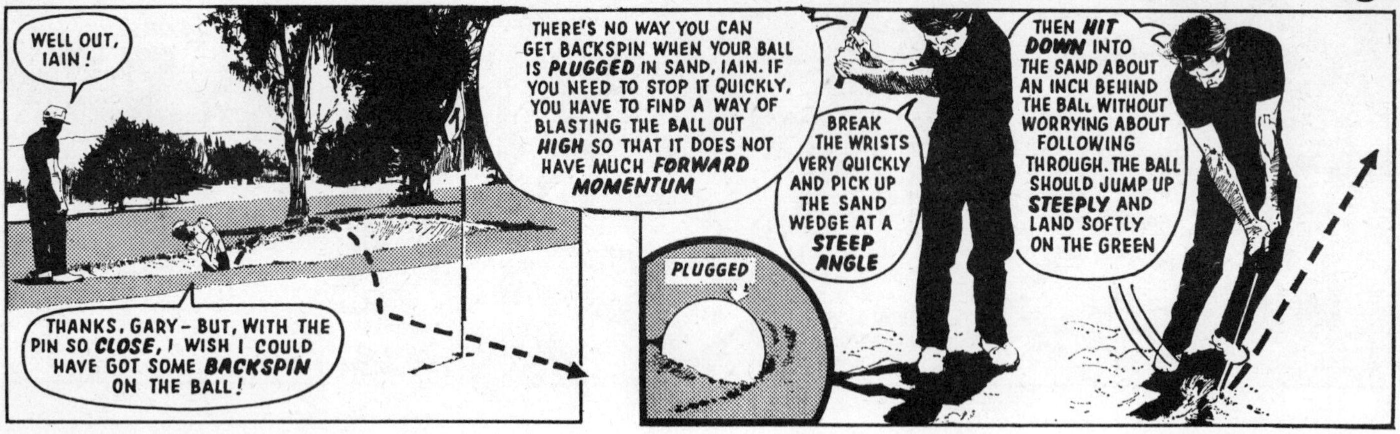

WELL OUT, IAIN!
THANKS, GARY - BUT, WITH THE PIN SO CLOSE, I WISH I COULD HAVE GOT SOME BACKSPIN ON THE BALL!
THERE'S NO WAY YOU CAN GET BACKSPIN WHEN YOUR BALL IS PLUGGED IN SAND, IAIN. IF YOU NEED TO STOP IT QUICKLY, YOU HAVE TO FIND A WAY OF BLASTING THE BALL OUT HIGH SO THAT IT DOES NOT HAVE MUCH FORWARD MOMENTUM
PLUGGED
BREAK THE WRISTS VERY QUICKLY AND PICK UP THE SAND WEDGE AT A STEEP ANGLE
THEN HIT DOWN INTO THE SAND ABOUT AN INCH BEHIND THE BALL WITHOUT WORRYING ABOUT FOLLOWING THROUGH. THE BALL SHOULD JUMP UP STEEPLY AND LAND SOFTLY ON THE GREEN

A bunker problem

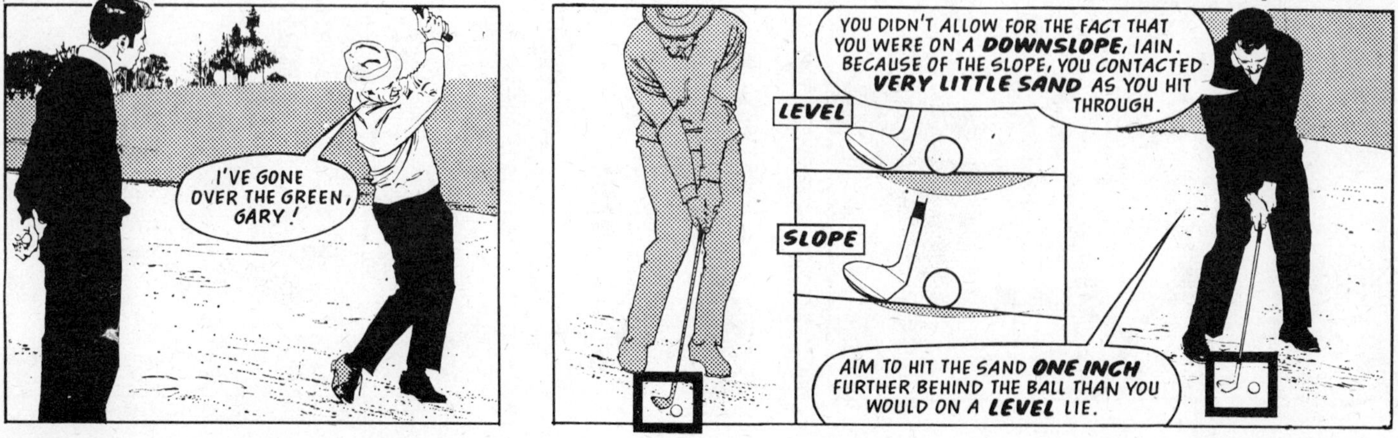

I'VE GONE OVER THE GREEN, GARY!
YOU DIDN'T ALLOW FOR THE FACT THAT YOU WERE ON A DOWNSLOPE, IAIN. BECAUSE OF THE SLOPE, YOU CONTACTED VERY LITTLE SAND AS YOU HIT THROUGH.
LEVEL
SLOPE
AIM TO HIT THE SAND ONE INCH FURTHER BEHIND THE BALL THAN YOU WOULD ON A LEVEL LIE.

Beware hard bunkers

YOU HAD A FULL BACKSWING AND A FULL FOLLOW-THROUGH WITH THE RESULT THAT YOU CAME DOWN VERY FAST INTO THE SHOT AND THE CLUB SKIDDED AND BOUNCED AT TREMENDOUS SPEED. NATURALLY, THE BALL SHOT OUT FURTHER THAN YOU WANTED IT TO!

WHEN THERE'S A SHORTAGE OF SAND AND THE GROUND IS VERY HARD, I TAKE A SHORTER BACKSWING IN ORDER TO CUT DOWN THE CLUBHEAD SPEED AND THE SPEED AT WHICH THE CLUB WILL BOUNCE AT THE BALL

Maintain the level

THAT IS A TERRIBLE LIE YOU HAVE IN THE BUNKER, TOM, AND YOU ARE APPROACHING THE SHOT ALL WRONG!
YOU WILL PROBABLY HIT THE BALL CLEAN BECAUSE YOUR LEGS ARE TOO STRAIGHT AND YOU ARE GRIPPING THE SAND-WEDGE TOO SHORT!
THIS IS ONE TIME WHEN THE CLUB MUST BE HELD RIGHT AT THE END. COME AS CLOSE AS YOU CAN TO THE BALL AND REALLY BEND THOSE KNEES.
MAINTAIN THE LEVEL OF THE KNEES AS YOU PLAY THE SHOT.
THIS ENABLES YOU TO STAY DOWN AND HIT BEHIND THE BALL.

Don't restrict your hands

YOU ARE SO CRAMPED, YOUR HANDS ARE ALMOST RESTING ON YOUR KNEES!
IAIN, YOU'RE 40 FEET FROM THE FLAG SO THIS IS A VERY LONG BUNKER SHOT - AND YOU ARE MAKING THE COMMON MISTAKES OF STANDING TOO CLOSE TO THE BALL AND GRIPPING THE CLUB FAR TOO SHORT!
NOW, WHEN YOU PLAY THE SHOT, YOUR KNEES GET IN THE WAY OF YOUR HANDS AND YOU ARE UNABLE TO HIT ACROSS THE BALL IN THE RECOMMENDED MANNER
FOR A LONG BUNKER SHOT I STAND FAR ENOUGH AWAY FROM THE BALL TO GIVE MY HANDS ROOM TO TRAVEL ACROSS THE BALL FROM OUT TO IN!
I PLAY THIS SHOT WITH A LONG, LAZY SWING, ACCELERATING THROUGH AND ACROSS THE BALL INTO A WIDE FOLLOW-THROUGH. IT IS IMPORTANT TO REMEMBER THAT, IN THE LONG BUNKER SHOT, THE RHYTHM MUST BE SLOW!

Short, medium and long bunker shots

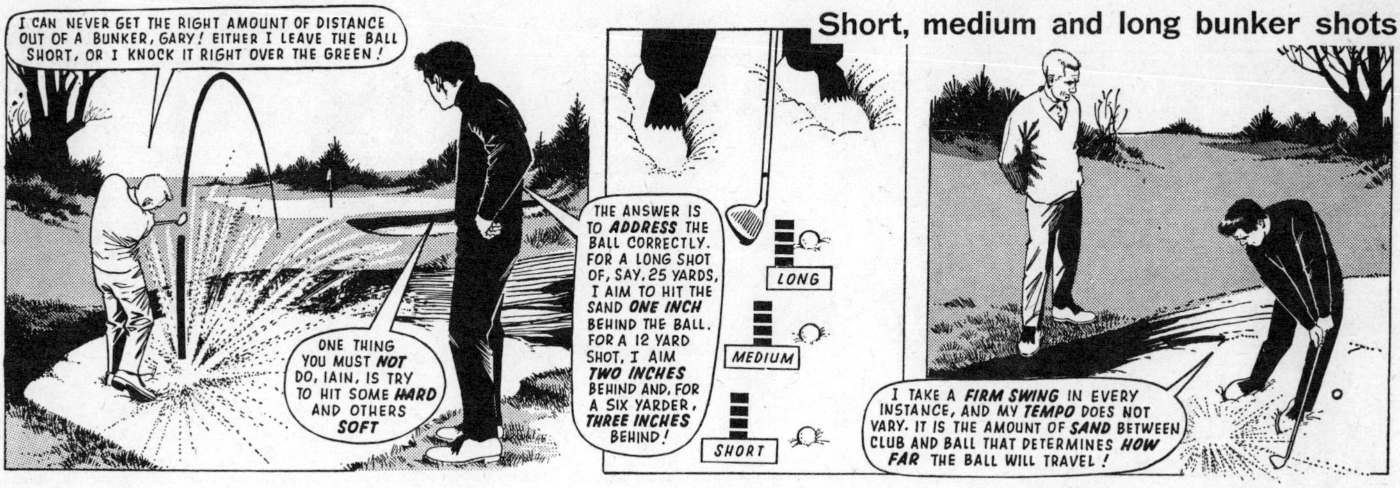
I CAN NEVER GET THE RIGHT AMOUNT OF DISTANCE OUT OF A BUNKER, GARY! EITHER I LEAVE THE BALL SHORT, OR I KNOCK IT RIGHT OVER THE GREEN!
ONE THING YOU MUST NOT DO, IAIN, IS TRY TO HIT SOME HARD AND OTHERS SOFT
THE ANSWER IS TO ADDRESS THE BALL CORRECTLY. FOR A LONG SHOT OF, SAY, 25 YARDS, I AIM TO HIT THE SAND ONE INCH BEHIND THE BALL. FOR A 12 YARD SHOT, I AIM TWO INCHES BEHIND AND, FOR A SIX YARDER, THREE INCHES BEHIND!
LONG
MEDIUM
SHORT
I TAKE A FIRM SWING IN EVERY INSTANCE, AND MY TEMPO DOES NOT VARY. IT IS THE AMOUNT OF SAND BETWEEN CLUB AND BALL THAT DETERMINES HOW FAR THE BALL WILL TRAVEL!

A long shot from a bunker

YOU WILL NEVER REACH THE GREEN WITH A 6-IRON, IAIN. TAKE A 4-WOOD
WHAT? A WOOD OUT OF A BUNKER?
YES, WHY NOT? THIS FAIRWAY BUNKER'S GOT NO REAL BANK TO IT SO, EVEN IF YOU TOP THE BALL, IT WILL RUN OUT ALL RIGHT... AND A TOPPED WOOD WILL NEARLY ALWAYS TRAVEL FURTHER THAN A WELL HIT 6-IRON
YOU MUST HIT THIS SHOT CLEANLY SO ADDRESS THE BALL OPPOSITE YOUR LEFT TOE. YOU WILL THEN STRIKE THE BALL ON THE UPSWING AND NOT GET TOO MUCH SAND BETWEEN IT AND THE CLUB FACE
ALSO REMEMBER TO SHUFFLE YOUR FEET INTO THE SAND SO THAT YOU HAVE A VERY FIRM FOOTING
HIT BALL CLEANLY

The toughest shot in golf

IT DIDN'T REACH THE GREEN, GARY!
DON'T BE TOO DESPONDENT, IAIN. YOU WERE FACED WITH THE TOUGHEST SHOT IN GOLF... THE LONG BUNKER SHOT. NOBODY IN THE WORLD CAN BLAST OUT FROM 60 YARDS AND CONSISTENTLY GET THE BALL WITHIN 10 FEET OF THE HOLE!
THIS IS ONE BUNKER SHOT WHERE I DO NOT USE A SAND WEDGE. AS I REQUIRE DISTANCE, I USE A PITCHING WEDGE WITH THE BLADE SQUARE TO THE TARGET, NOT OPEN. I ALSO ADDRESS THE BALL OPPOSITE MY RIGHT LEG AS THIS ENABLES ME TO HIT THE BALL LOWER AND THEREFORE FARTHER
I AM VERY CONSCIOUS OF THE NEED TO FOLLOW RIGHT THROUGH THE BALL. YOUR FOLLOW-THROUGH WAS MUCH TOO SHORT, IAIN
I THINK THESE FAIRWAY TRAPS 50-60 YARDS SHORT OF THE GREEN ARE VERY UNFAIR AS IT IS ONLY THE WEEKENDERS WHO VISIT THEM. WE HAVE MANY SUCH TRAPS IN SOUTH AFRICA. AND I BELIEVE THEY REFLECT BADLY ON THE OLD-TIME GOLF ARCHITECTS

Too much club

TOO MUCH CLUB, TOM!
IT'S ONLY AN 8-IRON, GARY!
FOR A LONG, FAIRWAY BUNKER SHOT, YOU SHOULD TAKE ONE CLUB LESS THAN YOU WOULD TAKE OFF TURF BECAUSE YOU WILL AUTOMATICALLY PLACE YOUR HANDS WELL IN FRONT OF THE BALL TO AVOID HITTING THE SAND BEHIND IT.
THIS SHUTS THE CLUBFACE AND TURNS A 9-IRON INTO AN 8-IRON.
9-IRON
AS THE BODYWEIGHT SHIFTS FORWARD, THE BALL IS SQUEEZED OUT AND FLIES IN A FAIRLY LOW TRAJECTORY
SQUEEZE

Getting height off a downslope

WHEN PLAYING OFF A DOWNSLOPE, IAIN, REMEMBER THAT THE BALL WILL TEND TO HAVE A LOW TRAJECTORY. SO, THE PROBLEM HERE IS TO GET ENOUGH HEIGHT TO CLEAR THE BUNKER
THEREFORE, I ADDRESS THE BALL WITH THE FACE OF MY SAND WEDGE OPEN AND THREE INCHES BEHIND THE BALL INSTEAD OF THE USUAL TWO
MY HANDS ARE IN FRONT OF THE BALL WHICH IS OPPOSITE MY RIGHT LEG. MY RIGHT KNEE IS IN
HANDS IN FRONT OF BALL
RIGHT KNEE IN
CLUB FACE OPEN
BALL OPPOSITE RIGHT LEG
I HIT DOWN INTO THE BALL AND GO THROUGH AS BEST I CAN WITH THE CLUB FACE OPEN, KEEPING MY HEAD VERY, VERY WELL DOWN
REMEMBER YOU WON'T BE ABLE TO GET THE BALL TO GO AS HIGH AS YOU WOULD LIKE, SO DON'T EXPECT IT TO STOP IMMEDIATELY! YOU MUST ALLOW FOR IT TO ROLL UP TO THE FLAG

Mind that slope

YOU HIT THAT BUNKER SHOT QUITE WELL, IAIN, BUT YOU MADE ONE BAD MISTAKE. YOU AIMED DIRECTLY AT THE PIN!
ON ALL SHOTS, WHEN THE BALL IS ABOVE THE LEVEL OF YOUR FEET, YOU MUST ALLOW FOR THE FACT IT IS GOING TO HOOK!
FOR A 20 YARD BUNKER SHOT LIKE THIS, I WOULD AIM ABOUT THREE YARDS TO THE RIGHT OF THE FLAG TO COMPENSATE FOR THE INEVITABLE HOOK
AN UPRIGHT SWING WILL MAKE ME HOOK THE BALL LESS, SO I GRIP MY SAND-IRON VERY, VERY SHORT
I PICK UP THE CLUB SHARPLY ON THE BACKSWING... IN OTHER WORDS, I COCK MY WRISTS IMMEDIATELY. NOW, ALL THAT REMAINS, IS TO MAKE SURE I GO RIGHT THROUGH THE SAND... NO QUITTING ON THE STROKE!

A simple way out of a bunker

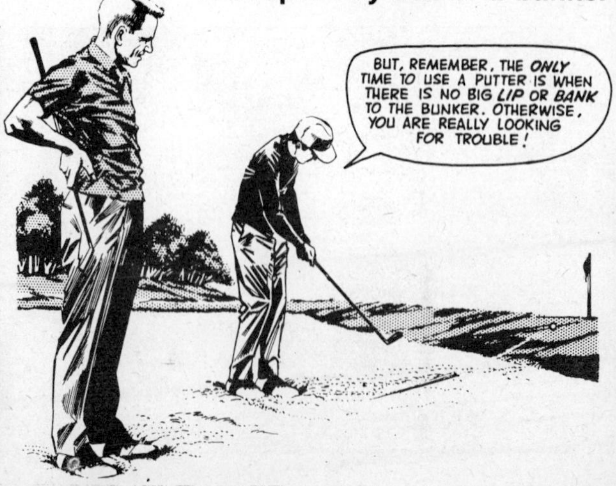

ALTHOUGH I PERSONALLY WOULD ALWAYS USE A SAND WEDGE AND BLAST OUT OF A BUNKER, YOU COULD HAVE GOT OUT OF THIS SHALLOW ONE QUITE SUCCESSFULLY USING A PUTTER

BUT, REMEMBER, THE ONLY TIME TO USE A PUTTER IS WHEN THERE IS NO BIG LIP OR BANK TO THE BUNKER. OTHERWISE, YOU ARE REALLY LOOKING FOR TROUBLE!

Putting out of a bunker

I PLAYED WITH GEORGE ARCHER IN A TOURNAMENT AT DORAL THIS YEAR, TOM, AND THREE TIMES HE PUTTED OUT OF A BUNKER AND LEFT THE BALL EXACTLY SIX FEET SHORT!
WELL, I'M IN GOOD COMPANY!
I AM SURE HE TOOK INTO CONSIDERATION THE FACT THAT THE SAND WOULD SLOW DOWN HIS BALL, BUT HE MAY NOT HAVE CONSIDERED THE SLOPE OUT OF THE BUNKER. THIS ALSO HAS A BRAKING EFFECT ON THE BALL.
YOU MUST REMEMBER BOTH FACTORS. GIVE IT A LITTLE EXTRA FOR THE SAND AND ADD A LITTLE BIT MORE FOR THE SLOPE.

Buried lie

WHEN THE BALL IS BURIED IN SAND, I ADDRESS IT IN THE CENTRE OF MY FEET WITH THE CLUB-FACE REASONABLY SQUARE—NOT TOO WIDE OPEN
MY HANDS ARE IN FRONT OF THE BALL SO THAT I CAN PICK UP THE CLUB SHARPLY AND HIT DOWN INTO THE SAND
WRISTS MUST BREAK QUICKLY
THIS IS ONE BUNKER SHOT WHERE I ONLY WANT A SHORT FOLLOW-THROUGH LIKE THIS
THERE IS NO WAY IN THE WORLD TO GET BACKSPIN OUT OF A BURIED LIE. THE SAND BETWEEN CLUB-FACE AND BALL ALWAYS IMPARTS TOPSPIN...
...SO I AIM TO POP THE BALL ONTO THE GREEN, AND ALLOW FOR IT TO RUN UP TO THE HOLE
FOLLOW THROUGH STOPS HERE

Let's have smooth bunkers

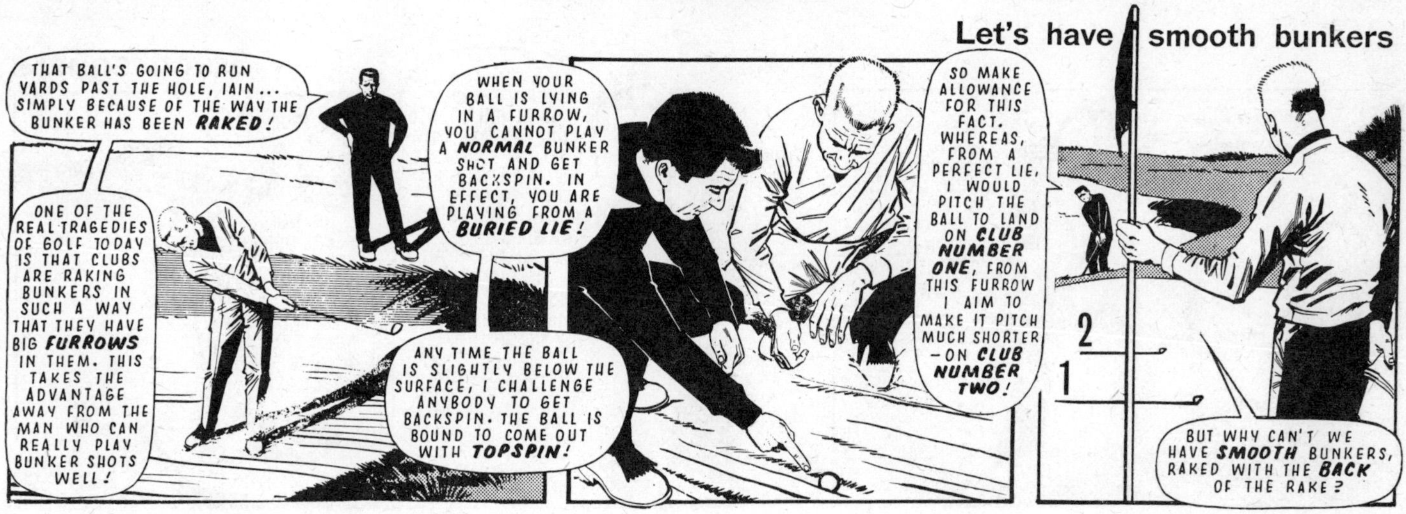

THAT BALL'S GOING TO RUN YARDS PAST THE HOLE, IAIN... SIMPLY BECAUSE OF THE WAY THE BUNKER HAS BEEN RAKED!
ONE OF THE REAL TRAGEDIES OF GOLF TODAY IS THAT CLUBS ARE RAKING BUNKERS IN SUCH A WAY THAT THEY HAVE BIG FURROWS IN THEM. THIS TAKES THE ADVANTAGE AWAY FROM THE MAN WHO CAN REALLY PLAY BUNKER SHOTS WELL!
WHEN YOUR BALL IS LYING IN A FURROW, YOU CANNOT PLAY A NORMAL BUNKER SHOT AND GET BACKSPIN. IN EFFECT, YOU ARE PLAYING FROM A BURIED LIE!
ANY TIME THE BALL IS SLIGHTLY BELOW THE SURFACE, I CHALLENGE ANYBODY TO GET BACKSPIN. THE BALL IS BOUND TO COME OUT WITH TOPSPIN!
SO MAKE ALLOWANCE FOR THIS FACT. WHEREAS, FROM A PERFECT LIE, I WOULD PITCH THE BALL TO LAND ON CLUB NUMBER ONE, FROM THIS FURROW I AIM TO MAKE IT PITCH MUCH SHORTER —ON CLUB NUMBER TWO!
2
1
BUT WHY CAN'T WE HAVE SMOOTH BUNKERS, RAKED WITH THE BACK OF THE RAKE?

SECTION SIX

Chipping

How to chip successfully

THE WORST THING YOU CAN DO WITH THESE LITTLE CHIP SHOTS FROM THE EDGE OF THE GREEN IS TO SCOOP THEM, IAIN
WHEN YOU BREAK YOUR LEFT WRIST LIKE THAT, YOU WILL NEARLY ALWAYS HIT BEHIND THE BALL AND FLUB THE SHOT
FAULT
THE WAY TO PLAY THIS SHOT IS TO HIT DOWN ON THE BALL, TRUSTING THE LOFT OF THE CLUB TO LIFT THE BALL INTO THE AIR
5-IRON
WHEN YOU ARE FURTHER BACK FROM THE GREEN, ALL YOU DO IS TAKE A MORE LOFTED CLUB. BUT IT DOES NOT MATTER WHETHER YOU ARE PLAYING A 5-IRON, A SEVEN OR A WEDGE – ON ALL CHIP SHOTS YOU MUST HIT DOWN!
5-IRON
7-IRON
WEDGE
I TELL YOU, IAIN, THIS TIP WILL REALLY HELP WEEKENDERS ROUND THE GREEN!

Stand square

ALTHOUGH IT IS ALL RIGHT TO STAND OPEN WHEN YOU CHIP, IAIN, I THINK IT IS PREVENTING YOU FROM MAKING SQUARE CONTACT WITH THE BALL
AS YOU ARE CHIPPING BADLY, I THINK YOU SHOULD CONCENTRATE ON GETTING YOUR FEET SQUARE TO THE INTENDED LINE. IF YOU HAVE TO HIT THE SHOT THREE FEET TO THE RIGHT OF THE FLAG THEN YOUR FEET SHOULD AIM THREE FEET TO THE RIGHT
IF THE SLOPE DEMANDS YOU START THE BALL OUT TWO FEET LEFT OF THE HOLE, THEN MAKE SURE YOUR FEET ARE AIMING TWO FEET LEFT

Open stance—not shoulders!

YOU'RE LEAVING YOUR CHIP SHOTS YARDS SHORT, IAIN, BECAUSE YOUR BODY IS TOO OPEN AT ADDRESS
I THOUGHT IT WAS CORRECT TO CHIP WITH AN OPEN STANCE, GARY?
AN OPEN STANCE, YES, BUT YOU ARE OPENING UP EVERYTHING TOO WIDE! A LINE ACROSS YOUR SHOULDERS POINTS FAR TOO MUCH LEFT OF TARGET. THIS MAKES YOU CUT ACROSS THE BALL SO MUCH IT'S HARD TO GET IT UP TO THE HOLE!
OPEN
WHEN CHIPPING, I MAKE SURE THAT ALTHOUGH MY FEET ARE OPEN, MY SHOULDERS AND HIPS ARE ONLY VERY SLIGHTLY OPEN. CONSEQUENTLY, I CAN GET SOME CRISPNESS INTO THE SHOT
OPEN

Consistent chipping

IAIN, YOU WILL NEVER CHIP WELL IF YOU ADDRESS THE SHOT WITH YOUR HANDS BEHIND THE BALL
THERE IS A STRONG LIKELIHOOD THAT THE FLANGE WILL CONTACT THE TURF BEHIND THE BALL. IF THIS HAPPENS THE CLUB WILL BOUNCE AND YOU WILL PROBABLY DUFF THE SHOT!
FLANGE
I KEEP MY HANDS WELL AHEAD OF THE BALL WHEN CHIPPING TO PREVENT THIS BOUNCING AND TO ENSURE THAT THE THIN, LEADING EDGE OF THE BLADE STRIKES THE BALL FIRST. THIS IS THE ONLY WAY TO GET CONSISTENCY IN CHIPPING!

Nail that left foot

MY CHIPPING IS TERRIBLY INCONSISTENT, GARY!
YOU'LL NEVER BE CONSISTENT AS LONG AS YOUR BODY IS LOOSE AS A GOOSE, IAIN! YOU WILL GET NO FIRMNESS IN YOUR SHOTS!
ALSO, BY HAVING YOUR WEIGHT FAVORING YOUR RIGHT SIDE YOU WILL BE INCLINED TO HIT THE BALL ON THE UPSWING
THROUGHOUT THE CHIP SHOT, I GET THE FEELING THAT MY LEFT FOOT IS NAILED TO THE GROUND AND MY ENTIRE WEIGHT IS ON IT
THE LEFT FOOT THEN BECOMES THE AXIS ROUND WHICH THE SWING REVOLVES. THIS FIRMS UP THE SWING AND KEEPS IT UNDER CONTROL. IT ALSO INSURES THAT I HIT DOWN ON THE BALL, INSTEAD OF SCOOPING!

A weak chipping grip

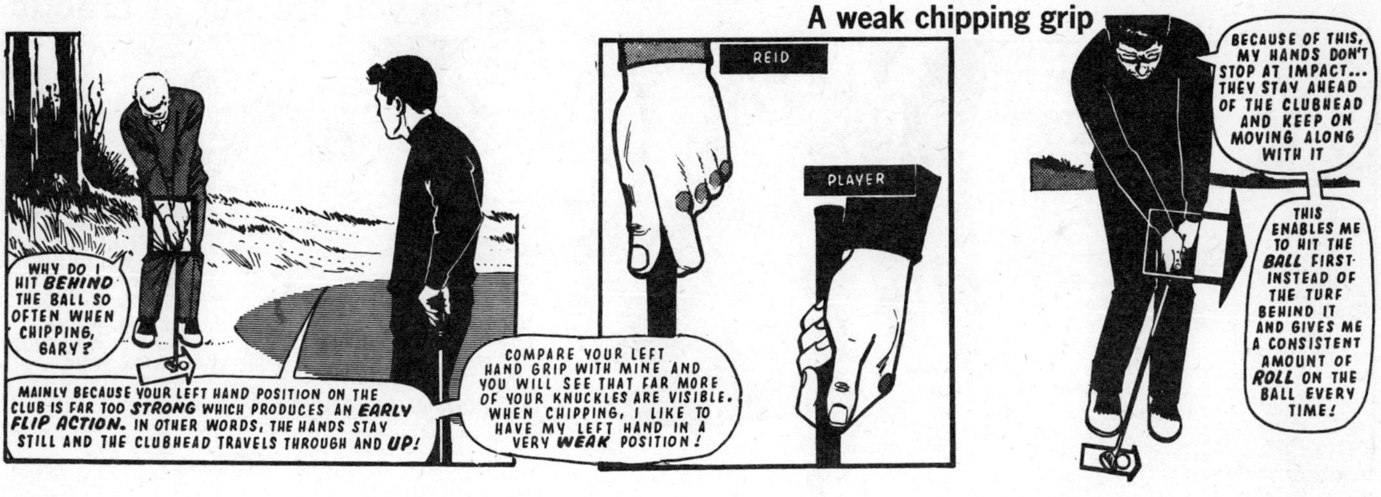

WHY DO I HIT BEHIND THE BALL SO OFTEN WHEN CHIPPING, GARY?
MAINLY BECAUSE YOUR LEFT HAND POSITION ON THE CLUB IS FAR TOO STRONG WHICH PRODUCES AN EARLY FLIP ACTION. IN OTHER WORDS, THE HANDS STAY STILL AND THE CLUBHEAD TRAVELS THROUGH AND UP!
REID
PLAYER
COMPARE YOUR LEFT HAND GRIP WITH MINE AND YOU WILL SEE THAT FAR MORE OF YOUR KNUCKLES ARE VISIBLE. WHEN CHIPPING, I LIKE TO HAVE MY LEFT HAND IN A VERY WEAK POSITION!
BECAUSE OF THIS, MY HANDS DON'T STOP AT IMPACT... THEY STAY AHEAD OF THE CLUBHEAD AND KEEP ON MOVING ALONG WITH IT
THIS ENABLES ME TO HIT THE BALL FIRST INSTEAD OF THE TURF BEHIND IT AND GIVES ME A CONSISTENT AMOUNT OF ROLL ON THE BALL EVERY TIME!

Two chipping methods

GARY, DO YOU THINK IT IS A GOOD THING TO CHIP STIFF-WRISTED LIKE THIS- OR SHOULD THERE ALWAYS BE A LITTLE BIT OF WRIST-BREAK?
STIFF WRISTS
I WOULDN'T LIKE TO BE ADAMANT ABOUT THIS, IAIN! PERSONALLY, I LIKE TO BREAK MY WRISTS BUT I DON'T SAY THAT IS THE ONLY WAY TO CHIP!
GOOD LIE
BAD LIE
STIFF WRISTS
HOWEVER, ONLY CHIP STIFF-WRISTED IF YOU HAVE A PERFECT LIE. IF YOU TRY TO DO IT WITH A BAD LIE, YOU WILL HIT THE MIDDLE OF THE BALL AND NOT GET HOLD OF IT PROPERLY!
WHEN YOUR BALL IS LYING BADLY, THERE IS ONLY ONE WAY TO CHIP ...YOU MUST BREAK YOUR WRISTS ON THE BACKSWING
WRIST BREAK
THEN, YOU WILL HIT DOWN ON THE BALL AND VERY EASILY CHOP IT OUT OF ITS BAD LIE

Chip with your hands

YOU HAVE SO MUCH BODY MOVEMENT WHEN YOU ARE CHIPPING, YOU ARE NOT USING YOUR HANDS AT ALL, IAIN!
IN ORDER TO HIT A SOLID CHIP, YOU MUST KEEP THE BODY STILL AND LET THE HANDS DO THE WORK
ANYONE WHO IS A POOR CHIPPER SHOULD TRY STANDING PIGEON-TOED
THIS CURTAILS THE BODY MOVEMENT AND ALLOWS THE ARMS TO CONTROL THE SHOT. THIS STANCE ALSO HELPS THE CLUBHEAD TO GO THROUGH VERY SQUARE

Chip as you putt

CORK
CHIPPING AND PUTTING ARE BASICALLY THE SAME ACTION. ANYONE WHO IS A POOR CHIPPER SHOULD PRACTISE WITH HIS 8-IRON TIED TO HIS PUTTER
ADDRESS TWO BALLS TOGETHER THEN CONCENTRATE SOLELY ON PUTTING BALL NUMBER ONE UP TO THE HOLE
1
2
IF YOU HIT YOUR PUTT WELL, YOU WILL FIND THAT YOU ALSO CHIP THE SECOND BALL WELL
THIS IS THE QUICKEST WAY TO PROVE TO YOURSELF THAT THE PUTTING ACTION IS IDEAL FOR CHIPPING

When you are out of practice

I FIND WHEN I AM OUT OF PRACTICE, GARY, THAT MY CHIPPING SUFFERS PARTICULARLY BADLY. I SEEM TO HIT EVERYTHING "FAT"!
YOU CERTAINLY HIT AN INCH BEHIND THAT ONE, IAIN!
LOOK HERE
WHEN YOUR CHIPPING IS A BIT RUSTY, IT PAYS TO GET THE HANDS WELL FORWARD. YOU SHOULD ALSO MAKE A CONSCIOUS EFFORT OF LOOKING AT THE FRONT OF THE BALL
THIS WILL DEFINITELY HELP YOU TO HIT THE BALL FIRST INSTEAD OF THE TURF BEHIND IT AND YOU WILL SOON REGAIN YOUR TOUCH AND YOUR CONFIDENCE

Don't ground your club

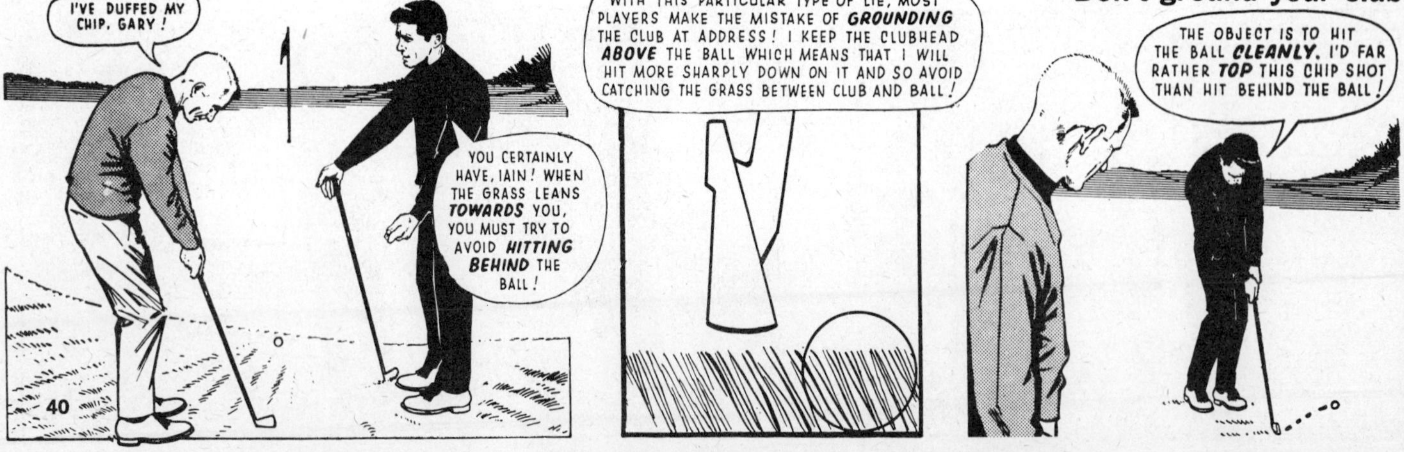

I'VE DUFFED MY CHIP, GARY!
YOU CERTAINLY HAVE, IAIN! WHEN THE GRASS LEANS TOWARDS YOU, YOU MUST TRY TO AVOID HITTING BEHIND THE BALL!
WITH THIS PARTICULAR TYPE OF LIE, MOST PLAYERS MAKE THE MISTAKE OF GROUNDING THE CLUB AT ADDRESS! I KEEP THE CLUBHEAD ABOVE THE BALL WHICH MEANS THAT I WILL HIT MORE SHARPLY DOWN ON IT AND SO AVOID CATCHING THE GRASS BETWEEN CLUB AND BALL!
THE OBJECT IS TO HIT THE BALL CLEANLY. I'D FAR RATHER TOP THIS CHIP SHOT THAN HIT BEHIND THE BALL!

A difficult chip shot

THAT WASN'T AN EASY CHIP SHOT, TOM! THE ROUGH GRASS STOPPED YOUR CLUBHEAD GOING THROUGH THE BALL!
THERE WAS A LOT OF ROUGH AROUND THE GREENS IN THE P.G.A. CHAMPIONSHIP AT WEST PALM BEACH THIS YEAR AND MY BROTHER-IN-LAW, BOBBY VERWEY, SUGGESTED I SHOULD PLAY THESE CHIPS WITH A SHORTER BACKSWING.
SHORT
BY REDUCING MY BACKSWING, I WAS SUBCONSCIOUSLY AWARE OF THE NEED TO HIT RIGHT THROUGH THE GRASS IN ORDER TO GET THE BALL UP TO THE HOLE. I PLAYED THIS SHOT PRETTY WELL IN THE TOURNAMENT.

A real tough one

YOU'VE GOT A DIFFICULT SHOT HERE, IAIN... PLAYING OFF A SEVERE DOWNSLOPE OVER A BUNKER. AND WITH THE FLAG ONLY TEN YARDS AWAY, BOY, THAT MAKES IT REALLY TOUGH!
BUT GIVE YOURSELF A CHANCE! DON'T ADDRESS THE BALL OPPOSITE YOUR LEFT LEG OR YOU'LL BE SURE TO HIT BEHIND IT AND DUFF THE SHOT
USING A SAND WEDGE, AS IT IS THE CLUB WITH MOST LOFT, I ADDRESS THE BALL OPPOSITE MY RIGHT LEG SO THAT I CAN MEET THE BALL FIRST
I PICK UP THE CLUB VERY SHARPLY ON THE BACKSWING AND HIT DOWN ON THE BALL. I THEN LET MY CLUB FOLLOW THE NATURAL SLOPE OF THE GROUND... IN OTHER WORDS, I GO LOW THROUGH THE BALL
DON'T EXPECT TO GET GREAT HEIGHT FROM THIS SHOT AS THE SLOPE OF THE GROUND HAS THE EFFECT OF TURNING A SAND WEDGE INTO ABOUT A 9-IRON!

Run your ball up to the hole

WHEN YOU ARE RIGHT ON THE EDGE OF THE GREEN, YOU SHOULD ALWAYS RUN THE BALL UP TO THE HOLE. THIS IS THE SAFETY SHOT
ANY GOLFER WHO PITCHES WITH A WEDGE OR 9-IRON FROM THE EDGE OF THE GREEN IS SIMPLY ASKING FOR TROUBLE, IAIN. SOMETIMES YOU WILL GET BACKSPIN ON YOUR BALL, AND SOMETIMES TOPSPIN! SO YOU NEVER KNOW WHETHER THE BALL IS GOING TO STOP OR RUN!
TAKE THE CLUB... SOMETIMES IT'LL BE A FOUR OR A FIVE-IRON... THAT WILL MAKE THE BALL PITCH ON THE FRONT EDGE OF THE GREEN, AND IT WILL RUN UP TO THE HOLE
IN THIS CASE, I WILL PLAY A CRISP LITTLE SHOT WITH A 6-IRON. I KNOW THAT THE BALL WILL RUN, AS I CANNOT POSSIBLY IMPART BACKSPIN!

Chipping from a depression

I DIDN'T THINK I HIT THAT CHIP VERY HARD, GARY, BUT IT'S RUN NINE FEET PAST!
YOUR BALL WAS LYING IN A SLIGHT DEPRESSION, IAIN. OBVIOUSLY, YOU CAUGHT SOME GRASS BETWEEN CLUBHEAD AND BALL WHICH, AS I HAVE TOLD YOU BEFORE, GIVES YOU TOPSPIN!

I ALSO TRY TO PITCH THE BALL A LITTLE SHORTER OUT OF A BAD LIE BECAUSE I CANNOT BE CERTAIN OF AVOIDING ALL THE GRASS BEHIND THE BALL!

Chipping out of long grass

WHEN YOU'RE IN LONG GRASS 'ROUND THE EDGE OF THE GREEN, YOU MUSTN'T SCOOP THE BALL OUT LIKE THAT, IAIN. YOU WON'T ACHIEVE CONSISTENTLY GOOD RESULTS THAT WAY
YOU'LL TEND TO GET LOTS OF GRASS SANDWICHED BETWEEN CLUBFACE AND BALL, AND YOU'LL NEARLY ALWAYS FLUFF THE SHOT
AT ADDRESS, I HAVE MY HANDS AHEAD OF THE BALL, AND MY WEIGHT FORWARD ON MY LEFT SIDE. THE REASON MY WEIGHT IS FORWARD IS TO MINIMIZE LEG AND BODY ACTION, AS THIS CHIP SHOT SHOULD BE PLAYED MAINLY WITH THE HANDS
WITH MY HEAD KEPT PARTICULARLY STEADY, AND MY HANDS DRIVING IN FRONT ALL THE TIME, I HIT DOWN AND THROUGH THE BALL
THIS GIVES ME A FIRM, CRISP SHOT AND ENSURES THAT I GET OUT OF THE GRASS CONSISTENTLY EVERY TIME

Chips that go to the right

WHY IS IT SO MANY OF MY CHIP SHOTS GO TO THE RIGHT, GARY?
THAT'S A COMMON FAULT OF THE HIGH-HANDICAP GOLFER, IAIN. IT IS CAUSED BY RISING UP ON THE SHOT!
WHEN YOU STRAIGHTEN UP, YOU ACTUALLY PULL AWAY FROM THE BALL WHICH MAKES YOU HIT IT WITH AN OPEN CLUBFACE. THEREFORE, THE BALL IS PUSHED TO THE RIGHT
CLUBHEAD TOO HIGH
WHEN CHIPPING, YOU MUST MAKE CERTAIN THAT YOU HIT THE BALL A DOWNWARD BLOW. TO ACHIEVE THIS, YOU MUST STAY DOWN... NO JUMPING UP!
IF YOU STAY DOWN AND HIT DOWN, YOUR CLUBHEAD WILL BE SQUARE, NOT OPEN, AT IMPACT AND THE BALL WILL TRAVEL STRAIGHT FORWARD
CLUBHEAD HUGS GROUND

SECTION SEVEN

Putting

Stand close

IF YOU STAND TOO FAR AWAY FROM THE BALL WHEN PUTTING, TOM, YOU ARE NOT ABLE TO SIGHT THE BALL CORRECTLY. ALSO, YOU WILL PROBABLY ROLL THE CLUB OPEN ON THE BACKSWING AND SHUT ON THE FOLLOW-THROUGH!
IDEALLY, YOU SHOULD STAND CLOSE ENOUGH SO THAT A VERTICAL LINE CAN BE DRAWN FROM YOUR EYE TO THE BALL.
THIS HELPS YOU TO AIM CORRECTLY AND AUTOMATICALLY KEEPS THE CLUBHEAD MORE SQUARE THROUGHOUT THE PUTTING STROKE.

Keep the putter low and slow

IT'S RIGHT TO HAVE YOUR HANDS IN FRONT OF THE BALL... WHEN PUTTING, TOM, BUT YOURS ARE TOO FAR IN FRONT
ALSO, BY HAVING YOUR WEIGHT ON YOUR LEFT SIDE, YOU WILL CHOP DOWN ON THE BALL AND HAVE NO FOLLOW-THROUGH
WEIGHT MUST BE EVENLY DISTRIBUTED. YOU MUST FEEL COMFORTABLE AND, ABOVE ALL, YOU MUST HAVE CONFIDENCE THAT YOU CAN MAKE THE PUTT
THE PUTTER MUST BE VERY CLOSE TO THE GROUND ON THE BACKSWING AND THE FOLLOW-THROUGH. SO REMEMBER, KEEP THE PUTTER LOW AND SLOW!

How to control the putter

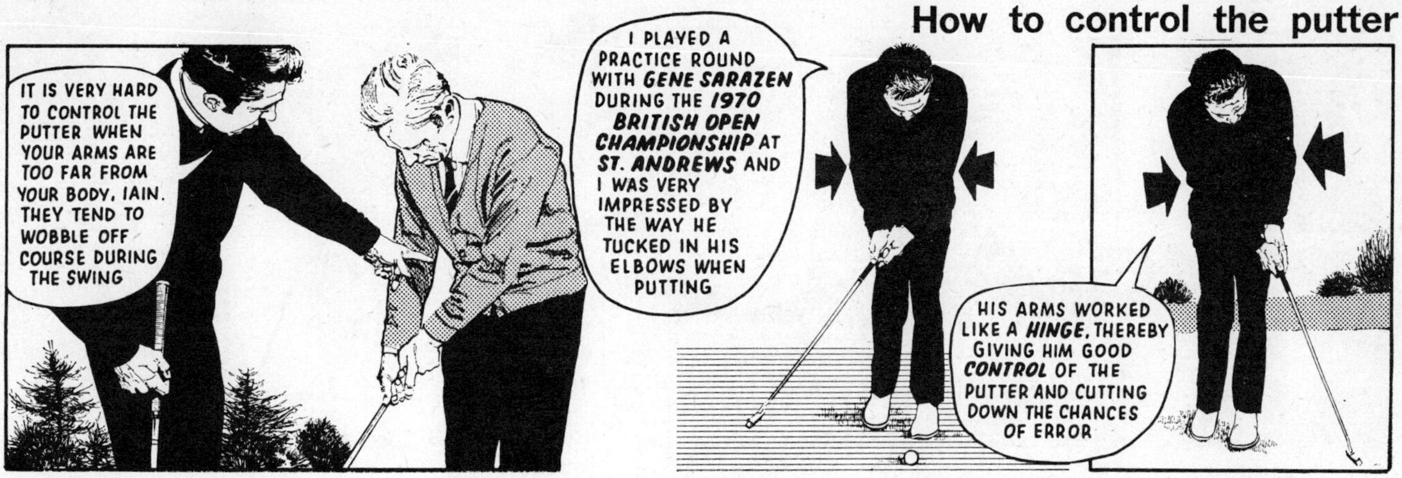
IT IS VERY HARD TO CONTROL THE PUTTER WHEN YOUR ARMS ARE TOO FAR FROM YOUR BODY, IAIN. THEY TEND TO WOBBLE OFF COURSE DURING THE SWING
I PLAYED A PRACTICE ROUND WITH GENE SARAZEN DURING THE 1970 BRITISH OPEN CHAMPIONSHIP AT ST. ANDREWS AND I WAS VERY IMPRESSED BY THE WAY HE TUCKED IN HIS ELBOWS WHEN PUTTING
HIS ARMS WORKED LIKE A HINGE, THEREBY GIVING HIM GOOD CONTROL OF THE PUTTER AND CUTTING DOWN THE CHANCES OF ERROR

Lock your body

YOU HAVE FAR TOO MUCH BODY MOVEMENT, IAIN. HOW CAN YOU EXPECT TO PUTT WELL?
HERE IS A TIP THAT WILL HELP YOU TO SINK THOSE VITAL PUTTS. FIRST, TAKE YOUR NORMAL STANCE
NOW LOCK YOUR BODY BY BENDING YOUR LEFT KNEE IN TOWARDS YOUR RIGHT
THIS REALLY CUTS DOWN BODY MOVEMENT AND IS ONE OF THE QUICKEST WAYS I KNOW TO IMPROVE YOUR PUTTING

Think positive, play positive

YOU MUST GET YOUR BALL UP TO THE HOLE, IAIN
BUT I'VE ALWAYS BEEN TOLD TO LEAVE IT A FOOT SHORT ON UPHILL PUTTS, GARY, SO THAT THERE'S NO CHANCE OF HAVING TO PUTT DOWNHILL!
WHAT A LOAD OF NONSENSE! IT'S LIKE BEING AFRAID TO HIT A SIX-IRON TO A WELL-GUARDED GREEN, SO YOU HIT A SEVEN-IRON SHORT, AND HOPE TO GET DOWN IN A CHIP AND A PUTT
WELL, IF YOU'RE GOING TO CHIP AND PUTT FOR A LIVING... YOU'LL STARVE!
I BELIEVE IN POSITIVE THINKING, SO I ALWAYS GIVE IT A GO! IF I'M GOING TO GET INTO TROUBLE, OKAY, I'LL GET INTO TROUBLE... BUT NEXT WEEK I'LL WIN!
ALL I WANT TO BE CONCERNED ABOUT IS WINNING, SO A NEGATIVE APPROACH IS NO DAMN GOOD AT ALL!

How to get the correct line

OCCASIONALLY, THERE ARE HIDDEN SLOPES WHICH THE NAKED EYE CAN'T DETECT, TOM, SO, IN ORDER TO FIND THE LINE, I USE MY PUTTER LIKE A SURVEYOR'S PLUMB LINE
SHOW ME HOW!
HOLD THE PUTTER PARALLEL TO THE FLAGSTICK WHICH MUST BE PERPENDICULAR. WITH ONLY YOUR MAJOR EYE* OPEN MAKE THE EDGE OF THE SHAFT CUT THE BALL IN HALF
NOW, THE GAP BETWEEN THE FLAGSTICK AND THE EDGE OF YOUR PUTTER SHOWS THE AMOUNT OF BORROW YOU MUST ALLOW FOR. THIS METHOD NEVER FAILS TO GIVE YOU THE RIGHT LINE
AIM HERE
* TO FIND YOUR MAJOR EYE, HOLD UP ONE FINGER IN LINE WITH A CERTAIN OBJECT. CLOSE EACH EYE IN TURN. WHEN YOU CLOSE YOUR MAJOR EYE, FINGER WILL APPEAR TO MOVE TO SIDE

Choose a little spot when putting

I THINK I READ THAT PUTT CORRECTLY, GARY, BUT WHEN I BENT OVER THE BALL TO PLAY IT, I JUST COULDN'T RETAIN A MENTAL PICTURE OF THE LINE
IT'S HARD TO KEEP A PICTURE OF THE WHOLE LINE IN YOUR HEAD, IAIN
MARK ON GRASS
WHEN YOU ARE LINING UP YOUR PUTT YOU SHOULD PICK OUT A LITTLE SPOT OR MARK ON THE LINE, NOT MORE THAN A FOOT IN FRONT OF YOU
THEN HIT THE BALL OVER THAT SPOT AND YOU WILL KNOW THAT YOU ARE STARTING THE BALL OUT ON THE RIGHT LINE
LOTS OF PEOPLE MAKE THE MISTAKE OF CHOOSING SPOTS 10 FEET OR SO AWAY. BUT, OBVIOUSLY, IT IS EASIER TO PICK OUT A SPOT AND HIT OVER IT WHEN IT IS WITHIN A FOOT OF WHERE YOU ARE STANDING

How to read a green

I CAN'T MAKE UP MY MIND WHICH WAY THIS GREEN SLOPES, GARY!
I'M NOT SURE EITHER, IAIN, BUT I WOULD PLUMP FOR A SLIGHT RIGHT TO LEFT BREAK
WHEN YOU HAVE DIFFICULTY READING A GREEN, IT IS A FAIR BET THAT IT SLOPES IN THE SAME DIRECTION AS THE NEIGHBORING TERRAIN. YOU CAN SEE THAT IT IS VERY DEFINITELY RIGHT TO LEFT. SO TAKE A CHANCE AND AIM FOR THE RIGHT LIP OF THE CUP
CONGRATULATIONS, IAIN! AT LAST, YOU'VE ACTUALLY DONE SOMETHING CORRECT!
IT'S IN!

Look closely at the hole

WHY DO YOU LOOK INTO THE HOLE BEFORE PUTTING, GARY?
I WANT TO KNOW WHICH SIDE OF THE HOLE IS WORN, AS THIS IS WHERE THE BALLS HAVE BEEN HITTING BEFORE DROPPING INTO IT! THIS CAN TELL ME HOW TO AIM AND HOW HARD TO HIT MY PUTT
THIS HOLE IS WORN AT THE RIGHT WHICH MEANS THAT PUTTS FROM THE LEFT HAVE BEEN TRAVELLING FAST AND HITTING THE FAR SIDE OF THE HOLE
FAST
ON THE OTHER HAND, PUTTS FROM THE RIGHT HAVE BEEN SLOWER. THEY HAVE JUST BEEN REACHING THE HOLE AND DROPPING IN
SLOWER
WORN HERE
PUTTS FROM ABOVE THE HOLE HAVE OBVIOUSLY BEEN PUSHED FROM RIGHT TO LEFT BY THE GRAIN
AIM
AND PUTTS FROM BELOW THE HOLE HAVE TURNED FROM LEFT TO RIGHT
AIM

Don't change your mind

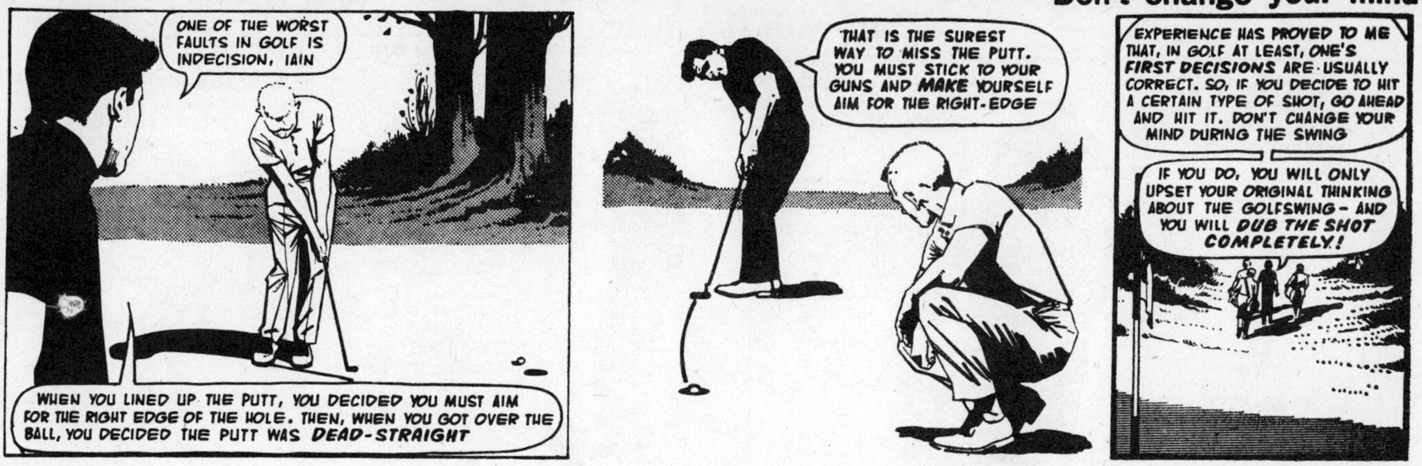

ONE OF THE WORST FAULTS IN GOLF IS INDECISION, IAIN
WHEN YOU LINED UP THE PUTT, YOU DECIDED YOU MUST AIM FOR THE RIGHT EDGE OF THE HOLE. THEN, WHEN YOU GOT OVER THE BALL, YOU DECIDED THE PUTT WAS DEAD-STRAIGHT
THAT IS THE SUREST WAY TO MISS THE PUTT. YOU MUST STICK TO YOUR GUNS AND MAKE YOURSELF AIM FOR THE RIGHT-EDGE
EXPERIENCE HAS PROVED TO ME THAT, IN GOLF AT LEAST, ONE'S FIRST DECISIONS ARE USUALLY CORRECT. SO, IF YOU DECIDE TO HIT A CERTAIN TYPE OF SHOT, GO AHEAD AND HIT IT. DON'T CHANGE YOUR MIND DURING THE SWING
IF YOU DO, YOU WILL ONLY UPSET YOUR ORIGINAL THINKING ABOUT THE GOLFSWING - AND YOU WILL DUB THE SHOT COMPLETELY!

Two lines and a dot

I'VE BEEN WATCHING YOU VERY CLOSELY ALL AFTERNOON, TOM. YOU ARE DEFINITELY NOT HITTING THE BALL WITH THE SAME PART OF THE PUTTER BLADE EVERY TIME.
YOU ARE ALSO AIMING BADLY.
EVERY GOLFER SHOULD FIND OUT WHERE THE SWEET SPOT IS ON HIS PUTTER AND MARK IT WITH A LITTLE DOT. THEN HE SHOULD DRAW TWO LINES ON HIS PUTTER TO HELP HIM AIM CORRECTLY
IF THE PUTT IS ON THE LEFT, THE LINES MUST AIM TO THE LEFT AND VICE VERSA. THIS IS A GREAT AID.

Paint your putter

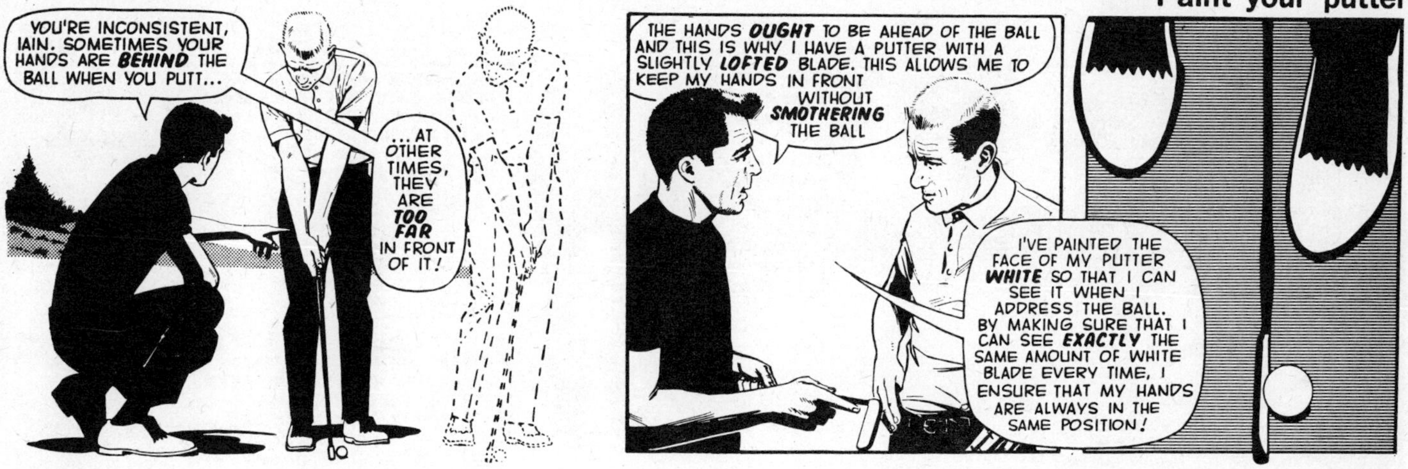

YOU'RE INCONSISTENT, IAIN. SOMETIMES YOUR HANDS ARE BEHIND THE BALL WHEN YOU PUTT...
...AT OTHER TIMES, THEY ARE TOO FAR IN FRONT OF IT!
THE HANDS OUGHT TO BE AHEAD OF THE BALL AND THIS IS WHY I HAVE A PUTTER WITH A SLIGHTLY LOFTED BLADE. THIS ALLOWS ME TO KEEP MY HANDS IN FRONT WITHOUT SMOTHERING THE BALL
I'VE PAINTED THE FACE OF MY PUTTER WHITE SO THAT I CAN SEE IT WHEN I ADDRESS THE BALL. BY MAKING SURE THAT I CAN SEE EXACTLY THE SAME AMOUNT OF WHITE BLADE EVERY TIME, I ENSURE THAT MY HANDS ARE ALWAYS IN THE SAME POSITION!

Is your aim good?

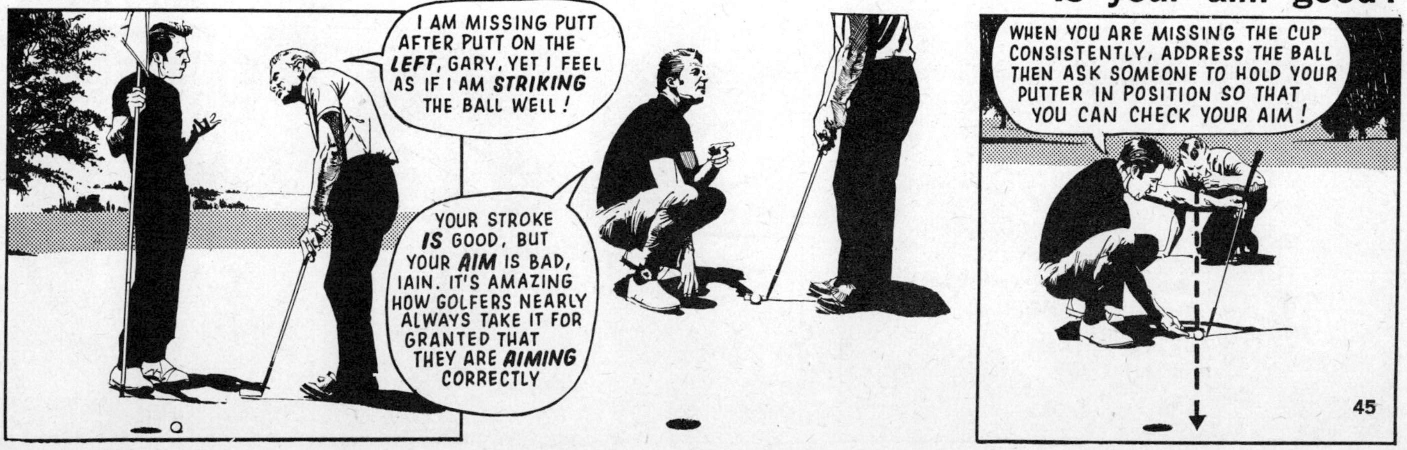

I AM MISSING PUTT AFTER PUTT ON THE LEFT, GARY, YET I FEEL AS IF I AM STRIKING THE BALL WELL!
YOUR STROKE IS GOOD, BUT YOUR AIM IS BAD, IAIN. IT'S AMAZING HOW GOLFERS NEARLY ALWAYS TAKE IT FOR GRANTED THAT THEY ARE AIMING CORRECTLY
WHEN YOU ARE MISSING THE CUP CONSISTENTLY, ADDRESS THE BALL THEN ASK SOMEONE TO HOLD YOUR PUTTER IN POSITION SO THAT YOU CAN CHECK YOUR AIM!

Putt with the match-play champion

YOU ARE STANDING OPEN, IAIN—AIMING LEFT OF THE HOLE!
THIS WILL TEND TO MAKE YOU TAKE THE PUTTER BACK OUTSIDE THE LINE
I BELIEVE YOU SHOULD STAND SLIGHTLY SHUT WHEN PUTTING. THE GREATEST PUTTER WHO EVER LIVED, BOBBY LOCKE, HAD A CLOSED STANCE
IN FACT, IF YOU ARE HAVING SEVERE PUTTING TROUBLE, IT'S NOT A BAD IDEA TO TURN YOUR BACK SLIGHTLY ON THE HOLE.

THIS HELPS YOU TO KEEP YOUR SHOULDERS SQUARE TO THE LINE AND TO TAKE THE CLUB BACK SLIGHTLY ON THE INSIDE. IT ALSO ENCOURAGES YOU TO LOOK LONGER AT THE BALL INSTEAD OF "PEEPING"!

Don't allow too much

LOOK AT THAT, GARY! I AIMED TWO INCHES TO THE RIGHT AND THE BALL DIDN'T COME IN AT ALL!
THAT'S THE TROUBLE WITH YOU WEEKENDERS! YOU'RE ALWAYS ALLOWING FOR SOMETHING, AND OFTEN THERE IS NO BREAK AT ALL!
IF YOU WOULD STOP ALLOWING SO MUCH AND TRICKLING THE BALL UP TO THE HOLE, YOU WOULD SINK MORE PUTTS! IT'S FAR BETTER TO AIM STRAIGHTER AND HIT THE BALL MORE BOLDLY!
HIT BOLDLY

Putt with rhythm

YOU'RE FOLLOWING-THROUGH NICELY, TOM, BUT YOU HAVE NO RHYTHM ON THE BACKSWING
YOU MUST COMPLETE THE BACKSWING BEFORE YOU START THE FORWARD SWING
FEEL SLIGHT PAUSE
WHEN JACK NICKLAUS WAS PREPARING FOR THIS YEAR'S P.G.A. IN FLORIDA, I TOLD HIM HE WASN'T TAKING THE PUTTER BACK SLOWLY ENOUGH, BUT THAT DIDN'T GIVE HIM THE ANSWER HE WAS LOOKING FOR
THEN DEAN BEMAN TOLD HIM TO COMPLETE HIS BACKSWING, WHICH COMES TO THE SAME THING, AND JACK PUTTED FANTASTICALLY WELL AND WON THE TOURNAMENT

Consistent putting

WHEN YOU "FAN" THE CLUBFACE OPEN, IAIN, IT IS DIFFICULT TO GET A CONSISTENT AMOUNT OF TOPSPIN ON THE BALL.
THE PUTTER SHOULD BE TAKEN BACK SQUARE. BOBBY LOCKE AND ARNOLD PALMER ARE THE BEST I HAVE EVER SEEN AT ACHIEVING THIS.
MANY PEOPLE "FAN" THE CLUB BECAUSE THEIR LEFT HAND IS IN A WEAK POSITION.
I BELIEVE THAT THE LEFT HAND SHOULD BE ABSOLUTELY SQUARE.
TOO WEAK
SQUARE
AS I'VE SAID BEFORE, THE PERFECT PUTTING RULE IS TO HAVE BOTH THUMBS STRAIGHT DOWN THE SHAFT.

A little wipe

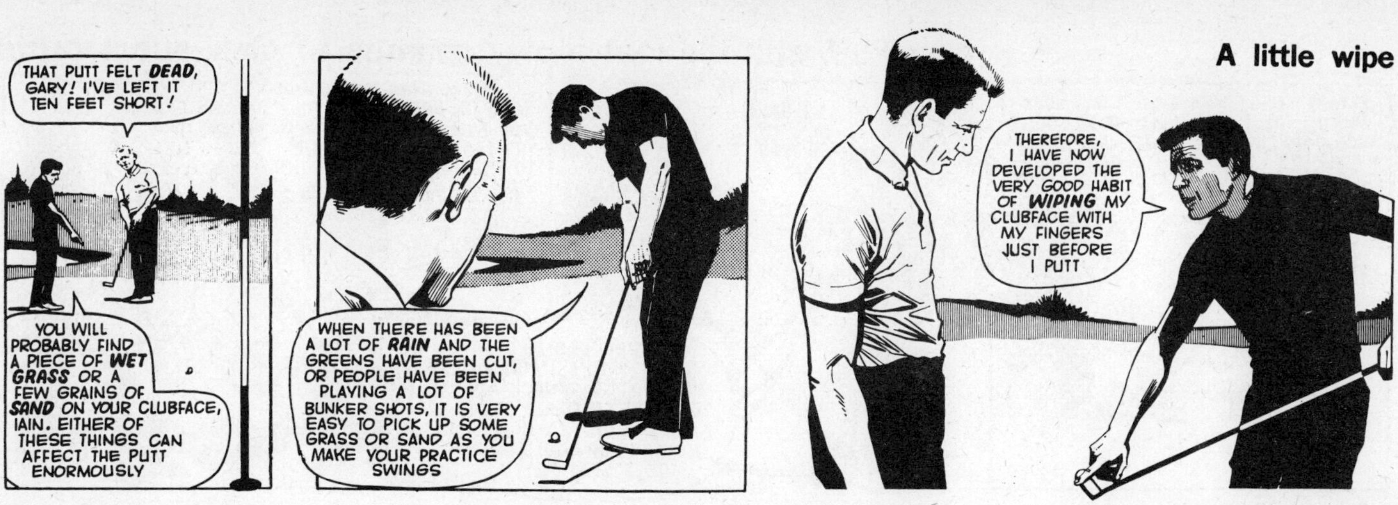

THAT PUTT FELT **DEAD**, GARY! I'VE LEFT IT TEN FEET SHORT!
YOU WILL PROBABLY FIND A PIECE OF **WET GRASS** OR A FEW GRAINS OF **SAND** ON YOUR CLUBFACE, IAIN. EITHER OF THESE THINGS CAN AFFECT THE PUTT ENORMOUSLY
WHEN THERE HAS BEEN A LOT OF **RAIN** AND THE GREENS HAVE BEEN CUT, OR PEOPLE HAVE BEEN PLAYING A LOT OF BUNKER SHOTS, IT IS VERY EASY TO PICK UP SOME GRASS OR SAND AS YOU MAKE YOUR PRACTICE SWINGS
THEREFORE, I HAVE NOW DEVELOPED THE VERY GOOD HABIT OF **WIPING** MY CLUBFACE WITH MY FINGERS JUST BEFORE I PUTT

Wash out that hole

OH, GARY! THESE **SHORT PUTTS** ARE KILLING ME!
YOU KNOW **WHY** YOU'RE MISSING THEM, IAIN? YOU'VE GOT YOUR EYE ON THE **BALL** AND THE **HOLE** AT THE SAME TIME
YOU'VE GOT TO **WASH OUT** THAT HOLE COMPLETELY!
LOOK, IAIN, WHEN I PUTT MY HEAD IS **TURNED AWAY** FROM THE HOLE. THAT PUTS THE HOLE OUT OF SIGHT AND OUT OF MIND—AND MAKES ME CONCENTRATE ENTIRELY ON **WATCHING THE BALL**!

Short putt—long putt

GARY, HAVE YOU HEARD THE THEORY THAT THE PUTTER SHOULD ALWAYS BE TAKEN BACK **TEN INCHES** AND THAT THE FOLLOW THROUGH SHOULD ALWAYS BE **SIX INCHES**?
I'VE ALSO HEARD IT SHOULD GO BACK **TEN INCHES** AND GO THROUGH **TWENTY**. BUT THESE THEORIES LEAVE ME COLD, IAIN. THE IMPORTANT THING WHEN PUTTING IS "FEEL" AND YOU CAN'T DESCRIBE **THAT** IN TERMS OF INCHES!
ON SHORT PUTTS, I WANT TO STRIKE THE BALL A FIRM, CRISP, DECISIVE BLOW, SO I TAKE A **SHORT** BACKSWING AND A **SHORT** FOLLOW-THROUGH
SHORT PUTTS — SHORT, CRISP ACTION
BUT ON LONG PUTTS, I WANT A SMOOTH, **STROKING** ACTION TO **ROLL** THE BALL UP TO THE HOLE, SO I TAKE BACK THE CLUB A **LONG** WAY WHICH AUTOMATICALLY GIVES ME A **SLOW** SWING WITH A LOT OF **RHYTHM**, AND A LONG FOLLOW-THROUGH
IF I HAD ONLY TAKEN A SIX INCH BACKSWING FOR THIS LONG PUTT MY ACTION WOULD HAVE BEEN DECIDEDLY **JERKY**!
LONG PUTTS — LONG STROKING ACTION

Listen for it!

IS THIS THE BEST KIND OF PUTTER, GARY?
THERE'S NO SUCH THING, TOM. EVERYBODY LIKES A DIFFERENT TYPE OF PUTTER. I PAID 50 DOLLARS FOR THAT ONE IN JAPAN, SO I'VE GOT TO KEEP USING IT TO TRY AND GET MY MONEY'S WORTH OUT OF IT!
I DON'T BELIEVE IN PUTTING WITH STIFF WRISTS. I THINK YOU SHOULD USE YOUR WRISTS JUST A LITTLE BIT
MANY GOLFERS **STILL** MAKE THE MISTAKE OF LIFTING THEIR HEADS BEFORE HITTING THE BALL —THOUGH THE OLDEST SECRET OF GOOD PUTTING IS TO KEEP YOUR HEAD DOWN UNTIL THE BALL IS **WELL AWAY**
AS FAR AS A **FOUR-FOOTER** IS CONCERNED, I **NEVER SEE** THE BALL GOING INTO THE HOLE... I ALWAYS **LISTEN** FOR IT!

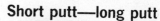

How to sink short putts

RETAIN YOUR GRIP ON THE CLUB, IAIN. I WANT TO SHOW YOU SOMETHING
WHATEVER IT IS, I HOPE IT WILL HELP ME TO SINK THESE THREE-FOOTERS, GARY!
SEE HOW EASILY I MANAGED TO PULL THE PUTTER OUT OF YOUR HANDS, IAIN? YOU WERE SO LOOSE AND FLIPPY-WRISTED THERE WAS NO WAY YOU COULD EVER HOLE THAT PUTT!
KEEP THE HANDS NICE AND FIRM ON SHORT PUTTS AND YOU WILL BE ABLE TO KEEP THE BLADE MORE SQUARE TO THE HOLE. NOW IT WON'T TURN ROUND ON YOU WHEN YOU STRIKE THE BALL!

Never up–never in!

WHENEVER YOU HAVE A PUTT OF OVER 15 FEET, IAIN, TRY TO GET THE BALL PAST THE HOLE. THERE ARE THREE GOOD REASONS FOR THIS ...
ONE, YOU HIT THE BALL MORE FIRMLY AND WITH MORE AUTHORITY, SO IT'S A BETTER PUTT. TWO, YOU GIVE THE BALL A CHANCE TO GO IN THE HOLE. NEVER UP, NEVER IN IS A VERY TRUE SAYING!
THREE, NINETY-NINE TIMES OUT OF A HUNDRED THE BALL WILL BREAK IN THE SAME DIRECTION ON THE RETURN PUTT —SO NOW YOU KNOW WHICH SIDE OF THE CUP TO AIM AT!

Chasing after the ball

THIS IS A 45 FOOT PUTT, IAIN! YET YOU HAVE FOLLOWED THROUGH NO FURTHER THAN I WOULD FOR A SIX FOOTER!
FOLLOW-THROUGH ENDS HERE
ON LONG PUTTS, I HAVE A LONG, SMOOTH BACKSWING
THEN, WHEN I STRIKE THE BALL, I KEEP MY PUTTER GOING THROUGH TO THE HOLE. I FEEL AS IF I AM TRYING TO HIT THE BALL AGAIN
CHASING AFTER THE BALL LIKE THIS IMPARTS A LOT OF TOPSPIN WHICH HELPS MAKE IT RUN UP TO THE HOLE!

Photograph those long putts

WHEN I HAVE A LONG PUTT OF ABOUT 40 FEET, NATURALLY I AM TRYING TO HOLE IT, BUT THE IMPORTANT THING IS TO LEAVE IT SO CLOSE TO THE HOLE THAT I WON'T THREE-PUTT!
A GREAT TIP ON THESE LONG PUTTS IS TO USE AN IMAGINARY STROKE! I LOOK AT THE HOLE AND IMAGINE I AM PUTTING TO IT SO THAT I GET THE FEEL OF THE DISTANCE RELAYED BACK INTO MY SUBCONSCIOUS
I DON'T LOOK AT THE BALL IN THESE PRACTICE PUTTS. I JUST LOOK AT THE HOLE. MY MIND PHOTOGRAPHS THE DISTANCE WHICH TELLS ME EXACTLY THE STRENGTH OF PUTT I NEED TO GET THE BALL UP TO THE HOLE
THEN I GET OVER THE BALL, LOOK AT THE HOLE ONCE MORE, AND CONCENTRATE ON ACTUALLY HITTING THE PUTT
HOW MANY PRACTICE SWINGS DO YOU RECOMMEND, GARY?
ON LONG PUTTS LIKE THIS, IAIN, I THINK YOU NEED THREE PRACTICE SWINGS... AND SEVERAL LOOKS AT THE HOLE

Long putts—don't jab!

WHY CAN'T I EVER GET THESE LONG PUTTS UP TO THE HOLE, GARY?
BECAUSE YOU JAB AT THEM, IAIN! YOU CAN'T EXPECT THE BALL TO RUN 40 FEET OR SO IF YOUR HANDS STOP OPPOSITE YOUR LEFT LEG
HANDS STOP
REID
NEXT TIME YOU ARE FACED WITH A LONG PUTT, CONCENTRATE ON TAKING YOUR HANDS RIGHT PAST THE EDGE OF YOUR PANTS. THIS WILL HELP YOU TO GET THE BALL UP TO THE HOLE

How to stop jabbing

YOU'RE JABBING YOUR PUTTS, IAIN, WHICH IS SOMETHING I'VE BEEN INCLINED TO DO ALL MY LIFE! PEOPLE KEEP TELLING ME THAT I MUST FOLLOW-THROUGH... BUT I NEVER FIND THAT HELPS BECAUSE THE FOLLOW-THROUGH IS ARTIFICIAL
I'VE WORKED ON THIS PROBLEM FOR YEARS AND I AM NOW CONVINCED THAT THE IMPORTANT THING IS TO SET YOURSELF UP PROPERLY
YOUR RIGHT SHOULDER IS TOO HIGH, YOUR RIGHT ARM TOO STRAIGHT AND YOU'VE TOO MUCH WEIGHT ON YOUR LEFT FOOT
NOWADAYS, I MAKE CERTAIN THAT MY RIGHT SHOULDER IS DOWN AND MY WEIGHT ONLY SLIGHTLY FAVORS MY LEFT SIDE. I GET THE FEELING THAT MY RIGHT FOREARM IS PARALLEL TO THE GROUND —ALTHOUGH ACTUALLY, IT ISN'T
NOW IT IS IMPOSSIBLE TO JAB THE BALL AND THE PUTTER GOES THROUGH NATURALLY WITHOUT MY HAVING TO MAKE ANY CONSCIOUS EFFORT TO FOLLOW-THROUGH

Bumpy greens

NOBODY COULD PUTT ON THIS GREEN, GARY— IT'S SO BUMPY!
YOU MAKE THINGS WORSE BY CHOPPING DOWN ON THE BALL, TOM. THE BUMPY GREEN SHOWS UP THE WEAKNESS IN YOUR PUTTING STROKE!
WHEN THE GREEN IS NOT TOO LEVEL YOU MUST TAKE THE PUTTER BACK EXTREMELY LOW. TRY TO SHAVE THE GRASS WITH THE BLADE
THIS WILL ENABLE YOU TO HIT THE BALL ON THE UPSWING SO THAT YOUR BLADE WILL IMPART TOPSPIN. THIS WILL START THE BALL ROLLING IMMEDIATELY AND KEEP IT HUGGING THE GRASS INSTEAD OF BOUNCING

A sloping 6-footer

I ALLOWED TOO MUCH FOR THE SLOPE, GARY!
AIM
FOR PUTTS INSIDE 6 FEET, UNLESS THERE IS A TREMENDOUS SLOPE, NEVER AIM OUTSIDE THE HOLE, TOM.
AIM FOR THE INSIDE OF THE HOLE AND I GUARANTEE YOU WILL SINK A LOT MORE.
AIM

Don't hook those putts

YOU MUST KEEP THE BLADE OF YOUR PUTTER ON THE LINE, IAIN!
THE MOMENT YOU ALLOW IT TO TURN OVER, YOU HOOK THE BALL!
REID
PLAYER
THERE IS A SIMPLE WAY TO GUARD AGAINST THIS. CONCENTRATE YOUR ATTENTION ON THE PALM OF YOUR RIGHT HAND. KEEP IT GOING THROUGH DIRECTLY TOWARDS THE HOLE AND YOU WILL AUTOMATICALLY KEEP THE BLADE ON LINE

Two-tier greens

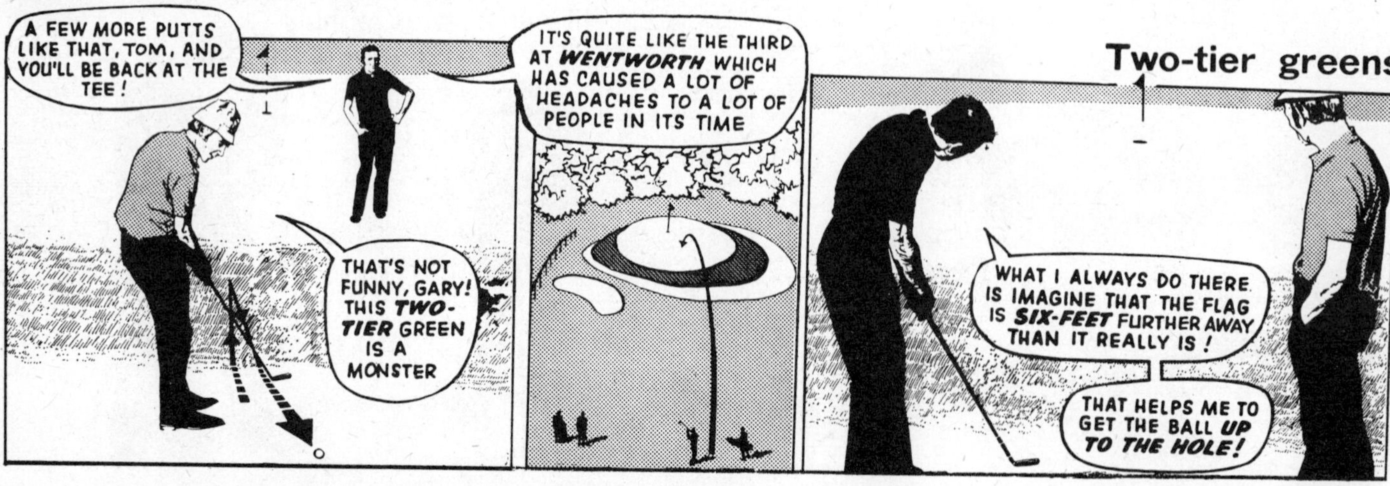

A FEW MORE PUTTS LIKE THAT, TOM, AND YOU'LL BE BACK AT THE TEE!
THAT'S NOT FUNNY, GARY! THIS TWO-TIER GREEN IS A MONSTER
IT'S QUITE LIKE THE THIRD AT WENTWORTH WHICH HAS CAUSED A LOT OF HEADACHES TO A LOT OF PEOPLE IN ITS TIME
WHAT I ALWAYS DO THERE IS IMAGINE THAT THE FLAG IS SIX-FEET FURTHER AWAY THAN IT REALLY IS!
THAT HELPS ME TO GET THE BALL UP TO THE HOLE!

Beware of the trees

I'D SAY THIS IS THE MOST DIFFICULT GREEN ON THE COURSE, GARY!
I AGREE, IAIN... IT'S BECAUSE IT LIES IN THE SHADE OF SEVERAL BIG TREES. GREENS LIKE THIS NEVER SEEM TO GROW SO WELL. THE GRASS DOESN'T KNIT TOGETHER, AND THIS MAKES THEM FAST.
ANOTHER PROBLEM IS THE LIGHT – OR LACK OF IT! WHEN YOU STEP OUT OF THE SUNSHINE ON TO A SHADY GREEN IT IS VERY DIFFICULT TO JUDGE DISTANCES. THEREFORE, WHEN I ADDRESS THE BALL, I TAKE A FEW MORE CAREFUL LOOKS AT THE HOLE THAN USUAL IN AN EFFORT TO IMPRINT THE DISTANCE ON MY SUBCONSCIOUS.
AUGUSTA – 10th GREEN
WEEKENDER AND PRO ALIKE SHOULD TAKE EXTRA CARE WHEN PUTTING ON A GREEN SURROUNDED BY TREES – FOR THIS IS WHERE HE'LL BE MOST LIKELY TO THREE-PUTT. THE 10th GREEN AT AUGUSTA, FOR EXAMPLE, IS A GREEN EVERYBODY HAS TROUBLE WITH!

Putting in the wind

THAT ONE WASN'T EVEN CLOSE, WAS IT, GARY?
I'M NOT SURPRISED, IAIN. THIS WIND HAD YOU SWAYING ALL OVER THE PLACE. AS I'VE SAID BEFORE, ONE OF THE MOST IMPORTANT THINGS WHEN PUTTING IS TO KEEP YOUR BODY STILL
IN ORDER TO MAINTAIN YOUR BALANCE, WHEN THE WIND IS BLOWING HARD, YOU HAVE GOT TO HAVE A WIDER STANCE. I INCREASE THE WIDTH OF MINE BY AT LEAST 12 INCHES
ANOTHER WAY TO CHEAT THE WIND ON THE PUTTING GREEN IS TO ADOPT THE ARNOLD PALMER STANCE WITH BOTH TOES POINTING INWARDS. THIS LOCKS THE KNEES AND KEEPS THE BODY VERY STILL, AND IS A GREAT WAY TO PUTT ON WINDY DAYS

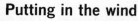

How to beat those problem putts

THAT'S ANOTHER RIGHT TO LEFT PUTT I'VE MISSED ON THE LEFT SIDE, GARY
PUTT BREAKS FROM RIGHT TO LEFT
AS YOU ARE HAVING DIFFICULTY IN KEEPING THE BALL OUT TO THE RIGHT ON THESE PUTTS, IAIN, YOU SHOULD TRY ADDRESSING THE BALL A BIT MORE TOWARDS THE CENTER OF YOUR STANCE
THIS WILL ENABLE YOU TO KEEP THE PUTTER BLADE GOING THROUGH TO THE RIGHT
FOR PUTTS THAT BREAK FROM LEFT TO RIGHT, DO THE OPPOSITE! ADDRESS THE BALL FURTHER FORWARD THAN USUAL, OPPOSITE YOUR LEFT TOE. THIS WILL HELP YOU KEEP THE BALL GOING TOWARDS THE LEFT

Grip short—grip long

YOU KNOW, TOM, YOU SHOULDN'T GRIP THE PUTTER THE SAME FOR A SIX FOOT PUTT AS FOR A 60 FOOTER!

FOR SHORT PUTTS, YOU SHOULD GET RIGHT OVER THE BALL. SO GRIP THE PUTTER SHORT.
BUT GRIP IT RIGHT AT THE END FOR LONG PUTTS. THEN YOU CAN GET A PENDULUM-LIKE STROKE.
SHORT PUTTS
LONG PUTTS

It pays to change your putting stance

THIS PUTT IS GOING TO BREAK QUITE A BIT FROM LEFT TO RIGHT, GARY
AND, LIKE MOST WEEKENDERS, YOU'LL PROBABLY MISS IT ON THE RIGHT, IAIN... UNLESS YOU DO SOMETHING TO KEEP THE BALL OUT TO THE LEFT
THIS IS WHAT TO DO. ADOPT A CLOSED STANCE, WITH YOUR LEFT FOOT IN FRONT OF YOUR RIGHT. THIS WILL GIVE YOU A BIT OF DRAW ON THE BALL WHICH WILL HELP KEEP IT OUT TO THE LEFT
CLOSED STANCE
FOR A RIGHT TO LEFT BREAK, ADOPT AN OPEN STANCE WITH RIGHT FOOT IN FRONT OF LEFT. THIS WILL HELP YOU FADE THE BALL AND KEEP IT OUT TO THE RIGHT
YOU KNOW, PUTTING'S JUST LIKE DRIVING, IAIN. CLOSE YOUR STANCE TO HOOK, OPEN IT TO SLICE!
OPEN STANCE

Improve your putting

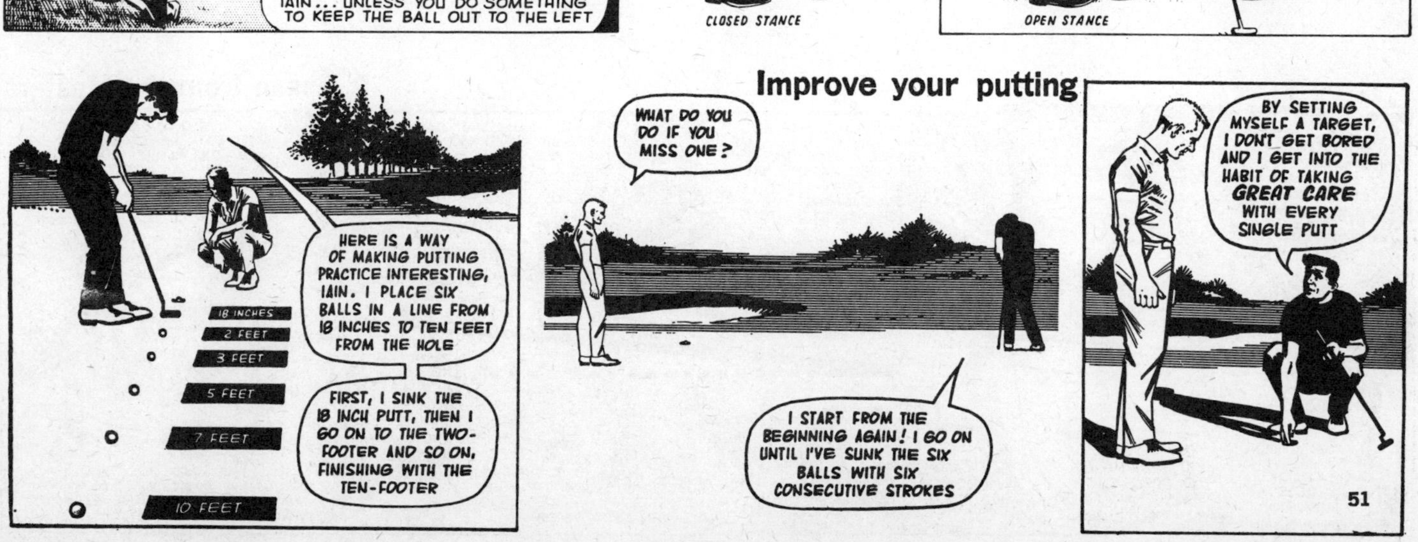
HERE IS A WAY OF MAKING PUTTING PRACTICE INTERESTING, IAIN. I PLACE SIX BALLS IN A LINE FROM 18 INCHES TO TEN FEET FROM THE HOLE
18 INCHES
2 FEET
3 FEET
5 FEET
7 FEET
10 FEET
FIRST, I SINK THE 18 INCH PUTT, THEN I GO ON TO THE TWO-FOOTER AND SO ON, FINISHING WITH THE TEN-FOOTER
WHAT DO YOU DO IF YOU MISS ONE?
I START FROM THE BEGINNING AGAIN! I GO ON UNTIL I'VE SUNK THE SIX BALLS WITH SIX CONSECUTIVE STROKES
BY SETTING MYSELF A TARGET, I DON'T GET BORED AND I GET INTO THE HABIT OF TAKING GREAT CARE WITH EVERY SINGLE PUTT

Cure those 'yips'

I WAS PLAYING WITH A MAN RECENTLY WHO HAS THE "YIPS" BOTH WHEN HE PUTTS AND WHEN HE CHIPS, GARY
THAT IS QUITE COMMON, IAIN!
IT IS NOW GENERALLY ACCEPTED THAT THE "YIPS" ATTACK THE FINER MUSCLES OF THE BODY. THESE ARE THE ONES THAT ARE MOST AFFECTED BY NERVES
THEREFORE, ANYONE WHO HAS THE "YIPS" SHOULD ADOPT AN ACTION WHICH WILL LEAVE THE HANDS AND THE WRISTS OUT OF THE SHOT
KEEP THE HANDS IN ONE PIECE AND ALLOW THE BIG MUSCLES TO SWING THE CLUB. TAKE THE CLUB BACK BY TURNING THE RIGHT HIP AWAY. BRING THE CLUB THROUGH BY TURNING THE LEFT HIP

When to concede a putt

WHEN IS IT GOOD TACTICS TO CONCEDE A PUTT IN MATCH PLAY, GARY?
WELL, IAIN, IT IS PSYCHOLOGICALLY EASIER TO PUTT FOR A HALF THAN FOR A WIN, THEREFORE I USUALLY CONCEDE A TWO-FOOTER IF MY OPPONENT NEEDS IT FOR A HALF. BUT, IF HE NEEDS IT FOR A WIN, I MAKE HIM PUTT!
I ALSO CONCEDE SHORT PUTTS MORE READILY IN THE EARLY STAGES OF A MATCH WHEN THEY ARE RELATIVELY EASY TO MAKE
HOWEVER, WHEN THE PRESSURE MOUNTS UP, THESE SHORT PUTTS BECOME TOUGHER, AND SUDDENLY MY OPPONENT FINDS HIMSELF WITH A TWO-FOOTER TO WIN THE HOLE!
HE KNOWS I'VE BEEN CONCEDING TWO-FOOTERS ALL DAY AND HE WONDERS IF HE WILL HAVE TO PUTT OR NOT. THIS CAN BE DISTRACTING
THEN, WHEN I SAY NOTHING, AND HE HAS TO PUTT OUT, THERE IS JUST THAT OUTSIDE CHANCE HE WILL BE SUFFICIENTLY DISTRACTED TO MISS THE PUTT!

SECTION EIGHT

Course Strategy

A lesson from the Masters

The 11th AUGUSTA
HOW YOU PLAN YOUR ATTACK ON A HOLE IS JUST AS IMPORTANT AS HOW YOU ACTUALLY PLAY THE STROKES. FOR EXAMPLE, LET'S TAKE A LOOK AT THE 11th HOLE AT AUGUSTA...
IN THE U.S. MASTERS TOURNAMENT, A LOT OF PEOPLE LIKE TO DRIVE UP THE RIGHT HAND SIDE OF THE FAIRWAY, THUS SHORTENING THE DISTANCE TO THE HOLE
THIS MEANS THAT ON THEIR NEXT SHOT THEY ARE AIMING DIRECTLY AT A POND, WHICH PUTS A GREAT STRAIN ON THEM. ALSO, BECAUSE OF THE GROUND SLOPE, THEY ARE LIABLE TO HOOK THEIR APPROACH SHOTS
I DRIVE DOWN THE LEFT, SO THAT I CAN THEN SHOOT AWAY FROM THE WATER. THE FACT THAT I NEED A 4-IRON TO THEIR 5 OR 6-IRON DOESN'T MAKE ALL THAT MUCH DIFFERENCE
THE GARY PLAYER ROUTE
THE SHORT ROUTE
SLOPE OF GROUND
WATER
WATER
IF I HIT A BAD SHOT, IT'S GOING TO BE AT LEAST ON THE FRONT EDGE OF THE GREEN. BUT IF THEY HOOK INTO THE WATER, THEY WILL MAKE A SIX, A SEVEN OR AN EIGHT!
SO, THE LESSON IS... WHENEVER POSSIBLE, GET INTO A POSITION FROM WHICH YOU CAN PLAY FOR THE GREEN WITHOUT SHOOTING TOWARDS A HAZARD

Give yourself a wide margin of error

The 13th AUGUSTA
YOU OFTEN FIND, IAIN, THAT IN ORDER TO GIVE YOURSELF A SIMPLE APPROACH SHOT TO THE GREEN, YOU HAVE TO DRIVE TO A SPOT ON THE FAIRWAY THAT IS PERILOUSLY CLOSE TO TROUBLE
ON THE 13th. AT AUGUSTA IT IS IMPORTANT TO LAND ON THE LEFT SIDE OF THE FAIRWAY... WHERE THE WATER AND BUSHES ARE!
BUT EVERYBODY GETS SCARED AND THEY AUTOMATICALLY DRIVE TO THE RIGHT OF THIS 50-YARD-WIDE FAIRWAY, AND SO GET FURTHER AWAY FROM THE HOLE
OR THEY AIM FOR THE MIDDLE WHICH GIVES THEM A MARGIN FOR ERROR OF ONLY 25 YARDS ON EACH SIDE. UNDER STRAIN, THAT'S NOT ENOUGH
WHAT I DO IS AIM FOR THE RIGHT SIDE AND HOOK THE BALL TOWARDS WHERE I WANT TO END UP. THIS GIVES ME A 50-YARD MARGIN FOR ERROR AND MEANS I HAVE THE WHOLE FAIRWAY TO PLAY FOR
13
AIM TO RIGHT
50-YARD-WIDE FAIRWAY
THIS WAY, I ALWAYS END UP IN THE LEFT HALF OF THE FAIRWAY. AND THERE'S NO DANGER, BECAUSE I CANNOT POSSIBLY HOOK THE BALL 50 YARDS!

Shoot away from trouble

ALL THE TROUBLE IS DOWN THE LEFT, TOM, YOU MADE THE MISTAKE OF TEEING UP AT THE RIGHT WHICH MEANT YOU WERE AUTOMATICALLY AIMING AT THE TREES... AND THAT'S WHERE YOU ENDED UP!
I ALWAYS TEE UP ON THE TROUBLE SIDE, AND YOU CAN SEE WHAT THE RESULT IS... I AM AUTOMATICALLY FACING AWAY FROM THE TREES WHICH MEANS I WILL BE SHOOTING AWAY FROM TROUBLE!

Join the tee set

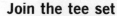

WHY DON'T YOU TEE UP YOUR BALL, IAIN?
I NEVER DO AT SHORT HOLES, GARY. I'M ALWAYS HOPING FOR A BIT OF BACKSPIN TO HOLD MY BALL ON THE GREEN
NO. 8 155 yds
BUT THAT'S NONSENSE, IAIN. WHEN YOU DON'T TEE UP, THERE IS A TENDENCY TO HIT BEHIND THE BALL, AND THIS GIVES YOU TOPSPIN!
I TEE UP MY BALL AT LEAST HALF-AN-INCH OFF THE GROUND AT EVERY SHORT HOLE... WHETHER I'M HITTING A 9-IRON OR A 4-WOOD!
BY USING A TEE-PEG I GET INCREASED BACKSPIN, BECAUSE I AM FAR MORE LIKELY TO HIT THE BALL FIRST
GOLF IS TOUGH ENOUGH AS IT IS, IAIN... SO, WHENEVER THE RULES ALLOW IT, TEE UP YOUR BALL!

Aim for the middle

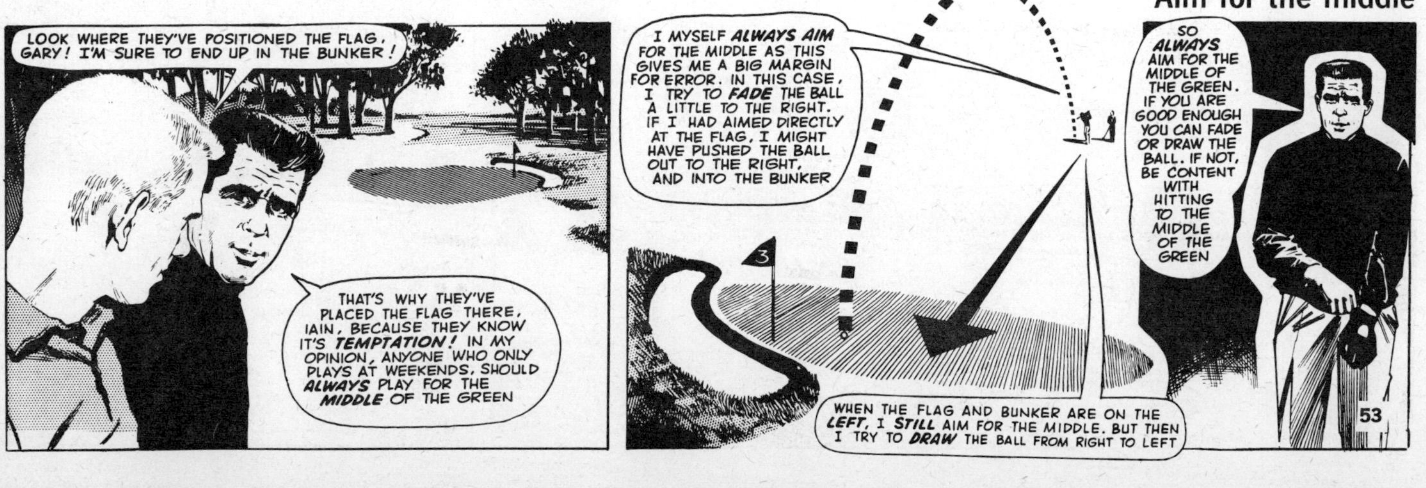

LOOK WHERE THEY'VE POSITIONED THE FLAG, GARY! I'M SURE TO END UP IN THE BUNKER!
THAT'S WHY THEY'VE PLACED THE FLAG THERE, IAIN, BECAUSE THEY KNOW IT'S TEMPTATION! IN MY OPINION, ANYONE WHO ONLY PLAYS AT WEEKENDS, SHOULD ALWAYS PLAY FOR THE MIDDLE OF THE GREEN
I MYSELF ALWAYS AIM FOR THE MIDDLE AS THIS GIVES ME A BIG MARGIN FOR ERROR. IN THIS CASE, I TRY TO FADE THE BALL A LITTLE TO THE RIGHT. IF I HAD AIMED DIRECTLY AT THE FLAG, I MIGHT HAVE PUSHED THE BALL OUT TO THE RIGHT, AND INTO THE BUNKER
3
WHEN THE FLAG AND BUNKER ARE ON THE LEFT, I STILL AIM FOR THE MIDDLE. BUT THEN I TRY TO DRAW THE BALL FROM RIGHT TO LEFT
SO ALWAYS AIM FOR THE MIDDLE OF THE GREEN. IF YOU ARE GOOD ENOUGH YOU CAN FADE OR DRAW THE BALL. IF NOT, BE CONTENT WITH HITTING TO THE MIDDLE OF THE GREEN

The safest place

FOR ONCE I HIT AS GOOD A SHOT AS YOU, GARY, AND IT KICKS OFF INTO A BUNKER! ISN'T THAT UNLUCKY?
NO, TOM, IT'S JUST BAD COURSE MANAGEMENT!
IF YOU PITCH IN FRONT OF THE GREEN THERE IS ALWAYS A CHANCE YOU WILL GET A BAD BOUNCE
GET INTO THE HABIT OF TAKING MORE CLUB AND PITCHING ON THE SAFEST AREA OF GROUND THERE IS – THE GREEN ITSELF!

Beware of the sand

THERE, GARY, I'VE HIT THREE BUNKER SHOTS. WHAT NOW?
I WANT YOU TO GO TO THE OTHER SIDE OF THE GREEN AND PLAY THREE CHIP SHOTS
THESE ARE MUCH CLOSER TO THE HOLE, TOM, AS I THOUGHT THEY WOULD BE
THIS LITTLE TEST MAY IMPRESS UPON YOU THE DANGERS OF SHOOTING FOR THE PIN WHEN THERE IS A BUNKER CLOSE TO IT
AS THE AVERAGE WEEKENDER'S CHIPPING IS MUCH BETTER THAN HIS SAND PLAY, HE SHOULD TRY TO ENSURE THAT, IF HE DOES MISS THE GREEN, HE MISSES IT ON THE SIDE THAT HAS NO BUNKER!
AIM HERE

Take care when playing a fade

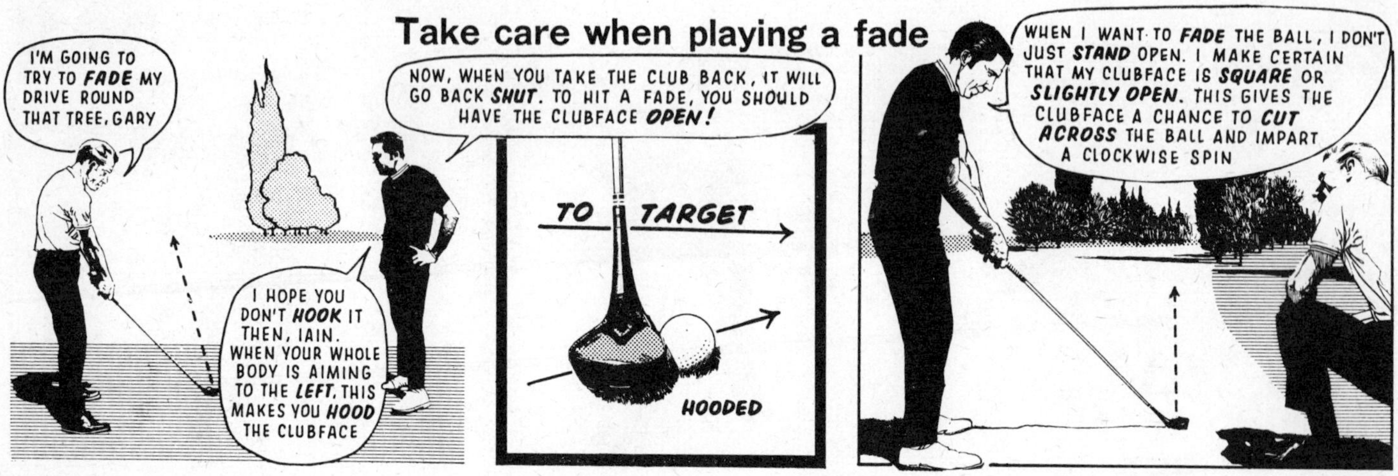
I'M GOING TO TRY TO FADE MY DRIVE ROUND THAT TREE, GARY
I HOPE YOU DON'T HOOK IT THEN, IAIN. WHEN YOUR WHOLE BODY IS AIMING TO THE LEFT, THIS MAKES YOU HOOD THE CLUBFACE
NOW, WHEN YOU TAKE THE CLUB BACK, IT WILL GO BACK SHUT. TO HIT A FADE, YOU SHOULD HAVE THE CLUBFACE OPEN!
TO TARGET
HOODED
WHEN I WANT TO FADE THE BALL, I DON'T JUST STAND OPEN. I MAKE CERTAIN THAT MY CLUBFACE IS SQUARE OR SLIGHTLY OPEN. THIS GIVES THE CLUBFACE A CHANCE TO CUT ACROSS THE BALL AND IMPART A CLOCKWISE SPIN

When you don't know where you're going...

YOU CAN'T SEE THE GREEN AT ALL FROM DOWN HERE...
AND THAT MAKES IT A BAD HOLE, IAIN. MODERN GOLF ARCHITECTS ALL AGREE THAT YOU SHOULD BE ABLE TO SEE THE GREEN FROM THE FAIRWAY, THE FAIRWAY FROM THE TEE
GOLF IS DIFFICULT ENOUGH WHEN YOU CAN SEE WHERE YOU'RE GOING!
HOWEVER, I CLIMB TO THE TOP OF THE RISE SO THAT I CAN SEE THE FLAG. I THEN TAKE THE SAME STANCE AS I WILL TAKE WHEN I ADDRESS MY BALL. I HOLD MY CLUB SO THAT IT POINTS TO THE BALL AND THE FLAG
NOW I PICK OUT A MARK ON THE GROUND THAT IS IN LINE WITH BALL AND FLAG. IT MIGHT BE A FLOWER OR A STONE...
BALL
TO FLAG
I WALK BACKWARDS DOWN THE HILL, KEEPING MY EYE ON THE MARK SO AS NOT TO LOSE IT...
...THEN I JUST GO AHEAD AND AIM TO HIT THE BALL RIGHT OVER THE MARK

How to be bright when it's breezy...

WHENEVER IT IS WINDY, IAIN, YOUR MARGIN OF ERROR IS REDUCED. A SHOT THAT WOULD NORMALLY BE FIVE YARDS OFF THE LINE WILL PROBABLY BE TEN YARDS OFF IN WIND
SO GRIP THE CLUB ABOUT TWO INCHES SHORTER THAN USUAL AND GIVE YOURSELF A MORE COMPACT SWING WHICH IS LESS LIABLE TO GET OUT OF CONTROL
I DON'T BELIEVE IN TRYING TO CUT THE BALL INTO A RIGHT-TO-LEFT WIND. IT'S HARD ENOUGH TO HIT THE SHOT STRAIGHT
DIRECTION OF WIND
I SIMPLY AIM TO THE RIGHT AND LET THE WIND BRING THE BALL IN
SIMILARLY, WHEN THE WIND IS LEFT TO RIGHT, I AIM LEFT OF TARGET. ALWAYS A NORMAL, STRAIGHT SHOT, YOU UNDERSTAND... NOTHING FANCY!
DIRECTION OF WIND

Crosswinds

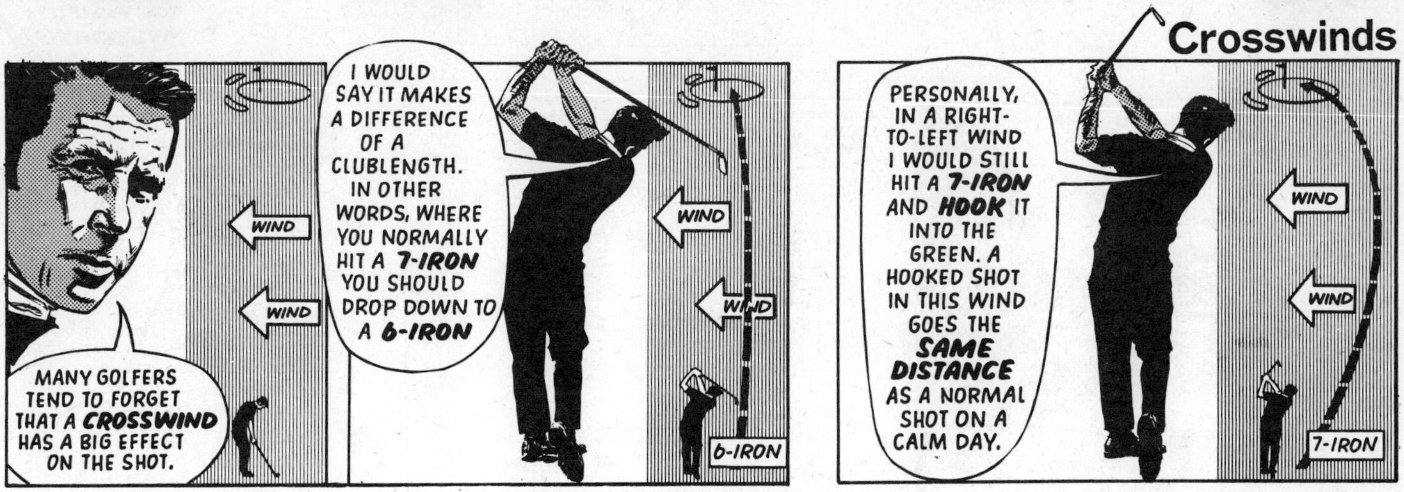
WIND
WIND
MANY GOLFERS TEND TO FORGET THAT A CROSSWIND HAS A BIG EFFECT ON THE SHOT.
I WOULD SAY IT MAKES A DIFFERENCE OF A CLUBLENGTH. IN OTHER WORDS, WHERE YOU NORMALLY HIT A 7-IRON YOU SHOULD DROP DOWN TO A 6-IRON
WIND
WIND
6-IRON
PERSONALLY, IN A RIGHT-TO-LEFT WIND I WOULD STILL HIT A 7-IRON AND HOOK IT INTO THE GREEN. A HOOKED SHOT IN THIS WIND GOES THE SAME DISTANCE AS A NORMAL SHOT ON A CALM DAY.
WIND
WIND
7-IRON

Fight the wind

I DIDN'T ALLOW ENOUGH FOR THE WIND, GARY!
GRIP GENTLY
IN A LEFT-TO-RIGHT WIND, TOM, YOU SHOULD GRIP MORE GENTLY WITH YOUR LEFT HAND AND MORE FIRMLY WITH YOUR RIGHT.
THIS ENCOURAGES THE RIGHT HAND TO CROSS OVER THE LEFT AT IMPACT WHICH PUTS HOOK SPIN ON THE BALL. THIS HELPS THE BALL FIGHT THE WIND.

Strangle the club

WIND
IN THIS RIGHT-TO-LEFT WIND, TOM, EVERY ONE OF YOUR SHOTS IS ENDING UP LEFT OF THE TARGET.
I KNOW, GARY! I'M REALLY HOOKING THEM TODAY!
THIS IS BECAUSE YOU ARE ALLOWING YOUR RIGHT HAND TO CROSS OVER THE LEFT AS YOU HIT THROUGH
IN THIS WIND, YOU MUST MAKE A CONSCIOUS EFFORT TO KEEP YOUR CLUBFACE POINTING TO THE HOLE.
STRANGLE THE CLUB WITH YOUR LEFT HAND AND RELAX THE RIGHT. THEN YOU WILL BE ABLE TO HOLD THE BALL UP INTO THE WIND AND KEEP THE SHOT UNDER CONTROL.

Don't fight the wind

PLAYING INTO THE WIND, IT IS NECESSARY TO KEEP THE BALL LOW. TO ACHIEVE THIS, I HAVE MY HANDS FURTHER IN FRONT OF THE BALL AT ADDRESS THAN NORMAL
DIRECTION OF WIND
WHEN THE WIND IS BEHIND ME, I PLAY THE BALL OFF MY LEFT HEEL IN ORDER TO HIT IT HIGH...
DIRECTION OF WIND
WITH A DRIVER, I TEE THE BALL HIGH... THE LONGER THE BALL STAYS IN THE AIR THE BETTER
WHAT I AM SAYING, IAIN, IS NEVER TRY TO DO COMPLICATED THINGS LIKE HOOKING INTO A LEFT TO RIGHT WIND...
ALWAYS USE THE WIND! DON'T FIGHT IT!

Don't take a divot

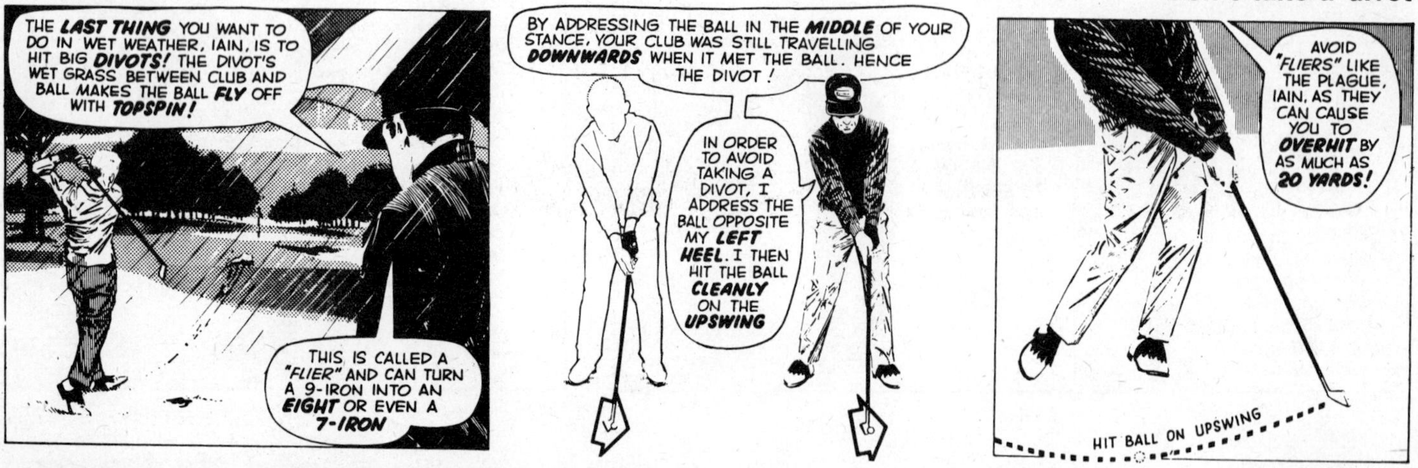

THE LAST THING YOU WANT TO DO IN WET WEATHER, IAIN, IS TO HIT BIG DIVOTS! THE DIVOT'S WET GRASS BETWEEN CLUB AND BALL MAKES THE BALL FLY OFF WITH TOPSPIN!
THIS IS CALLED A "FLIER" AND CAN TURN A 9-IRON INTO AN EIGHT OR EVEN A 7-IRON
BY ADDRESSING THE BALL IN THE MIDDLE OF YOUR STANCE, YOUR CLUB WAS STILL TRAVELLING DOWNWARDS WHEN IT MET THE BALL. HENCE THE DIVOT!
IN ORDER TO AVOID TAKING A DIVOT, I ADDRESS THE BALL OPPOSITE MY LEFT HEEL. I THEN HIT THE BALL CLEANLY ON THE UPSWING
AVOID "FLIERS" LIKE THE PLAGUE, IAIN, AS THEY CAN CAUSE YOU TO OVERHIT BY AS MUCH AS 20 YARDS!
HIT BALL ON UPSWING

Early morning golf

WHEN THE AIR IS COLD AND HEAVY, THE BALL DOESN'T GO SO FAR, SO THE EFFECT OF THE DAMP GRASS IS CANCELED!

When the ground is wet

YOU SEEM TO BE ADDRESSING THE BALL MUCH NEARER YOUR LEFT FOOT THAN USUAL, GARY!
THAT IS CORRECT, IAIN! AS THIS IS WET, MARSHY GROUND, I WANT TO HIT THE BALL MORE ON THE UPSWING. IF I POSITION IT FURTHER BACK, I WILL BE INCLINED TO GOUGE DOWN TOO DEEP AND TAKE A HUGE DIVOT
IN WET CONDITIONS, I ALSO CONCENTRATE ON LOOKING AT THE TOP OF THE BALL
THIS HELPS ME TO CONNECT WITH THE BALL FIRST AND HIT RIGHT THROUGH IT
IF I HIT BEHIND THE BALL, IT IS LIABLE TO SQUIRT OFF AT ANY OLD ANGLE AND IT WILL ALSO TRAVEL FURTHER THAN I WANT IT TOO!
HIT BALL FIRST

A par to win

IT'S THE STORY OF MY LIFE. I NEEDED A PAR 4 AT THE LAST HOLE TO WIN AND I TOOK A SIX!
WHEN YOU NEED A PAR TO WIN, YOU MUST MAKE SURE YOU RELEASE ON YOUR DRIVE. DON'T TRY TO STEER THE BALL SAFELY UP THE MIDDLE. GIVE IT A GOOD SOLID HIT
THEN, WHEN YOU PLAY YOUR APPROACH SHOT, DON'T TRY TO GO FOR THE FLAG WHEN IT IS IN A DIFFICULT POSITION. SHOOT FOR THE MIDDLE OF THE GREEN EVERY TIME
NOW YOU HAVE TWO PUTTS TO WIN. KEEP YOUR HEAD DOWN FOR A LONG, LONG TIME AND ALL SHOULD BE WELL

SECTION NINE

Club Selection

Weekenders are always short

WE COULD STAND AT THE BACK OF THIS, OR ANY GREEN ALL AFTERNOON, IAIN, AND I GUARANTEE WE WOULDN'T SEE A SINGLE WEEKENDER GET HIS BALL UP TO THE HOLE!
USUALLY, THE TROUBLE SPOTS ARE ALL AT THE FRONT OF THE GREEN AND NOT AT THE BACK — YET WEEKENDERS ARE ALWAYS SHORT OF THE FLAG!
YOU'LL BE SURPRISED HOW WELL YOU WILL PLAY!
THIS IS WHAT I WOULD ADVISE ALL YOU WEEKEND PLAYERS TO DO. NEXT TIME YOU PLAY, REMEMBER THERE IS A BACK TO THE GREEN, AND HIT ALL YOUR APPROACH SHOTS WITH ONE EXTRA CLUB THAN YOU WOULD NORMALLY TAKE. FOR EXAMPLE, IF YOU FEEL YOU SHOULD BE TAKING A 6-IRON, HIT A FIVE

How to choose the correct club

I CAN'T MAKE UP MY MIND WHETHER TO PLAY A SIX-IRON OR A SEVEN!
THAT SHOULD BE NO PROBLEM, IAIN. THIS IS YOUR HOME COURSE
I'VE ONLY PLAYED IT A COUPLE OF TIMES BUT I ALREADY KNOW THAT BUSH IS EIGHT IRON DISTANCE FROM THE GREEN. I'M 12 YARDS SHORT OF IT, SO I KNOW I NEED A SEVEN-IRON
AS A WEEKEND GOLFER PLAYS 90 PER CENT OF HIS GOLF ON HIS HOME COURSE, HE SHOULD PICK OUT SOME MARK OR OTHER WHERE HIS DRIVE NORMALLY FINISHES ON EVERY PAR FOUR AND PAR FIVE HOLE. HE SHOULD THEN PACE OUT THE DISTANCE FROM THERE TO THE GREEN, AND MAKE A NOTE OF IT. AFTER THAT HE SHOULD NEVER BE IN ANY DOUBT ABOUT WHICH CLUB TO USE
BUSH
10 YARDS SHORT
6 IRON
NORMAL DRIVE
140 YDS
7-IRON
10 YARDS LONGER
8 IRON
WEEKENDERS — ALLOW TEN YARDS DIFFERENCE BETWEEN EACH CLUB

Don't misjudge distances

I DIDN'T HAVE ENOUGH CLUB, GARY!
I THINK YOU WERE DECEIVED BY THE FACT THAT THERE ARE BIG TREES BEHIND THE GREEN. THIS ALWAYS MAKES THE FLAG SEEM CLOSER THAN IT REALLY IS, TOM!
IF, ON THE OTHER HAND, YOU ARE PLAYING TO A GREEN BATHED IN SHADOW, THAT MAKES THE HOLE SEEM A LOT FURTHER AWAY.
THE SAME APPLIES WHEN THE HORIZON IS VERY FLAT AND THERE ARE NO MOUNDS, TREES OR BUSHES BETWEEN YOU AND THE HOLE TO HELP YOU JUDGE YOUR DISTANCE. IN THIS SITUATION IT IS VERY EASY TO TAKE TOO MUCH CLUB!

One green—four clubs!

YOU'RE A BIT SHORT, IAIN. YOU SHOULD HAVE TAKEN A 6-IRON, NOT A SEVEN
BUT I ALWAYS HIT A 7-IRON AT THIS HOLE, GARY

ALWAYS? THAT IS GOING TO COST YOU A LOT OF SHOTS! A BIG GREEN LIKE THIS CAN CALL FOR ANYTHING FROM A 6-IRON TO A 9-IRON, DEPENDING ON THE POSITION OF THE FLAG
IF THE FLAG'S RIGHT AT THE BACK OF THE GREEN, YOU WILL NEED A SIX. IF IT'S AT THE FRONT, A 9-IRON WILL BE SUFFICIENT. SO ALWAYS LOOK FOR THE PIN-POSITION BEFORE YOU DECIDE WHICH CLUB TO TAKE!

6 IRON
7 IRON
8 IRON
9 IRON

The Texas Wedge

WHEN YOUR BALL IS LYING ON BARE GROUND JUST AT THE EDGE OF THE GREEN, IAIN, DON'T CHIP WITH A PITCHING WEDGE
MANY OF THE PRO'S DO THIS, BUT I CONSIDER IT POOR COURSE MANAGEMENT!

THE PUTTER IS DEFINITELY THE SAFEST CLUB TO USE OFF BARE GROUND
DON'T BE TOO PROUD TO TAKE OUT THE OLD TEXAS WEDGE!

Think positively

WHY DID YOU TAKE AN IRON OFF THE TEE, IAIN?
WELL, IT'S A PRETTY NARROW FAIRWAY, GARY. I DIDN'T WANT TO END UP IN THE TREES
THE ONLY TIME I BELIEVE IN TAKING AN IRON OFF THE TEE, EXCEPT AT PAR THREE HOLES, IS WHEN THERE IS A HAZARD RUNNING ACROSS THE FAIRWAY THAT I KNOW I CANNOT CARRY WITH MY DRIVER
I NOTICE LOTS OF PRO'S, ESPECIALLY IN SOUTH AFRICA, TAKE IRONS OFF THE TEE, AND I THINK THIS IS A NEGATIVE ATTITUDE. RIGHT AWAY THEY ARE ADMITTING DEFEAT, AND IT'S BOUND TO AFFECT THE SHOT
THINK POSITIVELY! IF YOU CAN HIT A 3-IRON STRAIGHT, YOU CAN HIT A DRIVER STRAIGHT! TAKE A MAN LIKE BYRON NELSON. HE WOULD NO MORE HAVE USED AN IRON OFF THE TEE WHEN A DRIVER WAS CALLED FOR THAN THE MAN IN THE MOON!
IF MY OPPONENT TAKES AN IRON OFF THE TEE, AND THEN I SMASH A DRIVER RIGHT DOWN THE MIDDLE, I FEEL SUPERIOR TO HIM... AND I KNOW THAT HE'S THINKING THAT TOO! THEREFORE, MY CHANCES OF WINNING ARE ENHANCED!

When greens are hard...

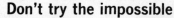

Don't try the impossible

Uphill-downhill

A low boring shot into the wind

On the fringe—putt or chip?

LOTS OF PLAYERS, TOM, NEVER KNOW WHEN TO PUTT AND WHEN TO CHIP FROM THE EDGE OF THE GREEN... BUT THERE ARE DEFINITE TIMES FOR EACH!
WHEN THE GRASS GROWS TOWARDS THE HOLE, TAKE YOUR PUTTER...
PUTT WITH THE GRAIN
WHEN IT GROWS THE OTHER WAY, YOU SHOULD ALWAYS CHIP! I'M CLOSE TO THE GREEN HERE, SO I'M USING A 6-IRON
IF I HAD PUTTED AGAINST THIS GRAIN, TOM, MY BALL WOULD HAVE BOUNCED, AND GONE OUT OF CONTROL
CHIP AGAINST THE GRAIN
IF EVER YOU ARE AT THE BOTTOM OF A BANK WITH THE FLAG POSITIONED JUST AT THE TOP, DON'T TRY TO CHIP OR PITCH... PUTT YOUR BALL UP TO THE HOLE!

Think ahead

I HAD A GREAT CHANCE TO WIN THIS FINAL HOLE, GARY, BUT I ALWAYS HIT MY WEDGE SHOTS BADLY UNDER PRESSURE.
DRIVER
WEDGE
INSTEAD OF TAKING A DRIVER OFF THE TEE, TOM, YOU SHOULD HAVE USED YOUR 3-WOOD.
3-WOOD
7-IRON
THEN YOU WOULD HAVE HAD A FULL 7- OR 8-IRON SHOT TO THE GREEN INSTEAD OF A THREE-QUARTER WEDGE SHOT. YOU MUST ALWAYS THINK AHEAD AND SET YOURSELF UP FOR THE SHOT YOU FEEL CONFIDENT ABOUT.

SECTION TEN

From The Rough

Meet the ball first

TOM, IF YOU ADDRESS THE BALL OPPOSITE YOUR LEFT HEEL IN LONG ROUGH, YOUR CLUBHEAD IS GOING TO MEET ALL THAT GRASS FIRST AND THEN THE BALL!
VITAL CLUB-HEAD SPEED IS GOING TO BE DISSIPATED BEFORE THE CLUBHEAD EVEN REACHES THE BALL
CLUBHEAD HAS TO CUT THROUGH GRASS BEFORE REACHING BALL
IN LONG ROUGH, YOU SHOULD ALWAYS ADDRESS THE BALL IN THE CENTER OF YOUR STANCE SO THAT THE CLUBHEAD CAN MEET THE BALL FIRST... AND FAST!
CLUBHEAD CONTACTS BALL BEFORE GRASS

How to play out of long rough

IN NORMAL SHOTS, IT IS CORRECT TO TAKE THE CLUB BACK IN ONE PIECE, KEEPING IT LOW. BUT, IN LONG ROUGH, THIS ACTION WILL CAUSE THE CLUB TO CATCH THE GRASS ON THE DOWNSWING
THE CLUB WILL TURN IN YOUR HANDS, AND YOU WON'T EVEN HIT THE BALL 20 YARDS
TOO LOW BACKSWING
STEEP BACKSWING
IN LONG ROUGH, I PICK UP THE CLUB VERY STEEPLY TO GET IT QUICKLY OUT OF THE GRASS
CHOP DOWN
I CAN THEN CHOP DOWN ON THE BALL AND AVOID GETTING MY CLUB TANGLED UP IN THE GRASS
I MAKE CERTAIN THAT I FOLLOW THROUGH COMPLETELY
WHEN YOU'RE IN LONG ROUGH, IAIN, THE TWO MOST IMPORTANT THINGS ARE, ONE, PICK UP THE CLUB SHARPLY LIKE THIS... AND, TWO, HIT RIGHT THROUGH THE BALL

Aiming in the rough

I'M YARDS OFF TARGET, GARY
WHENEVER A GOLFER HITS OUT OF THE ROUGH, THE TENDENCY IS FOR THE BALL TO GO TO THE LEFT, IAIN
THIS IS BECAUSE THE LONG GRASS TURNS THE CLUB OVER IN THE HANDS AND STOPS IT GOING STRAIGHT THROUGH
I STAND A LITTLE OPEN IN THE ROUGH WHICH HELPS ME TO KEEP THE CLUBFACE FROM CLOSING TOO MUCH
AND I ALSO AIM SLIGHTLY TO THE RIGHT OF TARGET
LEFT FOOT DRAWN BACK

Don't quit on the stroke

WITH ALL THIS THICK CLOVER AROUND, GARY, I'M GLAD THIS IS YOUR SHOT, NOT MINE
THE IMPORTANT THING TO REMEMBER IN THE ROUGH, TOM, IS NOT TO QUIT ON THE STROKE. OTHERWISE THE GRASS WILL CATCH HOLD OF YOUR CLUB. KEEP YOUR HANDS GOING RIGHT THROUGH THE BALL
MAKE CERTAIN THAT YOUR HEAD IS HELD ABSOLUTELY STILL AND THAT YOU DON'T LIFT IT BEFORE IMPACT
THEN WITH YOUR WEIGHT ON THE LEFT SIDE AND YOUR RIGHT KNEE IN...
...GO RIGHT THROUGH THE BALL... AND TAKE THE GRASS WITH YOU!

A rough tip

IF YOU STAND TOO UPRIGHT IN HEAVY ROUGH, TOM ...
... YOUR SWING WILL BE VERY FLAT AND YOU WILL HIT ALL THE GRASS BEFORE YOU HIT THE BALL
IN LONG ROUGH, I CROUCH OVER THE BALL SO THAT I CAN TURN MY LEFT SHOULDER UNDER MY CHIN MORE EASILY
THIS PICKS THE CLUB UP SHARPLY. NOW I WILL BE ABLE TO HIT THE BALL FIRST AND GET THROUGH THE GRASS

Beware that perched up ball...

THIS IS A BIT OF LUCK, GARY. I THOUGHT MY BALL WOULD BE BURIED IN THIS LONG ROUGH, BUT IT'S PERCHED UP NICELY ON THIS TUFT OF GRASS
IN SPITE OF ALL MY EXPERIENCE, I HAVE MANY, MANY TIMES FALLEN FOR THIS ONE MYSELF! THIS SEASON, IN A SOUTH AFRICAN TOURNAMENT, I DID EXACTLY WHAT YOU DID. IT IS VERY EMBARRASSING, AS THE BALL GOES NOWHERE
NOT SO LUCKY, IAIN. YOU'VE DONE EXACTLY WHAT I FEARED YOU'D DO... HIT COMPLETELY UNDERNEATH THE BALL!
WHAT YOU MUST DO IS TO ADDRESS THE TOP OF THE BALL WITHOUT PUTTING THE CLUB ON THE GROUND. THIS WILL MAKE YOU HIT THE BALL FIRST AND GET IT FLYING, INSTEAD OF MERELY SCYTHING THE GRASS IT'S SITTING ON
ADDRESS HERE

Chop down in long grass

THIS IS A SHOT WE HAVE TO PLAY MAINLY IN THE U.S. OPEN AND THE BRITISH OPEN WHERE, IF YOU OVERSHOOT THE GREEN, YOU FIND YOURSELF IN VERY LONG GRASS RIGHT NEXT TO THE EDGE OF THE GREEN
THE BEST THING TO DO IS TO PLAY IT LIKE A BUNKER SHOT AND AIM TWO INCHES BEHIND THE BALL
IN ORDER NOT TO GET ALL TANGLED UP WITH THE GRASS, I PICK UP MY SAND-IRON VERY SHARPLY. THEN I CAN CHOP DOWN THROUGH THE GRASS AND GET THE BALL UP AND OUT
BY AIMING TWO INCHES BEHIND THE BALL AND PLAYING IT JUST LIKE A BUNKER SHOT, ALL THE GRASS GOES UNDERNEATH THE BALL...
THEREFORE, YOU CANNOT HOPE FOR BACKSPIN. YOU MUST ALLOW FOR QUITE A BIT OF RUN ON YOUR BALL

Make allowance for "fliers"

WOULD YOU BELIEVE IT, GARY! I'VE GONE A DOZEN YARDS THROUGH THE GREEN..., WITH A 7-IRON!
YOU DIDN'T ALLOW FOR THE EXTRA DISTANCE YOU GET WHEN PLAYING OUT OF SHORT ROUGH!
YOU SEE, AT IMPACT, THE GRASS IS SQUASHED BETWEEN CLUBFACE AND BALL, WHICH SQUIRTS OUT WITH TOPSPIN. THIS IS CALLED A "FLIER", AND IT TRAVELS AT LEAST ONE CLUB LENGTH FURTHER
WHEN YOUR BALL LIES SLIGHTLY BELOW THE LEVEL OF THE GRASS, REMEMBER YOU'LL GET NO BACKSPIN... SO TAKE AN 8-IRON INSTEAD OF A 7, AND ALLOW FOR IT TO RUN UP TO THE HOLE

Coping with fliers

IT'S GONE 15 YARDS OVER THE GREEN, GARY!
YOU HIT A FLIER, IAIN, BECAUSE YOUR BALL WAS HALF-BURIED IN THE GRASS. WITH A LIE LIKE THAT YOU ARE ALWAYS CERTAIN TO GET A LOT OF TOPSPIN!
REID'S LIE
I TOLD YOU BEFORE THAT, WHEN YOU ARE IN LONG GRASS, YOU SHOULD TAKE ONE CLUB LESS THAN THE DISTANCE CALLS FOR. FOR EXAMPLE, IF YOU ARE 8-IRON DISTANCE FROM THE GREEN, TAKE A NINE
BUT, PLAYING IN AMERICA THIS YEAR, I HAVE DISCOVERED THAT THIS TENDS TO MAKE ME TRY TO HIT A BIT HARDER, WITH THE RESULT THAT I TAKE A BIGGER DIVOT WHICH GIVES ME EVEN MORE OF A FLIER!
I HAVE COME TO THE CONCLUSION THAT THE BEST WAY TO COMPENSATE FOR A FLIER IS TO TAKE ONE CLUB MORE THAN YOU WOULD FOR A NORMAL LIE AND TO HAVE ONLY A THREE-QUARTER BACKSWING
THREE-QUARTER SWING
IN OTHER WORDS, IF I AM 6-IRON DISTANCE FROM THE GREEN, I PLAY A SOFT LITTLE 5-IRON SHOT WITH THE RESULT THAT I TAKE A SMALLER DIVOT AND THE BALL COMES OUT CLEANER

Topping it!

WOW! I NEVER THOUGHT I WOULD HIT A 7-IRON THAT FAR, GARY!
YOU GOT A FLIER, IAIN! THIS FAIRWAY HASN'T BEEN CUT FOR SOME TIME AND YOUR BALL WAS LYING PRETTY LOW IN THE GRASS
AT ADDRESS, YOU HAD GRASS BETWEEN THE CLUBHEAD AND THE BALL—THAT IS WHY IT SQUIRTED OUT WITH SO MUCH OVERSPIN
WHEN THE FAIRWAY GRASS IS LONG, I DON'T GROUND MY CLUB. I ADDRESS ONLY THE UPPER PART OF THE BALL. THEN I REALLY TRY TO TOP THE SHOT, IN ORDER TO CUT DOWN THE AMOUNT OF GRASS I GET PINCHED BETWEEN CLUBHEAD AND BALL
DON'T WORRY, IAIN—YOU WON'T ACTUALLY TOP THE BALL! THAT IS A VERY DIFFICULT THING TO DO IN LONG GRASS!

How to get out of a ditch

I CAN'T GET THE BALL UP QUICKLY ENOUGH, GARY. I KEEP ON BASHING IT AGAINST THE BANK OF THIS DITCH
YOU SHOULDN'T HAVE YOUR WEIGHT EVENLY DISTRIBUTED FOR THIS TYPE OF SHOT, IAIN. AND YOU'VE GOT A LONG BACKSWING WITH NO WRIST BREAK WHICH CAUSES YOUR CLUB TO CATCH THE GRASS GOING BACK AND COMING DOWN!
BY HAVING MY WEIGHT FAVORING MY LEFT SIDE, I CAN PICK UP THE CLUB VERY SHARPLY ON THE BACKSWING, AND IT WON'T TANGLE UP IN THE GRASS
NOW I AM IN A POSITION TO CHOP DOWN ON THE BALL, AND THAT WILL GET IT UP AND OUT OF IT QUICKLY

How to play off a road

WHEN THE AVERAGE MAN FINDS HIS BALL SITTING ON A ROAD, HE IMAGINES HE'S IN BIG TROUBLE. HE FEELS THAT BECAUSE THE GROUND IS HARD, HE HAS TO SCOOP THE BALL UP, LIKE YOU'VE DONE, IAIN. AND LIKE YOU, HE WON'T GET DISTANCE
WELL, THE BALL MUST NOT BE SCOOPED UP! IT HAS GOT TO BE HIT DOWN INTO THE ROAD... DOWN AND THROUGH!
YOU CAN ONLY DO THIS IF YOU ADDRESS THE BALL CORRECTLY. THE WEIGHT MUST BE FORWARD ON THE LEFT LEG, AND THE HANDS MUST BE IN FRONT OF THE BALL
WHEN YOU ADDRESS THE BALL LIKE THIS, AND PUNCH INTO THE SHOT, YOU SOON DISCOVER THAT PLAYING OFF A ROAD IS REALLY ONE OF THE EASIEST SHOTS IN GOLF!

A MOMENT OF AGONY

He has traveled thousands of miles from his beloved South Africa.

He has lived out of a suitcase for as long as he can remember.

Home is a motel.

He has punished his muscles on the practice ground.

He has almost forgotten what his children look like.

And now the putts won't drop!

At a moment like this, the last thing Gary Player wishes to be is a professional golfer.

SECTION ELEVEN

Trouble Shots

Three golden rules

WAIT A MINUTE, IAIN! JUST BECAUSE YOU'VE GOT A BAD LIE THAT IS NO REASON TO TENSE UP! YOU ARE GRIPPING FAR TOO TIGHTLY AND YOUR LEGS ARE STRAIGHT AS RAMRODS
THERE ARE THREE GOLDEN RULES WHEN YOU HAVE A BAD LIE. FIRSTLY, YOU MUST RELAX AT ADDRESS. BEND THOSE KNEES
SECONDLY, MAKE A NICE SLOW TURN ON THE BACKSWING
THEN, THIRDLY, REALLY WHIP THAT CLUB THROUGH THE BALL AS FAST AS YOU CAN
FAST

The squeeze shot

I'VE LEFT IT SHORT AND OUT TO THE RIGHT, GARY!
YOU HIT BEHIND THE BALL, TOM!
WHEN YOUR BALL IS IN A DIVOT HOLE, THE WORST THING YOU CAN DO IS TO ADDRESS IT WITH AN OPEN CLUBFACE AND YOUR HANDS BEHIND THE BALL
YOU MUST SHUT THE CLUBFACE AND HAVE YOUR HANDS WELL AHEAD OF THE BALL. THIS WAY YOU WILL HIT THE BALL FIRST AND SQUEEZE IT OUT OF THE HOLE
THE BALL WILL FLY WITH A LOW TRAJECTORY AND A SLIGHT RIGHT TO LEFT DRAW!
SHUT

Watch that slope

TWO MAIN FAULTS, TOM. YOU'RE STANDING TOO FAR AWAY FROM THE BALL, AND YOU ARE AIMING DIRECTLY AT THE FLAG
WHEN THE BALL IS BELOW THE LEVEL OF THE FEET, IT HAS A TENDENCY TO GO TO THE RIGHT. BY STANDING TOO FAR AWAY FROM THE BALL, IT WILL GO EVEN MORE TO THE RIGHT!
AIM LEFT
I STAND AT LEAST SIX INCHES NEARER TO THE BALL THAN YOU DID. AND I AIM LEFT OF TARGET
MY BALL STARTS OFF TO THE LEFT OF THE FLAG BUT, WHEN IT LANDS, IT WILL BOUNCE TO THE RIGHT
THIS IS BECAUSE THE SLOPE OF THE GROUND AUTOMATICALLY MAKES ME PUT MORE CUT SPIN ON THE BALL THAN NORMALLY

The impossible shot!

THIS IS WHAT I CALL THE "IMPOSSIBLE SHOT", IAIN... WHEN YOUR BALL IS LYING RIGHT UP AGAINST THE BANK OF A FAIRLY STEEP BUNKER
EVEN I COULDN'T GET THAT BALL UP IN THE AIR QUICKLY ENOUGH TO CLEAR THE BANK IF I AIMED STRAIGHT FOR THE PIN
IT DOESN'T PAY TO BE TOO GREEDY IN THIS GAME OF GOLF. SOMETIMES YOU JUST HAVE TO ACCEPT THE FACT THAT YOU ARE GOING TO LOSE A STROKE!
FACED WITH THAT SHOT, I WOULD HAVE ACCEPTED THE FACT THAT I COULD NOT AIM AT THE FLAG, AND WOULD HAVE BLASTED OUT TO THE RIGHT OF IT
ALTHOUGH MY STANCE IS AWKWARD, I CAN AT LEAST GET THE BALL ONTO THE GREEN, AND I SHOULD BE DOWN IN TWO PUTTS... MAYBE EVEN ONE!

Playing off an up-slope

I THOUGHT I WOULD HAVE REACHED THE GREEN WITH AN 8-IRON, GARY!
YOU WOULD HAVE, IAIN... ON LEVEL GROUND! BUT AN UP-SLOPE ALWAYS MAKES THE BALL GO MUCH HIGHER THAN USUAL, AND SO YOU LOSE DISTANCE!
YOU ALSO MADE THE MISTAKE OF PLAYING THE BALL OFF YOUR LEFT HEEL WHICH MADE THE BALL GO HIGHER STILL!

AS THIS WOULD BE A 150 YARD 8-IRON SHOT TO THE GREEN OFF A NORMAL, FLAT LIE, I TAKE A 7-IRON TO ALLOW FOR THE EFFECT OF THE SLOPE
BECAUSE, ON AN UP-SLOPE, THE WEIGHT IS ON THE RIGHT LEG, ONE IS INCLINED TO "SCOOP" THE BALL. I COUNTERACT THIS, AND KEEP THE BALL FROM GOING TOO HIGH, BY HAVING MY HANDS IN FRONT OF THE BALL AND PLAYING IT OFF THE CENTER OF MY STANCE

When the ball is below your feet...aim left

REMEMBER WHAT I TOLD YOU ABOUT PLAYING OFF SLOPING GROUND, IAIN! THE BALL WILL ALWAYS TEND TO GO WHICHEVER WAY THE GROUND SLOPES
YOU MEAN, IT WOULD VEER TO THE RIGHT?
EXACTLY! AND BY AIMING DIRECTLY AT THE FLAG, YOU ARE NOT ALLOWING FOR THIS! IN ADDITION, YOU ARE GRIPPING THE CLUB SHORT. YOU ARE ALSO STANDING TOO FAR AWAY FROM THE BALL — BOTH COMMON MISTAKES.
I GRIP THE CLUB FULL, AND STAND CLOSER TO THE BALL THAN I DO ON LEVEL GROUND. THIS WAY I CAN GET OVER THE BALL BETTER. THEN ALL I DO IS TO SWING NORMALLY
ON A CALM DAY LIKE THIS, I AIM ABOUT TEN YARDS TO THE LEFT OF THE FLAG WHICH COMPENSATES FOR THE FACT THAT INEVITABLY, MY BALL IS GOING TO SLICE!
STANDING OVER THE BALL
AIMING LEFT OF PIN

Playing off a down slope

I HATE PLAYING OFF GROUND THAT SLOPES TOWARDS THE HOLE, GARY!
YES, IT'S VERY DIFFICULT, TOM. TO MAKE THINGS WORSE, YOU'RE ADDRESSING THE BALL OPPOSITE YOUR LEFT FOOT, THEREFORE THERE IS A LOT OF GROUND ABOVE THE LEVEL OF THE BALL WHICH WILL CAUSE YOU TO HIT BEHIND THE BALL
BY POSITIONING THE BALL OPPOSITE MY RIGHT LEG, THERE'S NOT SO MUCH GROUND ABOVE MY BALL, SO IT'S EASIER FOR ME TO HIT THE BALL FIRST
THE BEST TIP I CAN GIVE FOR ALL SLOPE SHOTS IS, REMEMBER THAT THE BALL ALWAYS TENDS TO GO IN THE DIRECTION OF THE SLOPE
HERE THE GROUND SLOPES DOWN, SO THE BALL WILL KEEP LOW. THERE'S NO GOOD TRYING TO HIT A 1-IRON HERE...
IF YOU TAKE A 5-IRON, THE SLOPE WILL TURN IT INTO A 4-IRON! VICE VERSA FOR RISING SLOPES

The shot that Palmer beat me with...

HOW DO YOU LIKE THAT, GARY! THE BEST DRIVE I'VE HIT ALL DAY AND IT BOUNCES OFF A STONE TO THE EDGE OF THE ROUGH
THAT'S GOLF, IAIN! BUT DON'T WORRY, THERE'S ALWAYS A WAY OUT
A FEW YEARS AGO IN THE CARLING EVENT AT OAKLAND HILLS, ARNOLD PALMER WAS FACED WITH THIS VERY SHOT ON THE LAST HOLE WHEN OUR SCORES WERE DEAD LEVEL. HE USED HIS HEAD, PLAYED THE SHOT PROPERLY AND HIS BALL ACTUALLY HIT THE FLAGSTICK. ARNIE GOT A THREE AND I TOOK FIVE!
WHAT PALMER DID, AND WHAT I ALWAYS DO IN THIS SITUATION, WAS TO TAKE THE CLUB BACK A LITTLE MORE INSIDE THE LINE THAN NORMAL TO AVOID GETTING IT ALL TANGLED UP WITH THE LONG GRASS
THE STANCE IS NORMAL AND SO IS THE FOLLOW-THROUGH. BUT, BECAUSE THE CLUB IS TAKEN BACK MORE INSIDE THE LINE THAN USUAL, REMEMBER THE BALL IS BOUND TO HOOK SLIGHTLY. SO MAKE ALLOWANCES

GARY PLAYER'S GOLF CLASS:

Playing out of water

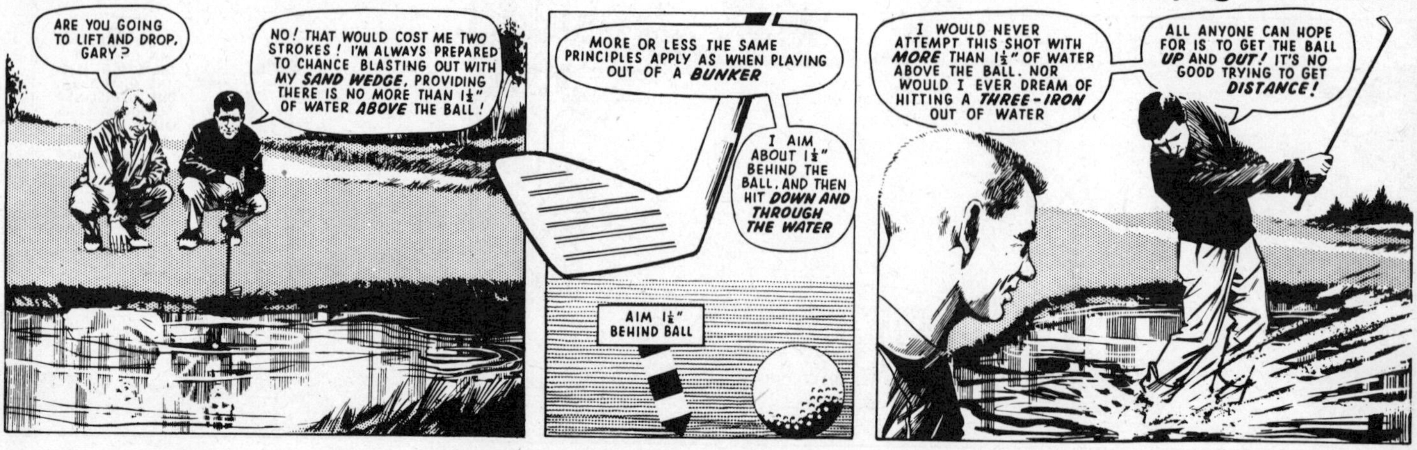

ARE YOU GOING TO LIFT AND DROP, GARY?
NO! THAT WOULD COST ME TWO STROKES! I'M ALWAYS PREPARED TO CHANCE BLASTING OUT WITH MY SAND WEDGE, PROVIDING THERE IS NO MORE THAN 1½" OF WATER ABOVE THE BALL!
MORE OR LESS THE SAME PRINCIPLES APPLY AS WHEN PLAYING OUT OF A BUNKER
I AIM ABOUT 1½" BEHIND THE BALL, AND THEN HIT DOWN AND THROUGH THE WATER
AIM 1½" BEHIND BALL
I WOULD NEVER ATTEMPT THIS SHOT WITH MORE THAN 1½" OF WATER ABOVE THE BALL. NOR WOULD I EVER DREAM OF HITTING A THREE-IRON OUT OF WATER
ALL ANYONE CAN HOPE FOR IS TO GET THE BALL UP AND OUT! IT'S NO GOOD TRYING TO GET DISTANCE!

Matty fairways

THIS IS A MATTY FAIRWAY, TOM. YOU MUST MAKE ALLOWANCES FOR IT.
DIVOT ROLLS OVER —DOESN'T FLY OUT
MATTY
YOU MUSTN'T CHOP DOWN AND DIG HUGE DIVOTS. TO AVOID THIS, ADDRESS THE BALL A LITTLE FURTHER FORWARD THAN YOU USUALLY DO.
HANDS SLIGHTLY BEHIND BALL.
ALSO, TRY TO HIT THE BALL A LITTLE BIT CLEANER. THIS WILL PREVENT YOU GETTING A FLYING SHOT TO THE GREEN.

How to play an impossible shot

THIS SHOT IS IMPOSSIBLE TO PLAY, GARY. I CAN'T GET A PROPER STANCE
NO, IAIN, IT'S NOT IMPOSSIBLE. LET ME SHOW YOU
STAND WITH YOUR BACK TO THE HOLE AND LINE UP THE SHOT BY LOOKING THROUGH YOUR LEGS...
THEN, LIFT UP THE CLUB STRAIGHT IN FRONT OF YOU...
AND CHOP DOWN ON THE BALL, PLAYING IT THROUGH YOUR LEGS
THIS SHOT IS NOT NEARLY SO DIFFICULT AS IT LOOKS, AND IT CAN BE A STROKE-SAVER!

Playing off a hard surface

HOLD IT, IAIN! I KNOW YOU ARE 7-IRON DISTANCE FROM THE GREEN, BUT TAKE AN 8-IRON OFF THIS PATH.
BOUNCE
WHEN THE CLUBHEAD HITS THE HARD SURFACE IT WILL BOUNCE AND SPRING OFF IT. THIS INCREASES THE CLUBHEAD SPEED THROUGH THE BALL.
SO, REMEMBER, WHEN YOU'RE HITTING OFF A TAR ROAD, A CEMENT ROAD OR ANY HARD SURFACE, TAKE ONE CLUB LESS THAN THE DISTANCE NORMALLY DEMANDS.
8-IRON
7-IRON

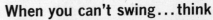

When you can't swing . . . think

I CAN'T SWING THE CLUB AT ALL HERE, GARY. I'LL JUST HAVE TO CHIP OUT BACKWARDS
I AGREE YOU CAN'T SWING RIGHT-HANDED, IAIN, BUT I THINK YOU CAN STILL MAKE THE GREEN AND SAVE A STROKE
AS YOUR LIE ISN'T TOO BAD, YOU CAN TAKE OUT YOUR PUTTER, AND SWING LEFT-HANDED
BE CAREFUL NOT TO TAKE A LONG BACKSWING AS YOU ARE NOT ACCUSTOMED TO SWINGING LEFT-HANDED
A SHORT BACKSWING WITH A LONG FOLLOW-THROUGH IS THE ANSWER.
YOU SEE, IT PAYS TO STOP AND THINK BEFORE DECIDING TO TOSS AWAY A VALUABLE STROKE!

A tough shot

THIS HAS GOT TO BE ONE OF THE HARDEST SHOTS IN GOLF, GARY—A 3-IRON OFF A DOWNSLOPE!
I AGREE, TOM!
I'M NEVER ABLE TO GET THE BALL UP IN THE AIR.
THAT IS BECAUSE YOU AIM TO THE RIGHT WHICH MAKES YOU SHUT THE CLUBFACE COMING INTO THE BALL.
I FIND IT PAYS TO STAND OPEN FOR THIS SHOT. THE BLADE IS THEN SLIGHTLY OPEN AT IMPACT, AND AN OPEN BLADE GIVES HEIGHT.

Hooking around trees

TO HOOK ROUND THESE TREES, I AIM TO THE RIGHT OF TARGET WITH A CLOSED STANCE... THAT IS, LEFT LEG IN FRONT OF RIGHT
I TAKE THE CLUB BACK INSIDE THE LINE. MY HANDS COME IN VERY CLOSE TO MY BODY WHICH GIVES ME AN EXAGGERATED PIVOT
ON THE DOWNSWING, MY CLUB TRAVELS INSIDE TO OUT. MY RIGHT HAND ROLLS OVER MY LEFT WHICH CLOSES THE CLUB-FACE AND IMPARTS RIGHT TO LEFT SPIN ON THE BALL
REMEMBER, IF YOU HIT FROM OUT TO IN YOU WILL SLICE... IN TO OUT AND YOU WILL HOOK!
PROVIDED HE HAS A REASONABLE LIE, THE AVERAGE PLAYER SHOULD NEVER BE AFRAID TO TRY THESE SHOTS!

Slicing around trees

I THINK I'LL TAKE AN AXE HERE, GARY. THESE TREES ARE IN MY WAY
NO NEED TO CUT 'EM DOWN, TOM. I'LL TEACH YOU HOW TO SLICE ROUND THEM
I AIM LEFT OF TARGET WITH AN OPEN STANCE — RIGHT LEG IN FRONT OF LEFT. THIS ENABLES ME TO TAKE BACK THE CLUB OUTSIDE THE TARGET LINE
NOTICE, ALSO, HOW I HAVE PICKED UP THE CLUB INTO A VERY UPRIGHT BACKSWING
UPRIGHT BACKSWING
LINE TO TARGET
INSIDE THE LINE
OUTSIDE THE LINE
NOW, ON THE DOWNSWING, MY CLUB TRAVELS FROM OUTSIDE THE LINE TO IN, CUTTING ACROSS THE BALL...
THIS IMPARTS A LEFT TO RIGHT SPIN ON THE BALL WHICH SLICES IT ROUND THE TREES

SECTION TWELVE

Tips For The Ladies

Ladies, shorten that backswing

SEE, IAIN, THERE'S A TYPICAL FAULT OF THE WOMAN GOLFER. WOMEN ARE SO SUPPLE, THEY TEND TO HAVE AN OVERLONG BACKSWING AND A VERY SHORT FOLLOW-THROUGH
BY TAKING THE CLUB TOO FAR BACK, THEY ARE UNABLE TO BUILD UP VERY MUCH CLUBHEAD SPEED THROUGH THE BALL
MY ADVICE TO ALL LADIES IS, DO NOT LET YOUR CLUB DROP BELOW A LINE PARALLEL TO THE GROUND, THEN YOU WILL BE ABLE TO GENERATE MUCH MORE CLUBHEAD SPEED THROUGH THE BALL
HERE, MY WIFE, VIVIENNE, IS DEMONSTRATING THIS VERY WELL. SHE HAS A GOOD WIND-UP, AND AN EXTREMELY LONG FOLLOW-THROUGH
SHE USES HER BACK AND LEG MUSCLES VERY WELL... WHICH IS IMPORTANT IF YOU WANT TO HIT THE BALL A LONG WAY. VIVIENNE HAS WHAT I CALL THE PERFECT GOLF SWING!

Advice for lady golfers

MANY LADY GOLFERS GRIP THE CLUB TOO TIGHTLY, IAIN. THIS GIVES THEM A MINI-BACKSWING WITH HARDLY ANY WRIST BREAK, AND A SHORT, SLUGGISH FOLLOW-THROUGH WITH, ONCE AGAIN, NO BREAKING OF THE WRISTS
NOW LOOK WHAT HAPPENS WHEN SHE GRIPS THE CLUB NO TIGHTER THAN SHE WOULD HOLD HER BOYFRIEND'S HAND! SHE GETS INTO A POSITION OF POWER ON THE BACKSWING WITH A FULL WRIST COCK
THEN SHE HITS RIGHT THROUGH THE BALL INTO A TREMENDOUS FOLLOW-THROUGH. THE DIFFERENCE IS LIKE NIGHT AND DAY!

A tip for the ladies

MANY PLAYERS, INCLUDING BOB ROSBURG AND ART WALL, USE THE "HAMMER" GRIP IN WHICH BOTH HANDS ARE PLACED TOGETHER ON THE SHAFT WITH NO OVERLAPPING OR INTERLOCKING OF THE FINGERS
THIS IS A VERY STRONG GRIP AND ONE WHICH I RECOMMEND TO LADY GOLFERS AS IT PRODUCES A TREMENDOUS AMOUNT OF CLUBHEAD SPEED
AS YOU PROBABLY KNOW, IAIN, IF YOU GIVE A CLUB TO A LADY FOR THE FIRST TIME, SHE'LL ALMOST CERTAINLY GRAB IT LIKE THAT ANYWAY!

Ladies, thump that heel down

SEE HOW THIS LADY IS UP ON HER TOES AS SHE COMES INTO THE BALL, IAIN? THAT'S ONE OF THE MOST COMMON FAULTS WITH WOMEN GOLFERS
SHE'S RIGHT IN THE HITTING AREA, THEREFORE HER LEFT HEEL SHOULD BE FLAT ON THE GROUND AND HER WEIGHT SHOULD BE TRANSFERRED ON TO HER LEFT SIDE
THIS TIME, SHE IS DOING WHAT I TOLD HER. SHE STARTED HER DOWNSWING BY THUMPING HER LEFT HEEL DOWN ON THE GROUND. AND THE IMPROVEMENT IN HER BODY ACTION IS TREMENDOUS
SHE'S GOT HER HEAD BEHIND THE BALL, AND HER BACK IS NICELY ARCHED. BY THUMPING HER HEEL DOWN SHE HAS GOT SOME GOOD LEG MOVEMENT INTO THE SWING INSTEAD OF JUST A DULL HAND ACTION
I REALLY RECOMMEND THIS HEEL-THUMPING... NOT ONLY TO WOMEN, BUT TO ANY MAN WHO'S HAVING TROUBLE WITH HIS SWING

SECTION THIRTEEN

Equipment

Check your clubs

I LOVE THE "FEEL" OF MY NEW DRIVER, GARY, BUT I SEEM TO BE SLICING MORE THAN USUAL!
I'M NOT SURPRISED, IAIN! THE FACE OF THIS CLUB IS SET OPEN! LET'S GO TO THE PRO-SHOP AND I'LL GET IT FIXED FOR YOU
FACE OPEN
THAT'S MUCH BETTER, IAIN. NOW, INSTEAD OF BEING OPEN, THE FACE IS SLIGHTLY HOOKED WHICH COUNTERACTS YOUR TENDENCY TO SLICE
GOLFERS ARE ONLY NOW BEGINNING TO REALIZE HOW IMPORTANT IT IS TO HAVE THE RIGHT GOLF CLUBS. MANY MANUFACTURERS ALL OVER THE WORLD ARE GIVING THEIR CLUBS A SLIGHT HOOK BECAUSE THE AVERAGE MAN SLICES
ON THE OTHER HAND, ARNOLD PALMER, WHO IS QUITE A HOOKER, HAS ALL HIS DRIVERS SET 'WAY OPEN. SO DON'T PLAY WITH CLUBS THAT ARE WRONG FOR YOU. GET YOUR PRO TO CHECK THEM AND RE-FACE THEM FOR YOU IF NECESSARY!
FACE CLOSED

The lie test

YOU KNOW, IAIN, THERE ARE PEOPLE WHO SLICE OR HOOK ALL THEIR LIVES, SIMPLY BECAUEE THE LIE OF THEIR CLUBS IS WRONG!
THESE CLUBS YOU'RE TRYING OUT TODAY WILL MAKE YOU HOOK BECAUSE THEY ARE TOO UPRIGHT FOR YOU—SEE, I CAN GET MY FINGER UNDERNEATH THE TOE OF THE CLUB!
TOO UPRIGHT
ON THE OTHER HAND, THIS CLUB IS TOO FLAT FOR YOU—THE HEEL IS OFF THE GROUND. THIS WILL MAKE YOU SLICE
TOO FLAT
THE MOST IMPORTANT THING TO CHECK WHEN BUYING CLUBS IS THAT THEY HAVE THE CORRECT LIE! THAT'S EVEN MORE IMPORTANT THAN SWINGWEIGHT!
CORRECT
MY OWN CLUBS ARE ONE DEGREE FLATTER THAN STANDARD WHICH IS SUITABLE FOR ANYONE UNDER 5'7". BETWEEN 5'7" AND 5'11", A STANDARD LIE IS CORRECT. ANYONE OVER 5'11" SHOULD HAVE A ONE DEGREE UPRIGHT CLUB
COUNTLESS PLAYERS USE CLUBS WITH THE WRONG LIE, AND THIS IS VERY SILLY BECAUSE A PROFESSIONAL CAN VERY EASILY PUT THEM RIGHT BY BENDING THEM
UNDER 5'7" ONE DEGREE FLAT
5'7"—5'11" STANDARD LIE
OVER 5'11" ONE DEGREE UPRIGHT

Thick grip—thin grip

ANY IDEA YET WHY I'M SLICING SO BADLY, GARY?
SORRY, IAIN! YOU'VE GOT ME STUMPED! YOUR STANCE IS FINE, YOU'RE GRIPPING THE CLUB PROPERLY... AH! ...WAIT! LET'S HAVE A LOOK AT YOUR CLUB...
THAT'S IT! THIS CLUB'S GRIP IS FAR TOO THICK FOR YOU! YOU ARE THEREFORE INCLINED TO HOLD THE CLUB IN THE PALM OF THE LEFT HAND WHICH WILL DEFINITELY CAUSE YOU TO SLICE
NOW THIS CLUB OF MINE SUITS YOU MUCH BETTER. BECAUSE IT IS THINNER, IT CAN LIE DIAGONALLY ACROSS THE LEFT HAND, RESTING HALF AN INCH BELOW THE LITTLE FINGER AND HALF AN INCH UP THE INDEX FINGER. CLOSE THE HAND AND YOU GET THE CORRECT LEFT HAND POSITION
IT IS ALSO BAD TO HAVE GRIPS THAT ARE TOO THIN. THEN YOU WILL TEND TO HOLD THE CLUB IN YOUR FINGERS WHICH WILL MAKE YOU HOOK
I THINK I COULD CURE ANY MAN WHO IS INCLINED TO HOOK SIMPLY BY THICKENING UP THE PART OF THE GRIP WHERE HIS LEFT HAND GOES

The secret of lighter clubs

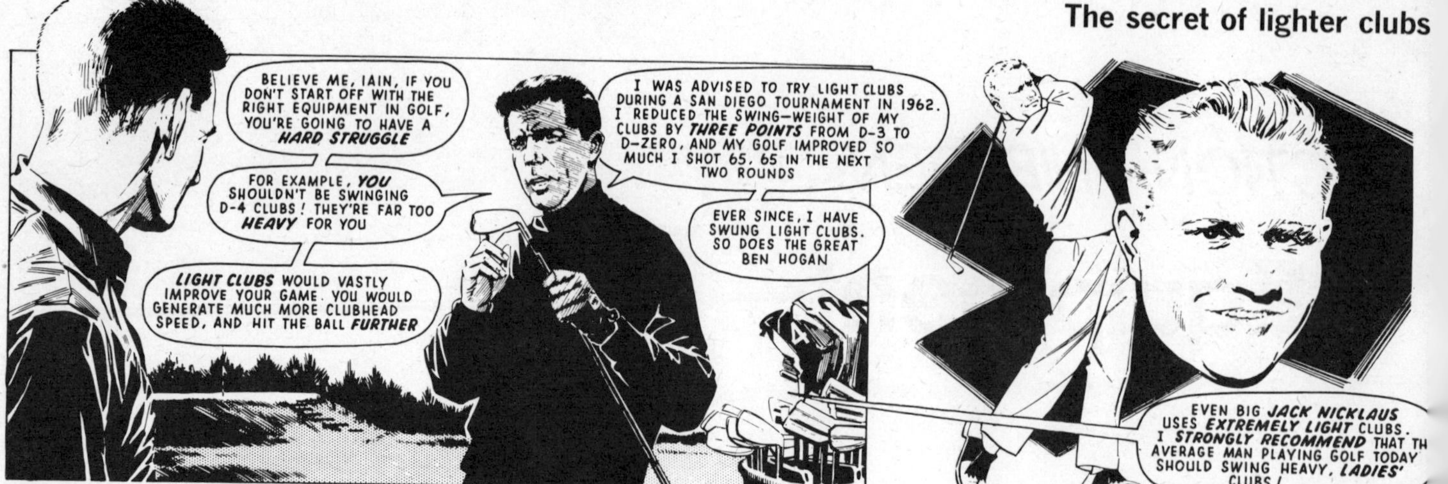

BELIEVE ME, IAIN, IF YOU DON'T START OFF WITH THE RIGHT EQUIPMENT IN GOLF, YOU'RE GOING TO HAVE A HARD STRUGGLE
FOR EXAMPLE, YOU SHOULDN'T BE SWINGING D-4 CLUBS! THEY'RE FAR TOO HEAVY FOR YOU
LIGHT CLUBS WOULD VASTLY IMPROVE YOUR GAME. YOU WOULD GENERATE MUCH MORE CLUBHEAD SPEED, AND HIT THE BALL FURTHER
I WAS ADVISED TO TRY LIGHT CLUBS DURING A SAN DIEGO TOURNAMENT IN 1962. I REDUCED THE SWING-WEIGHT OF MY CLUBS BY THREE POINTS FROM D-3 TO D-ZERO, AND MY GOLF IMPROVED SO MUCH I SHOT 65, 65 IN THE NEXT TWO ROUNDS
EVER SINCE, I HAVE SWUNG LIGHT CLUBS. SO DOES THE GREAT BEN HOGAN
EVEN BIG JACK NICKLAUS USES EXTREMELY LIGHT CLUBS. I STRONGLY RECOMMEND THAT TH AVERAGE MAN PLAYING GOLF TODAY SHOULD SWING HEAVY, LADIES' CLUBS!

Filing for height!

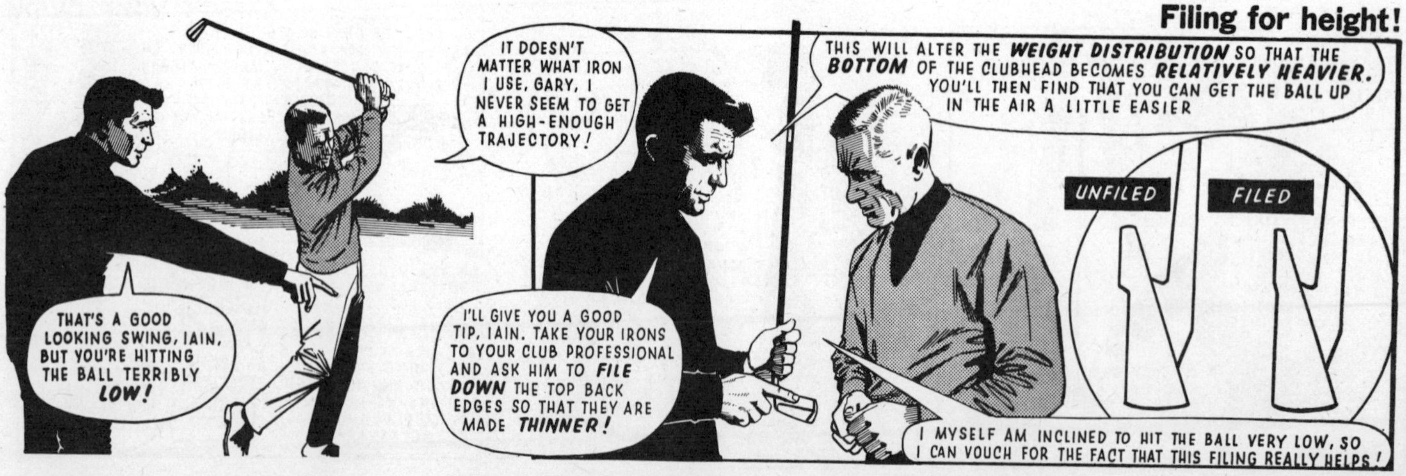

THAT'S A GOOD LOOKING SWING, IAIN, BUT YOU'RE HITTING THE BALL TERRIBLY LOW!
IT DOESN'T MATTER WHAT IRON I USE, GARY, I NEVER SEEM TO GET A HIGH-ENOUGH TRAJECTORY!
I'LL GIVE YOU A GOOD TIP, IAIN. TAKE YOUR IRONS TO YOUR CLUB PROFESSIONAL AND ASK HIM TO FILE DOWN THE TOP BACK EDGES SO THAT THEY ARE MADE THINNER!
THIS WILL ALTER THE WEIGHT DISTRIBUTION SO THAT THE BOTTOM OF THE CLUBHEAD BECOMES RELATIVELY HEAVIER. YOU'LL THEN FIND THAT YOU CAN GET THE BALL UP IN THE AIR A LITTLE EASIER
UNFILED
FILED
I MYSELF AM INCLINED TO HIT THE BALL VERY LOW, SO I CAN VOUCH FOR THE FACT THAT THIS FILING REALLY HELPS!

Large ball? Small ball?

MAN—I'VE SEEN YOU SLICE A FEW BALLS IN MY TIME, IAIN! BUT NEVER SO BAD AS THAT!
AND NOW I SEE WHY! YOU'RE PRACTICING WITH THE BIG BALL WHICH MEANS THAT EVERY MISTAKE YOU MAKE IS ACCENTUATED. THE AVERAGE WEEKENDER SHOULD STICK TO THE SMALL BALL, IAIN!
HOWEVER, I WOULD ADVISE PROS, TOP AMATEURS AND JUNIORS WHO WANT TO BECOME TOP-CLASS GOLFERS TO PRACTICE WITH THE BIG BALL BECAUSE IT IS MORE DIFFICULT TO USE. YOU CAN SOMETIMES HIT THE SMALL BALL BADLY AND GET AWAY WITH IT, BUT NOT SO WITH THE BIG BALL. THEREFORE, YOU LEARN TO STRIKE THE BIG BALL BETTER!
SLICE
HOOK
BIG BALL VEERS OFF LINE MORE BECAUSE ITS LARGER SURFACE ENCOUNTERS MORE AIR RESISTANCE

Three wedges

AS I FEEL THAT MOST OF THE SCORING IS DONE ROUND THE GREENS I ONLY CARRY TWO WOODS. THIS ALLOWS ME TO CARRY THREE WEDGES!
I HAVE A NORMAL SAND WEDGE WITH A BIG FLANGE FOR BUNKER SHOTS...
...A PITCHING WEDGE FOR FAIRWAY SHOTS 90 TO 120 YARDS OUT...
...AND A SPECIAL SAND WEDGE WITH A LOT OF LOFT BUT NO FLANGE FOR CHIPPING OVER TRAPS OR MOUNDS WHEN I WANT THE BALL TO STOP QUICKLY!
MY ADVICE TO THE AVERAGE WEEKENDER IS —CARRY THREE WEDGES, AND LEAVE YOUR 2-IRON IN THE CLUBHOUSE!
SAND WEDGE
PITCHING WEDGE
SAND WEDGE

A little dirt harms nobody, golfers excepted

IAIN, DON'T PUT YOUR CLUB AWAY LIKE THAT!
WHAT DO YOU MEAN?
THE GROOVES ARE THERE FOR A PURPOSE. THEY HELP YOU TO GET BACKSPIN ON YOUR BALL, SO YOU MUST KEEP THEM FREE OF DIRT
YOU MUST ALWAYS CLEAN THE CLUBFACE AFTER EVERY SHOT! TAKE A TEE-PEG AND RUB IT ALONG THE GROOVES LIKE THIS TO SCRAPE OUT ALL THE MUD
IT'S SURPRISING HOW MANY GOLFERS DON'T KEEP THEIR CLUBS CLEAN. I HAVE SEEN TOP PLAYERS LOSE TOURNAMENTS SIMPLY BECAUSE THEY DID NOT BOTHER TO CLEAN THE CLUBFACE AFTER EACH SHOT!

100 yards difference

I'VE HAD TO LAY UP SHORT OF THE WATER, GARY. IF ONLY MY TEE SHOT HAD BEEN A FEW YARDS LONGER, I COULD HAVE GONE FOR THE GREEN
WEDGE
4-IRON
DRIVE
REID
THAT PROVES A POINT THAT BOB GOALBY ONCE MADE. HE SAID THAT THERE IS SOMETIMES AS MUCH AS 100 YARDS ADVANTAGE FROM HITTING THE BALL 12 YARDS FURTHER!
3-WOOD
DRIVE
PLAYER
YOU NOW HAVE A 100 YARD WEDGE SHOT TO THE GREEN, WHEREAS I WILL BE PUTTING
IT CERTAINLY PAYS TO DO MUSCLE-BUILDING EXERCISES AND TO HAVE GOLF CLUBS THAT SUIT YOU. IF A MAN IS PLAYING WITH AN EXTRA-STIFF SHAFT WHEN HE SHOULD BE USING AN R-SHAFT, HE IS NOT GOING TO GET THE DISTANCE HE NEEDS

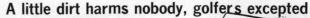

Don't slip!

MY FOOT KEEPS SLIPPING TODAY, GARY!
WHEN THE GROUND IS VERY HARD, I THINK IT'S A MISTAKE TO HAVE SPIKES IN YOUR HEELS
IF IT HASN'T RAINED FOR SEVERAL WEEKS I ALWAYS WEAR SHOES WITH RUBBER HEELS. I FIND THIS PREVENTS ME FROM SLIPPING
RUBBER
SPIKES
RUBBER HEELS ARE ALSO LESS TIRING ON THE FEET AND ARE IDEAL FOR OLDER PEOPLE WHO MIGHT BE AFRAID OF SLIPPING IN THE CLUBHOUSE— I'VE HEARD OF SOME VERY BAD ACCIDENTS LATELY

SECTION FOURTEEN

Practice

Analyze your round

EVEN THOUGH YOU SHOT 95, IAIN, THERE'S NO NEED TO BE DESPONDENT! YOU DROVE WELL, YOU HIT YOUR IRONS WELL AND YOU PUTTED WELL
BUT ONE CLUB CONTINUALLY LET YOU DOWN. YOU USED YOUR WEDGE EIGHT TIMES, AND PLAYED EIGHT BAD SHOTS!
YOU KEPT QUITTING ON THE BALL AND LEAVING IT SHORT. AT THE EIGHTH, FOR INSTANCE, YOU WERE ONLY 35 YARDS FROM THE GREEN YET YOU KNOCKED IT INTO THE SAND TRAP!
YOU QUIT ON EVERY WEDGE SHOT YOU PLAYED, INSTEAD OF GOING RIGHT THROUGH THE BALL AND FINISHING HIGH!
HANDS HIGH
SO ALWAYS ANALYSE YOUR ROUND WHENEVER YOU COME OFF THE LAST GREEN BECAUSE YOU WILL OFTEN DISCOVER THAT IT IS ONLY ONE CLUB THAT HAS LET YOU DOWN. THEN YOU CAN GO TO THE PRACTICE GROUND AND WORK ON THAT ONE SHOT

Try the sun cure

LIFTING THE HEAD IS THE BIGGEST FAULT THERE IS TOM IT RUINS MORE GOLF SHOTS THAN ANYTHING ELSE I KNOW.
YOU'VE GOT TO RID YOURSELF OF THIS DESIRE TO SEE WHERE THE BALL IS GOING.

GO ONTO THE PRACTICE GROUND IN THE EVENING AND HIT SHOTS INTO THE SUN. AS YOU CAN'T POSSIBLY FOLLOW THE FLIGHT OF THE BALL, YOU WON'T BE SO ANXIOUS TO JUMP UP.
THIS WILL REALLY MAKE YOU KEEP YOUR HEAD DOWN.

Slow down on the practice tee

YOU'RE CULTIVATING A VERY FAST, JERKY SWING, TOM, SIMPLY BECAUSE YOU HAVE YOUR PRACTICE BALLS IN FRONT OF YOU!
IMMEDIATELY YOU HIT ONE BALL YOU SCRAPE ANOTHER INTO POSITION AND HIT IT... YOU HIT BALL AFTER BALL WITHOUT THINKING! SLOW DOWN A BIT, OTHERWISE ALL YOUR RHYTHM WILL DISAPPEAR
I PRACTISE WITH THE BALLS BEHIND ME. AFTER EACH SHOT, I HAVE TO TURN ROUND AND SCOOP THE NEXT BALL INTO POSITION, WHICH TAKES QUITE A LOT OF TIME
THIS PREVENTS ME GETTING INTO A HURRIED, MECHANICAL ROUTINE. CONSEQUENTLY, I FIND THAT I SWING SLOWER, THINK BETTER, AND MAINTAIN MY RHYTHM

Every divot tells a story

OFTEN WHEN I HIT AN IRON SHOT TO THE FLAG, I CHECK TO SEE IF MY DIVOT MARK IS POINTING TO THE HOLE OR NOT. HERE THE DIVOT SHOWS I HAVE HIT FROM IN TO OUT— BECAUSE MY STANCE WAS TOO SHUT. THE RESULT WAS A BIG HOOK
CLOSED STANCE LEFT FOOT FORWARD
NOW, THIS DIVOT MARK SHOWS I HAVE SLICED THE BALL BY HITTING FROM OUT TO IN. MY STANCE WAS FAR TOO OPEN
OPEN STANCE LEFT FOOT BACK
WITH IRON SHOTS, I THINK A GOOD DIVOT SHOULD GO STRAIGHT TO THE TARGET. IF YOU CAN HIT YOUR IRON SHOTS STRAIGHT, IT'S BETTER FOR ALL TYPES OF CONDITIONS
SLICE
HOOK
RECENTLY, I WAS SLICING QUITE A BIT, AND I NOTICED MY DIVOTS WERE GOING ACROSS THE BALL, SO I ALTERED MY STANCE. THE DIVOTS STARTED GOING STRAIGHT FOR THE HOLE AND, IMMEDIATELY, I BEGAN HITTING THE BALL BETTER

Aid to memory

WEREN'T YOU GOING TO WORK ON KICKING YOUR RIGHT KNEE IN ON THE DOWNSWING, TOM? I DIDN'T SEE MUCH EVIDENCE OF IT DURING THAT ROUND!
OH! I COMPLETELY FORGOT, GARY!
YOU MUSTN'T RELY ON YOUR MEMORY, TOM! YOU SHOULD MAKE A NOTE ON THE BACK OF YOUR GLOVE OF THE THING YOU WANT TO WORK ON! THEN YOU WILL HAVE A CONSTANT REMINDER!
I DID THIS WHEN I WON THE U.S. OPEN. EVERY TIME I PULLED ON MY GLOVE, I WAS REMINDED TO SWING SLOW!
Slow

Aim at that bunker!

TOM, YOU SHOULDN'T STAND ON A PRACTICE TEE AND JUST SLOG AWAY. PRACTISE INTELLIGENTLY, OR YOU ARE WASTING YOUR TIME!
WHEN YOU PRACTISE A LOT WITHOUT A TARGET YOU CAN GET INTO VERY BAD HABITS WITH YOUR STANCE, WHICH IS YOUR AIMING. SO, I ALWAYS STICK A HOME-MADE FLAG INTO THE FAIRWAY AND SHOOT AT IT!
ANOTHER THING I USED TO DO A LOT WAS TO TRY TO HIT 7-IRON SHOTS INTO A BUNKER... AND I WOULDN'T GO HOME UNTIL I COULD KNOCK 45 OUT OF 50 BALLS INTO THE BUNKER!
IT'S ABSOLUTELY NECESSARY TO HAVE SOMETHING TO AIM AT, BECAUSE CHECKING YOUR STANCE IS JUST AS IMPORTANT AS PRACTISING YOUR SWING

How well do you hit the ball?

HERE IS A GREAT WAY OF TESTING WHETHER OR NOT YOU ARE HITTING THE BALL WELL, IAIN
I'VE PLACED THE BALL ON TOP OF THIS PIECE OF STRING. NOW GO AHEAD AND HIT THE BALL
YOU'VE TAKEN THE STRING WITH YOU, IAIN, WHICH MEANS YOU HAVE HIT BEHIND THE BALL. THIS RESULTS IN LOSS OF POWER, AND NO BACKSPIN
BY HITTING THE BALL FIRST— WHICH IS THE CORRECT WAY TO HIT IT —I DON'T EVEN TOUCH THE STRING. SEE, THE DIVOT STARTS BEYOND THE STRING
SPEND AN HOUR ON THIS EXERCISE, IAIN, AND I GUARANTEE YOUR STRIKING OF THE BALL WILL BE GREATLY IMPROVED

How to check your striking of the ball

WHAT EVERY GOLFER IS STRIVING FOR IS TO GET SOME BACKSPIN ON HIS SHOTS, AND I WOULD SAY THAT THE MAN WHO CAN DO THIS IS THE MAN WHO HITS THE BALL BEST
ONE OF THE BIGGEST FAULTS IS HITTING BEHIND THE BALL, THEREBY GETTING NO BACKSPIN
TO CHECK WHETHER OR NOT YOU ARE HITTING PROPERLY, PLACE A ROW OF TEE PEGS IN LINE WITH YOUR BALL, TOM, THEN HIT IT AND SEE WHERE YOUR DIVOT STARTS
SEE! YOUR DIVOT STARTS BEHIND THE PEGS INDICATING THAT YOU'VE HIT BEHIND THE BALL. MINE STARTS IN FRONT OF THE PEGS — THEREFORE MY SHOT HAD BACKSPIN AS I HAVE CLEARLY HIT THE BALL FIRST, AND THEN THE TURF
TOM
PLAYER

The greatest training

BEFORE WINNING THE BRITISH OPEN AT MUIRFIELD IN 1959 YOU PRACTISED HITTING SHOTS OFF THE BEACH, GARY. WAS THIS BUNKER PRACTICE?
NO, TOM, I HIT FULL IRON SHOTS OFF THE SAND TO ENSURE I WASN'T HITTING BEHIND THE BALL. THAT'S ONE OF THE WORST FAULTS IN GOLF
THE BEACH SAND IS VERY GOOD FOR TESTING THIS BECAUSE YOU'VE JUST GOT TO HIT THE BALL FIRST. IF YOU HIT BEHIND THE BALL IT WON'T GO ANYWHERE!
WHEN NO BEACH IS AVAILABLE I ADVISE PEOPLE TO PRACTISE HITTING FULL 7-IRON SHOTS OUT OF BUNKERS
THIS IS THE GREATEST TRAINING THERE IS! IT IS SOMETHING THAT WILL BE DONE A LOT IN THE FUTURE, AND IS WHY GOLF IS GOING TO GET BETTER AND BETTER!

THE KING OF SPIN

No golfer gets more backspin on his ball than Gary Player. His approach shots to the green take two forward bounces then, on the third bounce, they check. Often the ball spins back six feet or more.

In order to get backspin, the ball must be hit *before* the turf. Player's divot mark starts an inch or two closer to the hole than where his ball was sitting.

"The *better* you hit the ball," says Player, "the more backspin you get!"

SECTION FIFTEEN

Exercises

Develop Rhythm, Feel and Timing

Head down, follow through

IAIN, I HAVE TOLD YOU COUNTLESS TIMES THAT, IN THE GOLF SWING, THE TWO MOST IMPORTANT THINGS ARE HEAD DOWN AND FOLLOW-THROUGH! BUT LOOK AT YOU — NO FOLLOW-THROUGH AT ALL!
IF YOU DON'T FOLLOW-THROUGH, HOW CAN YOU FORCE THE BALL TO THE HOLE?
HERE IS A GREAT EXERCISE THAT WILL REALLY TEACH YOU TO FORCE THE BALL TO THE HOLE. FIRST, TAKE A TINY BACKSWING TO HERE...
STOP!
THEN, SLOWLY FOLLOW-THROUGH INTO THIS POSITION AND HOLD IT FOR A FEW SECONDS
STOP!
FROM THERE, FORCE YOUR ARMS THROUGH SLOWLY INTO THE FULL FOLLOW-THROUGH AND HOLD THAT FOR A FEW SECONDS
YOU MAY FIND THIS VERY DIFFICULT AT FIRST, BUT PERSEVERE — IT'S IDEAL FOR TONING UP THE GOLF MUSCLES!

Quiet hands

MANY GOLFERS HAVE POOR RHYTHM BECAUSE THEY ALLOW THEIR HANDS TO COME INTO PLAY TOO EARLY!
QUIET
QUIET
MY HANDS ARE ABSOLUTELY QUIET ON THE TAKEAWAY
QUIET
WHEN THEY REACH WAIST HIGH, THEY ARE STILL QUIET
ACTIVE
AT THE TOP OF THE SWING THEY ARE STILL MERELY HOLDING ON TO THE CLUB
ONLY WHEN THEY COME DOWN TO WAIST LEVEL DO THEY COME TO LIFE. THEN THEY ZIP RIGHT THROUGH THE BALL INTO A HIGH FOLLOW-THROUGH!
ACTIVE

Build up your golfing muscles

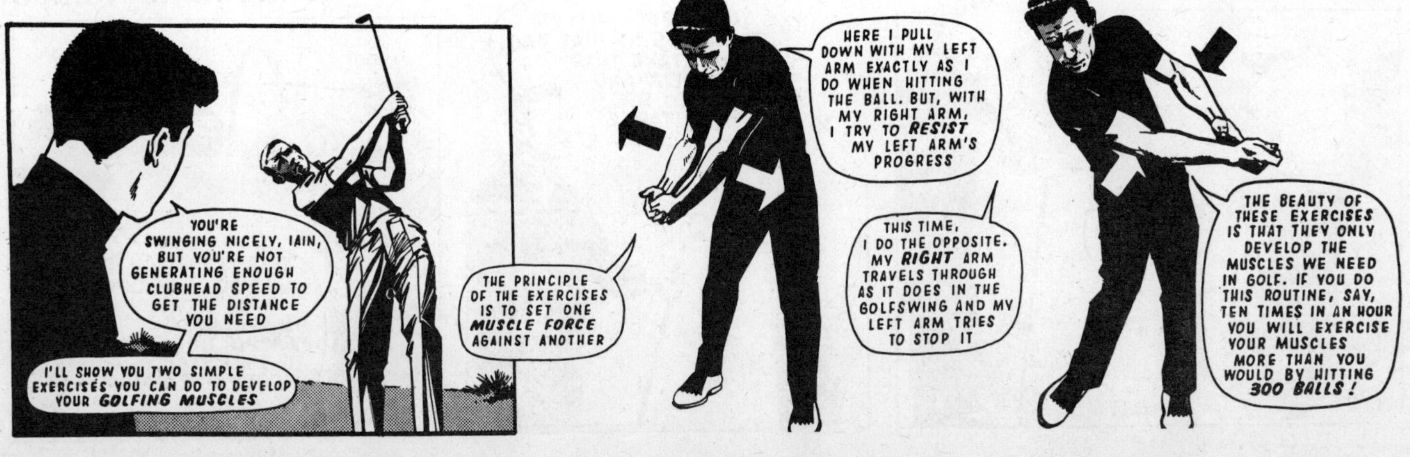

YOU'RE SWINGING NICELY, IAIN, BUT YOU'RE NOT GENERATING ENOUGH CLUBHEAD SPEED TO GET THE DISTANCE YOU NEED
I'LL SHOW YOU TWO SIMPLE EXERCISES YOU CAN DO TO DEVELOP YOUR GOLFING MUSCLES
THE PRINCIPLE OF THE EXERCISES IS TO SET ONE MUSCLE FORCE AGAINST ANOTHER
HERE I PULL DOWN WITH MY LEFT ARM EXACTLY AS I DO WHEN HITTING THE BALL. BUT, WITH MY RIGHT ARM, I TRY TO RESIST MY LEFT ARM'S PROGRESS
THIS TIME, I DO THE OPPOSITE. MY RIGHT ARM TRAVELS THROUGH AS IT DOES IN THE GOLFSWING AND MY LEFT ARM TRIES TO STOP IT
THE BEAUTY OF THESE EXERCISES IS THAT THEY ONLY DEVELOP THE MUSCLES WE NEED IN GOLF. IF YOU DO THIS ROUTINE, SAY, TEN TIMES IN AN HOUR YOU WILL EXERCISE YOUR MUSCLES MORE THAN YOU WOULD BY HITTING 300 BALLS!

Greater clubhead speed

WHY ARE YOU STANDING SO NARROW, GARY?
THIS IS AN EXERCISE I RECOMMEND FOR THE PRACTICE TEE, TOM!
WHEN I HIT THE BALL, MY RIGHT KNEE GOES PAST MY LEFT KNEE
IT'S AMAZING HOW MUCH EXTRA CLUBHEAD SPEED THIS CREATES
THIS EXERCISE ALSO HELPS ME TO MAINTAIN BALANCE IN THE SWING
WHEN I'M OUT ON THE COURSE, I STAND A LITTLE BIT WIDER, BUT I STILL TRY TO GET THE FEELING THAT MY RIGHT KNEE IS GOING PAST MY LEFT

How to relax

TOM, TAKE A BIG BREATH AND THEN EXHALE SLOWLY
THAT'S MUCH BETTER. NOW YOU ARE FAR MORE RELAXED—ALL THE TENSION HAS GONE
IF YOU START OFF TENSE YOUR SWING IS GOING TO BE TENSE AND UNRHYTHMICAL
WHEN WAITING FOR MY TURN TO PUTT, I TAKE PLENTY OF DEEP BREATHS. THESE CALM ME DOWN AND GIVE ME AN OPPORTUNITY TO DO MY JOB PROPERLY

How to cultivate "feel"

TO PLAY GOLF SUCCESSFULLY, IT IS IMPORTANT TO HAVE WHAT WE CALL "FEEL"
FOR EXAMPLE, I CAN DESCRIBE MY METHOD OF CHIPPING TO A HOLE THAT'S 30 FEET AWAY, BUT HOW CLOSE YOU GET TO THE HOLE WILL DEPEND UPON YOUR SENSE OF "FEEL"
TRY THIS EXERCISE, IAIN. HIT HALF A DOZEN 7-IRON SHOTS TO THE GREEN, THEN TAKE OUT YOUR 5-IRON
7-IRON
5-IRON
THEN, HOLDING THE CLUB A LITTLE SHORTER THAN USUAL, TRY AND HIT THE SAME DISTANCE WITH YOUR FIVE AS YOU DID WITH YOUR SEVEN!
I CAN'T TEACH YOU "FEEL", BUT I GUARANTEE THIS EXERCISE WILL HELP YOU TO CULTIVATE IT!

Automatic tempo

HOW CAN I IMPROVE MY TEMPO, GARY?
YOU'VE BEEN HITTING 7-IRONS TO THAT BAG, TOM. TAKE THIS 5-IRON AND HIT TO THE SAME TARGET
THIS IS ALL YOU HAVE TO DO TO GET WHAT I CALL AUTOMATIC TEMPO. THIS IS ONE TIP THAT REALLY WORKS LIKE MAGIC

How to develop "feel"

WHEN I WAS AT SCHOOL, I COULDN'T PRACTICE MY GOLF EVERY DAY, SO WHAT I USED TO DO WAS STAND ON A LITTLE MAT IN MY ROOM AND HAVE ABOUT 100 SWINGS EVERY NIGHT BEFORE I WENT TO BED
THIS MEANT THAT WHEN I DID PLAY AT WEEKENDS, I ALREADY HAD THE "FEEL" OF THE CLUB, AND IT DIDN'T SEEM STRANGE IN MY HANDS. WEEKENDERS PLEASE COPY!
IN TOURNAMENTS, I LIKE TO SWING A CLUB BETWEEN SHOTS AS IT'S GOOD TO KEEP THE "FEEL" OF THE CLUB IN YOUR HANDS DURING A GAME
BUT IF I HIT, SAY, A 4-WOOD ON TO THE GREEN, I IMMEDIATELY ASK MY CADDIE TO GIVE ME MY PUTTER . . .
I DON'T WANT TO WALK TO THE GREEN WITH A 4-WOOD IN MY HANDS. I WANT TO GET ACCUSTOMED TO THE "FEEL" AND THE WEIGHT OF MY PUTTER LONG BEFORE I REACH THE GREEN

Developing 'feel'

YOU'LL OFTEN SEE PROFESSIONAL GOLFERS, WHEN THEY'VE GOT A BIT OF TIME TO SPARE, BOUNCING A BALL ON A WEDGE OR SAND IRON, IAIN
THIS IS A VERY USEFUL EXERCISE WHICH DEVELOPS BALL SENSE AND GOOD "FEEL." AND ANYTHING THAT CULTIVATES "FEEL" HAS GOT TO BE GOOD FOR YOUR GOLF
THIS IS ALSO GOOD FOR YOUR EYE AND TEACHES YOU TO HIT THE BALL IN THE MIDDLE OF THE CLUB
BUT DON'T BE FAST AND JERKY! YOU MUST BOUNCE THE BALL VERY SLOWLY AND RHYTHMICALLY AS A REMINDER THAT RHYTHM IS ONE OF THE ESSENTIAL INGREDIENTS OF A GOOD GOLFSWING!

The art of timing

MANY BAD GOLF SHOTS CAN BE TRACED BACK TO ONE BASIC CAUSE... BAD TIMING!
WHEN WE SWING TOGETHER, IAIN, YOU ARE IN SUCH A HURRY THAT YOU ARE STARTING YOUR DOWNSWING JUST AS I AM COMPLETING MY BACKSWING!
THEREFORE, BY THE TIME I AM HALF WAY THROUGH MY DOWNSWING, YOU HAVE ALREADY STRUCK THE BALL! YOU MUST SLOW DOWN, IAIN. MAKE YOUR SWING SMOOTH, NOT FAST AND JERKY!
YOU DON'T GIVE YOUR SHOULDERS TIME TO MAKE A COMPLETE TURN
IN OTHER WORDS, YOU START YOUR DOWNSWING BEFORE YOU REACH THE TOP OF YOUR BACKSWING
GET TO THE TOP OF YOUR BACKSWING BEFORE YOU START DOWN. OTHERWISE YOU WILL GET WHAT IS CALLED A "SNATCH". AND THAT CAN CAUSE ANY BAD SHOT IN GOLF

How to keep your balance

WATCH YOUR BALANCE, IAIN! YOU'RE CONTINUALLY FALLING BACK ON THESE LONG-IRON SHOTS!
I USED TO DO THIS A LOT MYSELF, AND ONE OF THE THINGS THAT HELPED ME MOST WAS HITTING PRACTICE SHOTS WEARING ORDINARY LEATHER-SOLED SHOES INSTEAD OF SPIKES!
WITH ORDINARY SHOES, I HAVE TO MAKE A SPECIAL CONSCIOUS EFFORT TO STAY IN BALANCE. I CAN'T HIT THE BALL SO HARD, BUT THAT DOESN'T MATTER
WHEN I'M AT HOME, I OFTEN GO OUT IN THE EVENINGS AND HIT A FEW 5-IRONS LIKE THIS, MERELY TO REMIND ME TO STAY IN BALANCE!

How to regain your rhythm

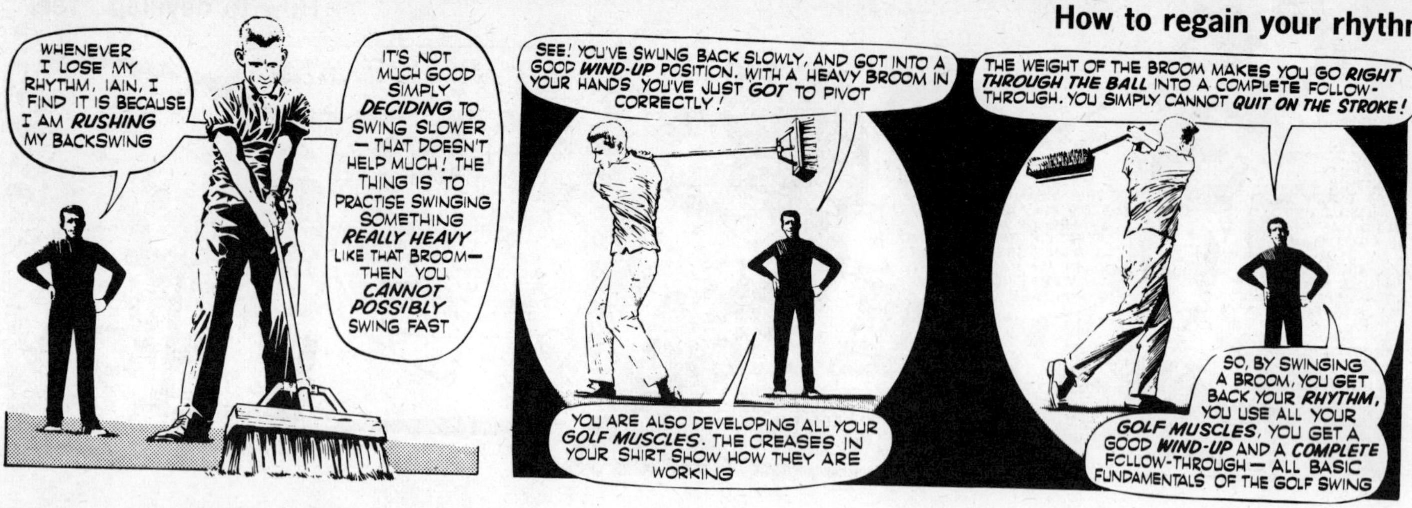

WHENEVER I LOSE MY RHYTHM, IAIN, I FIND IT IS BECAUSE I AM RUSHING MY BACKSWING
IT'S NOT MUCH GOOD SIMPLY DECIDING TO SWING SLOWER — THAT DOESN'T HELP MUCH! THE THING IS TO PRACTISE SWINGING SOMETHING REALLY HEAVY LIKE THAT BROOM— THEN YOU CANNOT POSSIBLY SWING FAST
SEE! YOU'VE SWUNG BACK SLOWLY, AND GOT INTO A GOOD WIND-UP POSITION. WITH A HEAVY BROOM IN YOUR HANDS YOU'VE JUST GOT TO PIVOT CORRECTLY!
YOU ARE ALSO DEVELOPING ALL YOUR GOLF MUSCLES. THE CREASES IN YOUR SHIRT SHOW HOW THEY ARE WORKING
THE WEIGHT OF THE BROOM MAKES YOU GO RIGHT THROUGH THE BALL INTO A COMPLETE FOLLOW-THROUGH. YOU SIMPLY CANNOT QUIT ON THE STROKE!
SO, BY SWINGING A BROOM, YOU GET BACK YOUR RHYTHM, YOU USE ALL YOUR GOLF MUSCLES, YOU GET A GOOD WIND-UP AND A COMPLETE FOLLOW-THROUGH — ALL BASIC FUNDAMENTALS OF THE GOLF SWING

The need for rhythm

YOU HIT THREE CHIP-SHOTS FROM THE SAME SPOT, IAIN, AND JUST LOOK AT THEM!
1
2
3
YOU KNOW THAT RHYTHM IS ESSENTIAL IN LONG SHOTS, BUT YOU DON'T SEEM TO APPRECIATE THAT IT'S EQUALLY IMPORTANT WHEN CHIPPING OR PUTTING!
1
2
3
YOUR TROUBLE WAS THAT YOU JERKED THE CLUB BACK FROM THE BALL SO FAST THAT YOU LOST ALL SENSE OF "FEEL" AND RHYTHM. THIS IS INDICATED BY THE FACT THAT YOUR HANDS WENT TO A DIFFERENT LEVEL EACH TIME
HAD YOU PLAYED THE SHOTS RHYTHMICALLY YOUR HANDS WOULD HAVE GONE TO THE SAME SPOT EVERY TIME
SO TAKE THE CLUB BACK SMOOTHLY AND ALWAYS MAKE SURE THAT YOU COMPLETE YOUR BACKSWING BEFORE YOU START YOUR DOWNSWING

The "Three S" cure

ALL GOLFERS OCCASIONALLY LOSE THEIR RHYTHM, TOM. WHEN THIS HAPPENS TO ME, I TRY THE 3S CURE ON THE PRACTICE GROUND
I SWING SLOWER
SLOW
SHORT
I SWING SHORTER...
...AND I HIT SOFTER. I CAN REALLY RECOMMEND THIS TREATMENT
SOFT

Hit the ball 15 yards further

NOW THAT YOU ARE ANCHORING YOUR HEAD AND LETTING YOUR WEIGHT GO FORWARD, IAIN, YOU HAVE GOT A VERY GOOD-LOOKING SWING
BUT I'M STILL NOT GETTING MUCH DISTANCE, GARY!
LIKE MOST WEEKENDERS, YOU NEED TO STRENGTHEN YOUR HANDS, WRISTS, AND FOREARMS. WHEN YOU HAVE FINISHED READING YOUR PAPER IN THE EVENING TAKE TWO PAGES AND CRUMPLE THEM UP WITH THE FINGERS OF ONE HAND
KEEP AT IT UNTIL YOU'VE CRUMPLED THE PAPER INTO A TIGHT BALL AND YOUR HANDS ARE ACHING
IF YOU DO THIS EVERY NIGHT WITH BOTH HANDS, I GUARANTEE IN THREE MONTHS YOU WILL HIT THE BALL FIFTEEN YARDS FURTHER!

Strengthening the left hand

YOU HAVE NO TENSION IN YOUR LEFT HAND WHATSOEVER, IAIN. YOUR HAND IS ACTUALLY OPEN AT THE TOP OF THE SWING AND YOUR ARM BENT!
IN ORDER TO CONTROL THE CLUB PROPERLY, THE LEFT HAND MUST REMAIN FIRMLY SHUT AND THE LEFT ARM MUST BE EXTENDED
A GOOD EXERCISE IS TO SWING WITH THE LEFT HAND ONLY HOLDING THE CLUB
THIS WILL STRENGTHEN YOUR LEFT HAND AND ALSO GIVE YOU THE FEELING OF A STRAIGHT LEFT ARM. ACTUALLY HIT A FEW BALLS ONE-HANDED. YOU WILL BE SURPRISED HOW WELL YOU CAN DO THIS!

A strong left hand

VICTOR HIT THE BALL REALLY WELL TODAY, GARY!
VIC HAS A BUILT-IN ADVANTAGE, TOM! SEE, HE IS SIGNING HIS CARD WITH HIS LEFT HAND, YET HE SWINGS RIGHT-HANDED
THE LEFT HAND IS THE GUIDING HAND IN THE SWING AND IT'S A POSITIVE HELP IF IT IS STRONGER THAN THE RIGHT! AS WELL AS GUIDING THE CLUB CORRECTLY, VIC GETS GOOD EXTENSION THROUGH THE BALL BECAUSE HIS LEFT HAND IS SO STRONG!
HOWEVER, DON'T DESPAIR, TOM! YOU CAN BUILD UP THE STRENGTH OF YOUR LEFT HAND AS I DO-BY SQUEEZING A RUBBER BALL!

Stretch yourself

I CAN SEE YOU ARE JUST BEGINNING TO PLAY AGAIN AFTER A LONG WINTER LAY-OFF, IAIN! YOUR SWING IS SHORT AND CRAMPED!
IT WILL TAKE YOU SOME TIME TO GET YOURSELF BACK INTO SHAPE!
IT'S SILLY TO ALLOW YOUR MUSCLES TO TIGHTEN UP WHEN YOU CAN QUITE EASILY KEEP THEM SUPPLE
ALL YOU NEED TO DO IN ORDER TO MAINTAIN YOUR SWING-LENGTH DURING THE WINTER IS TO HAVE SOME STRETCHING EXERCISES IN YOUR ROOM OR GARDEN
REMEMBER, THE BIGGER THE SWING ARC, THE FURTHER YOU HIT THE BALL - THERE IS NO QUESTION ABOUT IT!
TAKE YOUR CLUB BACK TO TOUCH A WALL OR TREE AT FULL STRETCH. THEN PRACTICE THE FOLLOW-THROUGH IN THE SAME MANNER

He Almost Tossed a Championship Away

Golf is a game of high drama, fickle in its treatment of those who participate.

Golf raises a man up one minute and hurls him down the next.

Golf makes a man old before his time.

And nowhere is golf more cruel, more heartless than on the putting green. It is there that strong men weep.

When Gary Player left his approach putt stone dead on the final hole of the 1968 British Open Championship at Carnoustie, his most dangerous opponent, Jack Nicklaus, knew—and the thousands who thronged the eighteenth green knew—that Gary had won it.

Bubbling over with delight, Player ran towards his ball. As the great crowd cheered, and Vivienne Player hurriedly clambered into the reserved stand to witness her husband's moment of triumph, Gary had only one thought in his mind.

Words spoken to him many years ago by fellow-South African, Bobby Locke:

"Gary if ever you have a tap-in putt to win a major championship, mark your ball and let your opponent putt out. This will give you the honor of putting last."

It seemed like a good idea to the excited Player who had battled Carnoustie's strong sea breezes all week for the honor of winning the Open for a second time. Then, suddenly, like a man who has had a vision of impending disaster, Player stopped in his tracks, a few feet from his ball! His heart beat quickened. Beads of cold sweat sent a shiver down his back.

Almost too late, Player remembered that the continuous putting rule was in operation throughout the Championship. If he lifted the ball, he would suffer a one-stroke penalty! Then, if Nicklaus sank *his* putt for a tie, the Championship that was surely Player's by right might be snatched from his grasp in a play-off.

It was as if golf were trying to complete a tragic "double" that year, for only three months previously Roberto De Vicenzo had denied himself the title of U.S. Master Golfer by the simple expedient of signing an incorrect scorecard.

Fortunately for Player, he recovered his poise, shrank back from golfing suicide—and holed the putt!

SECTION SIXTEEN

Common Faults and Cures

Don't keep your shoulders straight

IF YOU DON'T HAVE THE CORRECT SHOULDER ACTION IN GOLF, THERE IS NO WAY YOU CAN PLAY CONSISTENTLY WELL

MY RIGHT SHOULDER IS LOWER THAN MY LEFT AT ADDRESS. THIS ALLOWS ME TO GET MY RIGHT SHOULDER UNDERNEATH MY CHIN WHEN I HIT THE BALL, WHICH IS VERY IMPORTANT
BY HAVING THE CORRECT SHOULDER POSITION AT ADDRESS, MY CLUB STAYS ON A GOOD LINE...

THE ARC OF YOUR SWING WILL BE FLAT, AND ROUND YOUR BODY, WHEREAS MINE WILL BE STRAIGHT BACK AND STRAIGHT THROUGH!

The most important thing

I'VE BEEN WATCHING YOU PRACTISE, IAIN, AND YOU HAVE BEEN CONCENTRATING ON YOUR STANCE, YOUR WAGGLE, YOUR TAKEAWAY...
BUT, NOT ONCE HAVE YOU TAKEN A REAL HARD LOOK AT THE BALL JUST BEFORE STARTING THE CLUB BACK
THAT IS THE MOST IMPORTANT THING TO REMEMBER. IT HELPS YOU TO STAY DOWN ON THE SHOT AND TO MAKE GOOD CONTACT WITH THE BALL!

Hold that head position

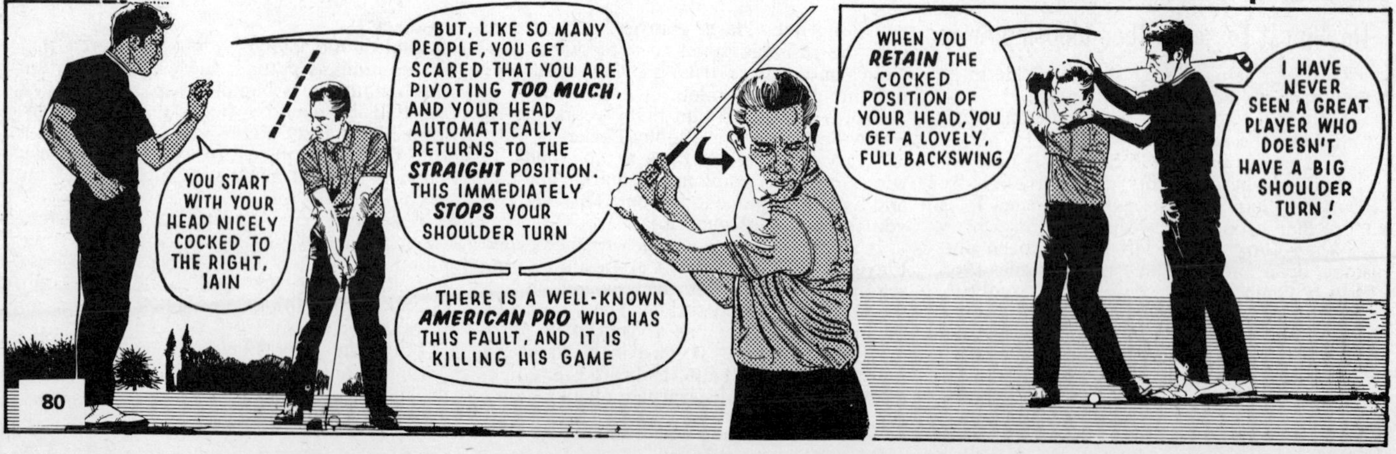

YOU START WITH YOUR HEAD NICELY COCKED TO THE RIGHT, IAIN
BUT, LIKE SO MANY PEOPLE, YOU GET SCARED THAT YOU ARE PIVOTING TOO MUCH, AND YOUR HEAD AUTOMATICALLY RETURNS TO THE STRAIGHT POSITION. THIS IMMEDIATELY STOPS YOUR SHOULDER TURN
THERE IS A WELL-KNOWN AMERICAN PRO WHO HAS THIS FAULT, AND IT IS KILLING HIS GAME
WHEN YOU RETAIN THE COCKED POSITION OF YOUR HEAD, YOU GET A LOVELY, FULL BACKSWING
I HAVE NEVER SEEN A GREAT PLAYER WHO DOESN'T HAVE A BIG SHOULDER TURN!

Changing gear

THIS SUDDEN WRIST BREAK AND SPEEDY TAKEAWAY IS KILLING YOUR GAME, TOM
THINK OF THE SWING IN TERMS OF DRIVING A CAR. YOU NEVER GO FAST IN REVERSE GEAR, SO TAKE THE CLUB BACK SLOWLY
REVERSE
NEUTRAL
THEN, YOU WOULDN'T CHANGE STRAIGHT FROM REVERSE INTO FORWARD GEAR! PUT YOUR SWING INTO NEUTRAL BY KEEPING YOUR HANDS PASSIVE FOR THE FIRST TWO FEET OF THE DOWNSWING
FROM THERE, YOU CAN ENGAGE FORWARD GEAR AND REALLY LET IT RIP!
FORWARD

A cure for fast swingers

ONE REASON YOU'RE SO VERY FAST ON THE BACKSWING, IAIN, IS YOU ARE MUCH TOO TENSE AT ADDRESS
YOU'RE SO TENSE, YOU ARE PUSHING THE CLUBHEAD DOWN INTO THE GROUND! AS YOU BEGIN YOUR BACKSWING, THE CLUB WILL BE RELEASED WITH A FAST, FLICK-LIKE ACTION
MY ADVICE TO ANY FAST SWINGER WHO FINDS DIFFICULTY IN SLOWING DOWN HIS BACKSWING IS TO ADDRESS THE BALL WITH THE CLUB OFF THE GROUND
TRY THIS, IAIN, AND YOU WILL FIND YOU CAN TAKE BACK THE CLUB MUCH MORE SLOWLY AND SMOOTHLY AS THERE IS NO INITIAL RESISTANCE TO OVERCOME

A glove tip

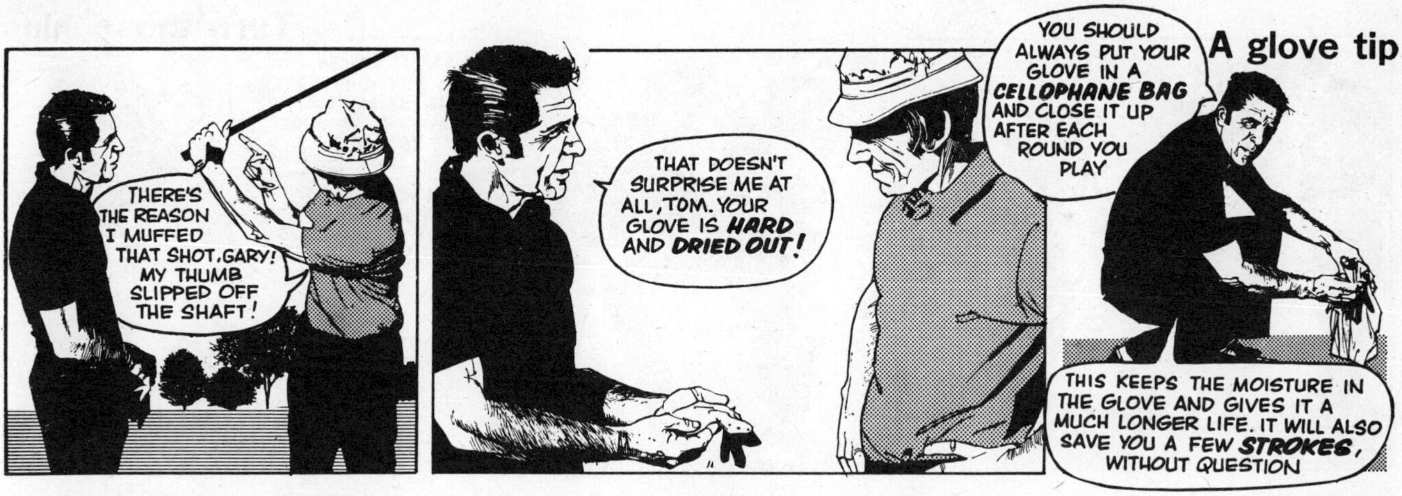

THERE'S THE REASON I MUFFED THAT SHOT, GARY! MY THUMB SLIPPED OFF THE SHAFT!
THAT DOESN'T SURPRISE ME AT ALL, TOM. YOUR GLOVE IS HARD AND DRIED OUT!
YOU SHOULD ALWAYS PUT YOUR GLOVE IN A CELLOPHANE BAG AND CLOSE IT UP AFTER EACH ROUND YOU PLAY
THIS KEEPS THE MOISTURE IN THE GLOVE AND GIVES IT A MUCH LONGER LIFE. IT WILL ALSO SAVE YOU A FEW STROKES, WITHOUT QUESTION

Watch your thumb

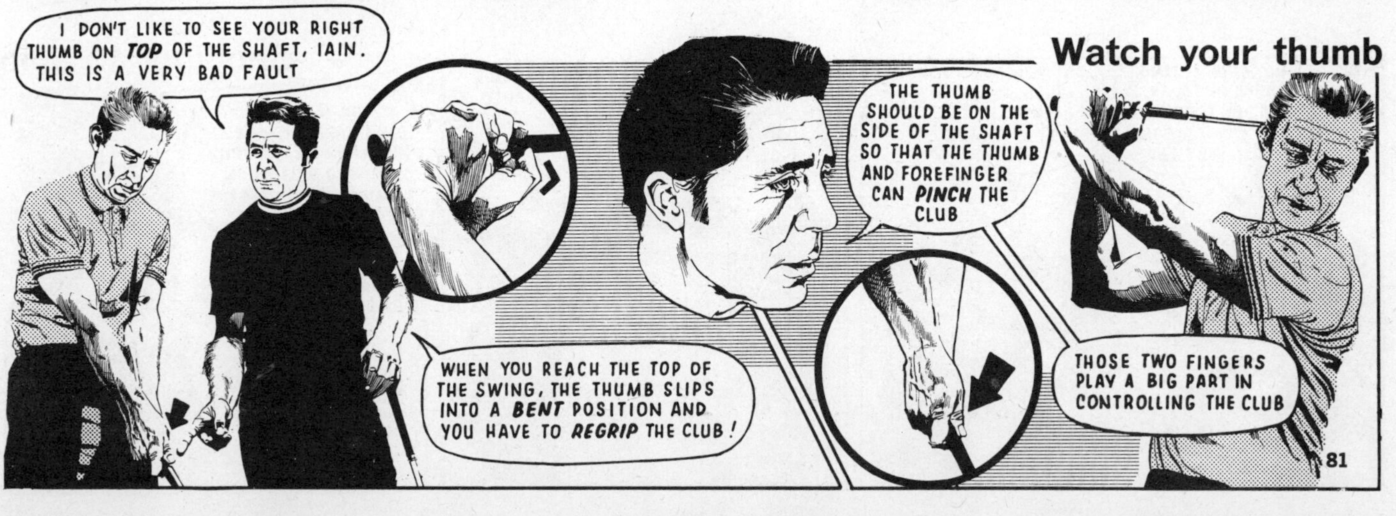

I DON'T LIKE TO SEE YOUR RIGHT THUMB ON TOP OF THE SHAFT, IAIN. THIS IS A VERY BAD FAULT
WHEN YOU REACH THE TOP OF THE SWING, THE THUMB SLIPS INTO A BENT POSITION AND YOU HAVE TO REGRIP THE CLUB!
THE THUMB SHOULD BE ON THE SIDE OF THE SHAFT SO THAT THE THUMB AND FOREFINGER CAN PINCH THE CLUB
THOSE TWO FINGERS PLAY A BIG PART IN CONTROLLING THE CLUB

Don't swing out!

IAIN! YOU ARE TAKING THE CLUB BACK 'WAY OUTSIDE THE LINE. THIS IS WHY YOU ARE SLICING YOUR FAIRWAY WOODS!
WHEN PRACTISING, IT IS A GOOD IDEA TO PLACE A BAG, OR SOME SUCH THING, JUST OUTSIDE THE BALL
THIS WILL SOON GET YOU OUT OF THE HABIT OF GOING BACK ON THE OUTSIDE, WHICH IS ONE OF THE WORST FAULTS THERE IS!

In search of more power

THIS GIVES YOU A GOOD WIND-UP AND PUTS YOU IN A POSITION OF POWER AT THE TOP OF THE SWING

Turn those hips

IAIN, YOU ARE STILL TAKING THAT CLUB BACK OUTSIDE THE LINE, AND THAT IS WHY YOU SLICE SO MUCH!
ADDRESS THE BALL ONCE AGAIN AND I WILL SHOW YOU A DEFINITE MOVEMENT THAT WILL HELP YOU OVERCOME THIS TROUBLE
SEE WHAT HAPPENS WHEN I TURN YOUR HIPS FOR YOU! THE CLUB GOES BACK ON THE INSIDE! THAT IS THE SECRET, IAIN – MAKE SURE THOSE HIPS TURN!
WHEN YOU TURN YOUR HIPS ON THE BACKSWING, YOUR BODY GETS WOUND UP TIGHT LIKE A CLOCK!
NOW YOU ARE ABLE TO UNWIND MUCH BETTER, AND YOUR CLUB WHIPS RIGHT THROUGH THE BALL!

Shoulder to chin

Don't be flat

IT IS A GOOD THING TO BE IN THE SWING PLANE RATHER THAN OUT OF IT, IAIN, BUT YOU ARE SWINGING FAR TOO FLAT
THERE IS NO WAY YOU CAN COME INTO THE BALL CORRECTLY!
BECAUSE YOU BREAK YOUR WRISTS TOO EARLY, YOU BREAK THE CLUB RIGHT OFF THE LINE! SO THEN YOU GET FLAT!
ALTHOUGH SOME PROS ADVOCATE AN EARLY WRIST BREAK, I HAVE NEVER SEEN A GREAT PLAYER WHO DOES THIS
TAKE YOUR CLUB, ARMS AND HANDS BACK AS ONE UNIT AND YOU WILL KEEP THE CLUB LONGER ON THE LINE. THEREFORE, YOUR SWING WILL BE IN A BETTER PLANE

Perfecting the takeaway

MY BACKSWING DOESN'T FEEL GOOD, GARY. I DON'T KNOW WHAT I'M DOING WRONG!
IT'S THAT OLD FAULT, TOM—BREAKING YOUR WRISTS AND TAKING THE CLUB OUTSIDE THE LINE
PRETEND YOU HAVE A PUTTER IN YOUR HANDS THEN TAKE THE CLUB BACK EXACTLY AS YOU WOULD FOR A LONG PUTT
THIS WILL KEEP YOUR BLADE CLOSE TO THE GROUND AND ENCOURAGE A SMOOTH, RHYTHMICAL TAKEAWAY
ONCE YOU GET THE TAKEAWAY RIGHT, THE REST OF THE BACKSWING WILL TAKE CARE OF ITSELF

The power arc

YOUR ARC IS TOO FLAT, TOM, AND THERE IS NO WIDTH TO IT. YOU'LL NEVER HIT THE BALL FAR SWINGING LIKE THAT.
WIDE ARC
I HAVE YET TO SEE A BIG HITTER WHO DOESN'T HAVE A WIDE BACKSWING ARC, UNLESS HE IS PHENOMENALLY STRONG.
BOBBY COLE HAS A WONDERFULLY WIDE ARC. SO HAS NEW ZEALANDER JOHN LISTER WHO IS ONE OF THE LONGEST HITTERS I HAVE EVER SEEN.

Don't obscure the ball

WHEN YOU RAISE YOUR LEFT SHOULDER ON THE BACKSWING, TOM, IT OBSCURES YOUR VIEW OF THE BALL AND ALSO MAKES YOU COCK YOUR WRISTS TOO EARLY
MAKE THE LEFT SHOULDER TURN UNDER THE CHIN AND KEEP THE CLUBHEAD CLOSE TO THE GROUND
THIS ENABLES YOU TO WATCH THE BALL MORE EASILY AND YOU GET A BETTER POSITION WITH YOUR HANDS MORE UNDERNEATH THE CLUB

The shoulder regulator

I KNOW I'VE BEEN SWINGING TOO FLAT, GARY, BUT I SIMPLY CAN'T PUT MY HANDS INTO THE RIGHT PLANE
YOU SHOULDN'T TRY TO DO IT WITH YOUR HANDS, IAIN. THE SWING PLANE IS DETERMINED BY THE SHOULDER TURN
TOO FLAT
TOO UPRIGHT
IF I DROP MY LEFT SHOULDER AND TILT IT UNDERNEATH MY CHIN, I GET AN UPRIGHT PLANE
UPRIGHT
IF I TURN THE SHOULDER MORE PARALLEL TO THE GROUND I GET A FLATTER PLANE
FLAT
THE CORRECT AND QUICKEST WAY TO ALTER THE PLANE OF YOUR SWING IS BY THE LEFT SHOULDER

Smooth and tranquil

THAT IS A TERRIBLE SHOULDER TURN, TOM. YOUR SWING IS AS FLAT AS A DOLLAR BILL. THE STRAIN OF SWINGING LIKE THAT HAS FORCED YOUR HANDS OPEN.
THE MINUTE YOU PUT PRESSURE ON YOUR BODY AND FEEL TENSE, YOU PUT AN EXTRA STRAIN ON YOUR HANDS.
IN ORDER THAT YOUR HANDS CAN HANG ON AND FUNCTION PROPERLY, THE SWING MUST BE SMOOTH AND TRANQUIL WITH THE SHOULDER TURNING EASILY UNDERNEATH THE CHIN.
SAM SNEAD STILL DOES THIS BETTER THAN ANYONE. HIS IS THE MOST RHYTHMICAL SWING IN THE WORLD.

How not to swing flat

YOU ARE SWINGING VERY FLAT, IAIN! YOUR CLUB IS LAID OFF TO THE LEFT OF THE TARGET AND YOUR LEFT WRIST IS IN A VERY FLAT POSITION!
WILL I TRY TO TAKE MY HANDS HIGHER THEN, GARY?
NO, IAIN. THAT IS A MISTAKE MANY PEOPLE MAKE. THEY ARE TOLD THEY ARE SWINGING FLAT SO THEY TRY TO SWING MORE UPRIGHT. IT IS MUCH BETTER TO GET YOUR HANDS UNDERNEATH THE SHAFT THAN TO THINK ABOUT SWINGING MORE UPRIGHT!
SIMPLY BY ENSURING THAT YOUR HANDS ARE UNDERNEATH THE SHAFT, YOU ARE NOW IN A PERFECT POSITION WITH YOUR CLUBHEAD POINTING TO THE TARGET. YOUR ACTUAL BACKSWING WAS THE SAME AS BEFORE!
ONCE YOU GET YOUR HANDS UNDERNEATH THE SHAFT, YOU WILL NEVER BE IN A FLAT POSITION

If you're a "flailer" read on...

I KNOW I KEEP TELLING YOU TO TAKE THE DRIVER BACK IN ONE PIECE, IAIN, BUT YOU'RE ALMOST AT THE TOP OF YOUR BACKSWING AND YOU STILL HAVEN'T COCKED YOUR WRISTS!
THIS MEANS YOU WILL BREAK THEM ON THE DOWNSWING. WE CALL THIS A "FLAIL", AND IT IS A VERY BAD FAULT WHICH GIVES YOU A SLOPPY, INCONSISTENT ACTION
IN ALL SHOTS FROM 100 YARDS DOWNWARDS, THE WRISTS SHOULD BE COCKED VERY EARLY.. CHIPPING, PUTTING, BUNKER SHOTS, THE LOT!
BUT WITH THE DRIVER, THE BEST TIME TO COCK THE WRISTS IS WHEN YOUR HANDS REACH THE LEVEL OF YOUR WAIST!

Cock your wrists

THAT IS NOT A BACKSWING AT ALL, IAIN! IF YOU DON'T COCK YOUR WRISTS YOU WON'T GET ANY POWER IN THE SHOT
THE REASON YOUR WRISTS DON'T COCK IS YOU GRIP THE CLUB FAR TOO TIGHTLY, AS IF YOUR HANDS WERE IN A VICE. THIS MAKES YOU FREEZE AND STIFFEN UP! YOU MUST RELAX YOUR GRIP
RELAX
RELAX
RELAX
RELAX
ALSO, AS YOU TEND TO BE STIFF-WRISTED, PRACTISE YOUR BACKSWING WITH A SMALL WEIGHT OR STONE TIED TO THE END OF THE CLUB
THIS WEIGHT WILL HELP TO BREAK YOUR WRISTS AT THE TOP OF THE SWING AND HELP YOU TO GET THE CORRECT FEELING OF THE WRIST COCK

How to cock your wrists

IAIN, YOU ARE IN SUCH A HURRY TO START YOUR DOWNSWING, YOUR WRISTS DON'T GET A CHANCE TO COCK!
YOU MUST NOT START THE DOWNSWING IMMEDIATELY YOUR ARMS HAVE COMPLETED THEIR BACKSWING MOVEMENT...
YOU MUST ALLOW THE CLUBHEAD TO CONTINUE ITS BACKWARD JOURNEY! IT IS THIS MOMENTUM OF THE CLUBHEAD, AFTER THE ARMS HAVE STOPPED, WHICH COCKS THE WRISTS!

To pause...or not to pause

YOU MUSTN'T PAUSE AT THE TOP OF THE BACKSWING, IAIN. YOU'VE GOT TO HAVE NERVES OF STEEL TO DO THAT AS IT BREAKS THE NATURAL RHYTHM OF THE SWING
BUT MANY TOP PLAYERS, INCLUDING TOMMY ARMOUR AND MAX FAULKNER HAVE WRITTEN THAT A PAUSE IS A GOOD THING, GARY
I KNOW THEY HAVE, BUT I DON'T SEE THEM DOING IT THEMSELVES! IF YOU WATCH THE PERFECT RHYTHM OF A CLOCK'S PENDULUM IT GOES LEFT AND RIGHT, LEFT AND RIGHT. IT DOESN'T GO LEFT STOP AND RIGHT, LEFT STOP AND RIGHT!
THE ONLY TOP PLAYER I EVER SAW WITH A DEFINITE PAUSE WAS CARY MIDDLECOFF. BUT HOGAN, SNEAD, NICKLAUS AND PALMER— THE FOUR GREATEST PLAYERS I'VE EVER SEEN— ALL HAVE SMOOTH SWINGS WITH NO PAUSE!
Nº9
342YDS
4

Hold on! Don't overswing!

HORIZONTAL
A LONG BACKSWING IS VERY GOOD, IAIN, PROVIDED THE CLUB REMAINS UNDER CONTROL. BUT YOU ARE OVERSWINGING, THEREBY BUCKLING YOUR LEFT ARM AND OPENING UP YOUR LEFT HAND
HORIZONTAL
IT'S ALL RIGHT FOR THE CLUB TO REACH THE HORIZONTAL, OR EVEN SLIGHTLY LOWER, AS LONG AS YOU CAN KEEP YOUR LEFT ARM STRAIGHT AND YOUR HAND CLOSED. THIS REQUIRES VERY SUPPLE WRISTS
SO CONCENTRATE ON KEEPING YOUR ARM STRAIGHT AND YOUR LEFT HAND CLOSED. THIS AUTOMATICALLY SHORTENS YOUR BACKSWING AND HELPS YOU KEEP CONTROL OF THE CLUB

Keep control of the club

IT IS A FAULT, IAIN. IT SHOWS THAT YOU ARE LETTING THE CLUB DROP WAY BELOW HORIZONTAL AND ARE CONSEQUENTLY LOSING CONTROL OF IT!
I CAN SEE THE CLUBHEAD FROM THE CORNER OF MY EYE EVERY TIME I SWING, GARY. IS THIS GOOD OR BAD?
KEEP YOUR LEFT HAND CLOSED AT THE TOP AND TRY TO HAVE A STRAIGHT LEFT ARM. THIS WILL SHORTEN YOUR SWING AND HELP YOU CONTROL THE CLUB

Wide arcs, long shots

IN GOLF, A STRAIGHT LEFT ARM IS AN ABSOLUTE NECESSITY, IAIN. YOUR ELBOW IS BUCKLED AND YOUR ARM BENT!
AS SOON AS YOUR LEFT ARM IS BENT, THE ARC OF YOUR BACKSWING BECOMES VERY NARROW
MIND YOU, YOUR LEFT ARM DOESN'T HAVE TO BE RIGID, IAIN, BUT IT MUST BE STRAIGHT
AND DON'T FORGET THIS... THE WIDER YOUR ARC, THE FARTHER YOU'LL HIT THE BALL!

Try some splints

LOOK AT YOUR LEFT ARM, IAIN! YOU'LL NEVER HIT A LONG BALL IF YOU ALLOW IT TO BUCKLE!
ANY GOLFER WHO HAS DIFFICULTY KEEPING HIS LEFT ARM STRAIGHT SHOULD TRY SWINGING IN SPLINTS! ALL THAT'S NEEDED IS A COUPLE OF PIECES OF WOOD AND SOME STRING!
PRACTICE A FEW BACKSWINGS NOW AND AGAIN AND YOU WILL SOON GET THE FEELING OF SWINGING WITH A STRAIGHT LEFT ARM
BUT DON'T TRY TO FOLLOW-THROUGH, IAIN — OR YOU'LL REALLY HURT YOURSELF!

Laying the club of

YOU HAD A VERY FLAT SWING WHEN YOU FIRST CAME TO BRITAIN, GARY...
THAT'S RIGHT, TOM. I WAS SO SCARED OF HOOKING, I DEVELOPED A SLICER'S GRIP WHICH MADE ME SWING VERY FLAT
THIS IS HOW I USED TO SWING, "LAYING THE CLUB OFF" LIKE SO MANY WEEKENDERS. IN OTHER WORDS, THE CLUB IS NOT POINTING TO THE TARGET AT THE END OF THE BACKSWING
ALSO, MY LEFT WRIST IS ON TOP OF THE CLUB
I CORRECTED MY SWING SIMPLY BY GRIPPING THE CLUB CORRECTLY WITH THE TWO "V'S" POINTING TO MY RIGHT SHOULDER
NOW WHEN I TAKE THE CLUB BACK, IT POINTS TO WHERE I AM AIMING, AND MY LEFT WRIST IS UNDERNEATH THE CLUB
POINTS TO TARGET
ADMITTEDLY, A SHORT MAN SWINGS FLATTER THAN A TALL MAN... BUT I DEFINITELY USE TO BE A LITTLE TOO FLAT!

Inside and up!

YOU ARE LAYING THE CLUB OFF, IAIN. IN OTHER WORDS, IT IS POINTING WAY LEFT OF TARGET AT THE TOP OF YOUR SWING. THIS WILL MAKE YOU SLICE THE BALL
THE CLUB SHOULD POINT TO THE TARGET
A GOOD WAY TO ACHIEVE THIS IS TO TAKE THE CLUB BACK SLIGHTLY ON THE INSIDE TO ABOUT HERE...
THEN, TAKE THE CLUB STRAIGHT UP. THIS HELPS YOU TO GET YOUR HANDS UNDER THE SHAFT, AND THE CLUB WILL DEFINITELY POINT MORE TOWARDS THE TARGET

The perfect wrist position

GARY, SEVERAL OF OUR READERS HAVE WRITTEN TO ASK WHAT IS THE CORRECT POSITION OF THE WRISTS AT THE TOP OF THE BACKSWING, AND HOW CAN THEY CHECK THAT THEY ARE GETTING INTO THIS POSITION?
ALL THEY HAVE TO DO, IAIN, IS TO SLIP A RULER OR PENCIL UNDERNEATH THEIR WATCH STRAPS AND TAKE A SWING. IF THIS IS THE RESULT, THE WRISTS ARE TOO FLAT
HERE, THE POSITION OF THE RULER SHOWS THAT THE WRISTS ARE TOO FAR UNDERNEATH THE SHAFT
PERFECT
BUT THIS TIME THE RULER LIES STRAIGHT ACROSS MY WRIST AND THE BACK OF MY HAND. THIS INDICATES THE PERFECT WRIST POSITION

A tip for tall men

JOHN HAS A VERY FLAT SWING, GARY
HE HAS HARDLY ANY ARC AT ALL, IAIN. THAT IS WHY HE IS A SHORT HITTER!
LIKE MOST TALL MEN, HE STANDS TOO FAR AWAY FROM THE BALL. THIS IS WHERE THE BALL OUGHT TO BE POSITIONED
NOW HE WILL BE ABLE TO LIFT HIS HANDS HIGHER ON THE BACKSWING, HE WILL GET A BIGGER ARC AND BETTER WEIGHT TRANSFERENCE COMING INTO THE BALL...
AND MUCH MORE CLUBHEAD SPEED

Three faults—one cure

1
2
3
THREE FAULTS HERE, TOM. YOU ARE RAISING YOUR LEFT HEEL AS YOU COME INTO THE BALL, YOU ARE FALLING BACK AND YOU ARE HITTING EARLY.
THERE IS ONE CURE FOR ALL THREE MISTAKES AND THAT IS TO IMAGINE THERE IS A TEE-PEG UNDER YOUR LEFT HEEL AT THE TOP OF THE BACKSWING.
START THE DOWNSWING BY THUMPING THE PEG INTO THE GROUND WITH YOUR HEEL.
3
2
1
TONY LEMA WAS A GREAT BELIEVER IN THIS AND, WITHOUT A DOUBT, IT IS A GOOD WAY OF SHIFTING YOUR WEIGHT TO YOUR LEFT SIDE.

Keep the heel down

YOU'RE LIFTING YOUR HEEL TOO HIGH ON THE BACKSWING IAIN. THIS IS AS BAD A FAULT AS THERE IS IN GOLF
I'M NOT SAYING IT'S BAD TO LIFT YOUR LEFT HEEL A COUPLE OF INCHES, BUT WHEN YOU LIFT IT AS HIGH AS YOU HAVE, THERE'S NO WAY YOU CAN CONSISTENTLY HIT THE BALL STRAIGHT!
YOU DEVELOP TREMENDOUS BODY SWAY WHICH MEANS YOU WON'T TAKE THE CLUB BACK ON THE SAME LINE EVERY TIME. NOR WILL YOU BRING YOUR HEEL BACK TO THE POSITION IT WAS IN AT ADDRESS
HERE I AM HITTING A 4-IRON AND YOU CAN SEE THAT MY LEFT HEEL NEVER LEAVES THE GROUND. I BELIEVE THAT ALL PRO'S SHOULD KEEP THE LEFT HEEL DOWN FOR EVERY SINGLE SHOT, AS THIS GIVES THE BODY A CERTAIN TENSION THAT IS NEEDED TO GENERATE POWER
HOWEVER, THIS RATHER DIFFICULT TECHNIQUE WON'T SUIT SOME AMATEURS AS THEY CANNOT PRACTISE AS MUCH AS THE PROS. SO EXPERIMENT, AND FIND OUT WHAT IS RIGHT FOR YOU!

Don't straighten that right leg

YOU ADDRESS THE BALL QUITE WELL, TOM, WITH YOUR KNEES NICELY FLEXED
HOWEVER, AS YOU GO BACK, YOU STRAIGHTEN THAT RIGHT LEG AND GET NO HIP TURN OR SHOULDER TURN WHATSOEVER. YOUR BACKSWING IS BADLY RESTRICTED, YOUR HEAD IS LIFTED UP OFF THE BALL AND YOU HAVE NO WRIST COCK!
AS SOON AS YOU STRAIGHTEN YOUR LEG, YOUR SPINE STIFFENS UP AND YOU LOSE ALL FLEXIBILITY AND SUPPLENESS
BY KEEPING THE RIGHT LEG BENT, MY SHOULDERS TURN, MY HIPS TURN, MY WRISTS COCK AND MY HEAD REMAINS ABSOLUTELY ON THE SAME LEVEL!

Winding up from the knee

THAT ONE DIDN'T GO FAR, DID IT, GARY?
I CAN TELL YOU JUST WHY, TOM...YOU DIDN'T WIND UP PROPERLY!
SEE, ON THE BACKSWING, YOUR LEFT KNEE IS POINTING DIRECTLY AT THE BALL. NOW THAT'S NOT GOOD
IT MUST POINT BEHIND THE BALL, OTHERWISE YOU CAN'T WIND UP YOUR BODY CORRECTLY, AND THE BODY IS LIKE A SPRING—YOU WIND IT UP AND IT UNWINDS ITSELF! SO IT'S IMPORTANT TO WIND IT UP CORRECTLY!

Shifting the weight

PROPER WEIGHT TRANSFERENCE IS ONE OF THE SECRETS OF GOLF, TOM... AND YOU HAVEN'T GOT IT! LOOK AT YOUR BACKSWING...
YOUR RIGHT KNEE IS ABSOLUTELY RIGID DURING YOUR WIND-UP, AND YOUR WEIGHT IS STILL ON YOUR LEFT SIDE...
NOW LOOK AT MY WIND-UP! MY RIGHT KNEE IS BENT AND MY WEIGHT NOW FAVORS MY RIGHT SIDE!
IF YOU FAIL TO SHIFT YOUR WEIGHT TO YOUR RIGHT SIDE WHEN TAKING THE CLUB BACK AND TO TRANSFER IT BACK TO THE LEFT ON THE DOWNSWING, THE RESULT CAN BE ANYTHING FROM A HOOK, SLICE, "TOP," SKYBALL —OR WHAT HAVE YOU!

Beating a sway

YOU ARE A CHRONIC SWAYER, TOM. YOUR HEAD MOVES AT LEAST A FOOT ON THE BACKSWING
I WANT YOU TO PRACTICE FOR AN HOUR WITH YOUR RIGHT FOOT TURNED IN AS FAR AS POSSIBLE
BY LOCKING YOURSELF LIKE THIS, YOU WILL GET THE FEELING OF SWINGING WITHOUT SWAYING. WHEN YOU GO OUT ON THE COURSE AGAIN, STAND NORMALLY

Nail that shoe

ROLLING YOUR RIGHT FOOT ON THE BACKSWING, MAKES YOU SWAY OFF THE BALL, IAIN
NOTICE HOW MY RIGHT FOOT IS PINNED TO THE GROUND. THIS PRODUCES THE TENSION IN MY HIP THAT WILL HELP ME UNLEASH THE CLUBHEAD AT THE BALL WITH TREMENDOUS SPEED
WHEN YOU ROLL, YOU GET NO TENSION AT ALL!
TENSION
THROUGHOUT THE BACKSWING, YOU MUST FEEL AS IF YOUR SHOE IS NAILED TO THE GROUND!

Sway no more

YOU'VE TOLD ME OFTEN THAT MY RIGHT LEG MUST NOT SWAY OUT TO THE SIDE ON THE BACKSWING, GARY...
BUT THIS IS EASIER SAID THAN DONE! WHEN I TRY TO KEEP IT STILL, I SEEM UNABLE TO WIND-UP PROPERLY!
YOU MUST GET THE FEELING OF WHAT IT IS LIKE TO SWING CORRECTLY, TOM...
... AND THE BEST WAY TO GET THIS IS TO ADDRESS THE BALL WITH YOUR RIGHT LEG UP AGAINST A LOW BENCH WHICH WILL PREVENT YOUR LEG SWAYING WHEN YOU TAKE A SWING
NOTE THE BIG SHOULDER WIND-UP I AM ABLE TO GET WITHOUT MY RIGHT LEG MOVING AN INCH!
PRACTICE LIKE THIS UNTIL YOUR BODY HAS LEARNED WHAT THE CORRECT MOTION FEELS LIKE— THEN RELY ON MUSCLE MEMORY!

Don't tilt your hips

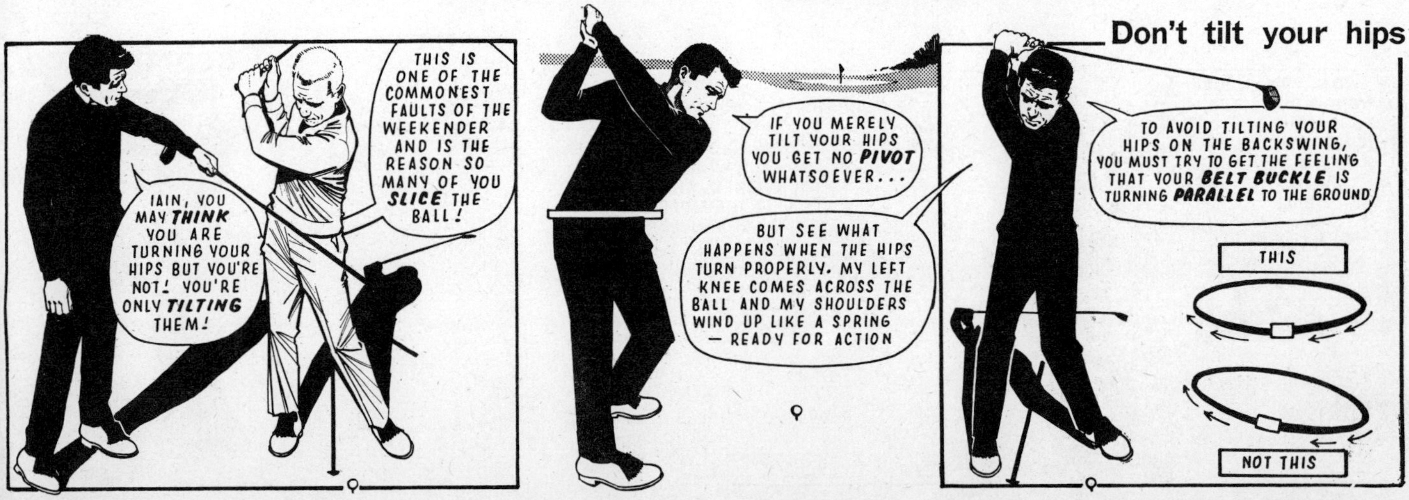

IAIN, YOU MAY THINK YOU ARE TURNING YOUR HIPS BUT YOU'RE NOT! YOU'RE ONLY TILTING THEM!
THIS IS ONE OF THE COMMONEST FAULTS OF THE WEEKENDER AND IS THE REASON SO MANY OF YOU SLICE THE BALL!
IF YOU MERELY TILT YOUR HIPS YOU GET NO PIVOT WHATSOEVER...
BUT SEE WHAT HAPPENS WHEN THE HIPS TURN PROPERLY. MY LEFT KNEE COMES ACROSS THE BALL AND MY SHOULDERS WIND UP LIKE A SPRING — READY FOR ACTION
TO AVOID TILTING YOUR HIPS ON THE BACKSWING, YOU MUST TRY TO GET THE FEELING THAT YOUR BELT BUCKLE IS TURNING PARALLEL TO THE GROUND
THIS
NOT THIS

Beware the extra sweater

YOU HAVE NO WIDTH TO YOUR BACKSWING, TOM!
GOLFERS TEND TO SHORTEN THEIR SWINGS IN COLD WEATHER. THIS IS BECAUSE MUSCLES ARE NOT AS SUPPLE AS USUAL. THE FACT THAT YOU ARE WEARING TWO SWEATERS ALSO MAKES IT HARDER FOR YOU TO MAKE A GOOD BACKSWING TURN
YOU MUST MAKE AN EXTRA SPECIAL EFFORT TO GET A BIG PIVOT IN COLD WEATHER OTHERWISE YOUR RHYTHM WILL BE AFFECTED AND YOU WON'T HIT THE SAME SHOTS AS YOU DO UNDER NORMAL CONDITIONS.

Don't spill your power

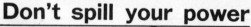

HITTING EARLY IS ONE OF THE BIG FAULTS IN GOLF
THE LATE HIT IS THE SECRET OF DISTANCE AND ACCURACY!
HITTING LATE
A GOOD WAY OF ACHIEVING THIS LATE HIT IS TO IMAGINE YOU HAVE AN UNCORKED BOTTLE OF WINE IN YOUR HANDS
TRY TO KEEP THE WINE IN THE BOTTLE AS LONG AS POSSIBLE ON THE DOWNSWING

How to develop the late hit

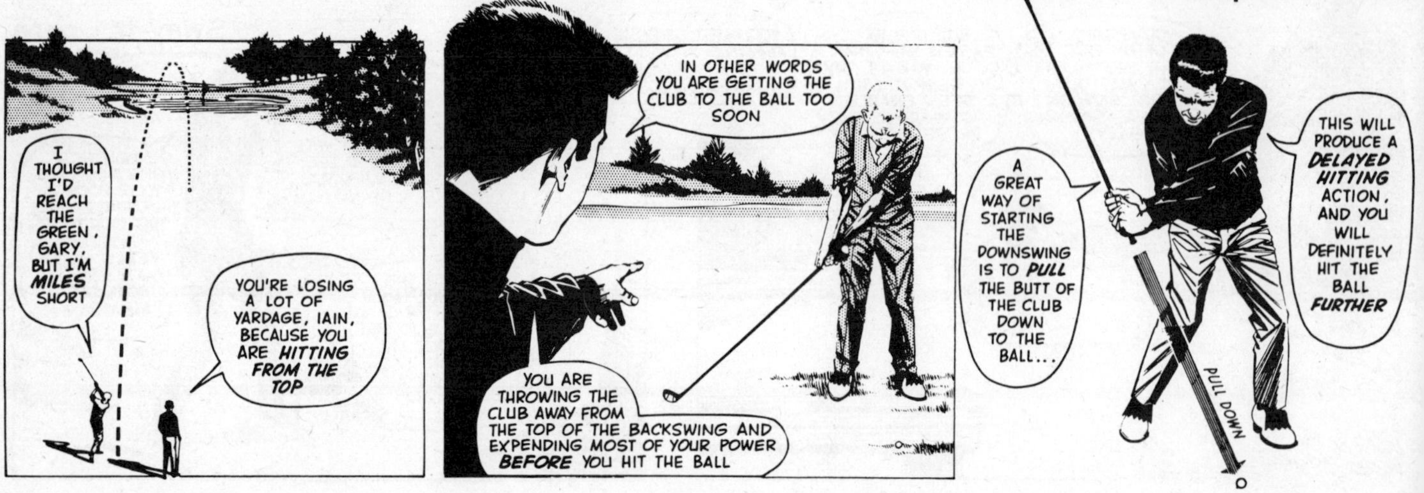

I THOUGHT I'D REACH THE GREEN, GARY, BUT I'M MILES SHORT
YOU'RE LOSING A LOT OF YARDAGE, IAIN, BECAUSE YOU ARE HITTING FROM THE TOP
IN OTHER WORDS YOU ARE GETTING THE CLUB TO THE BALL TOO SOON

THIS WILL PRODUCE A DELAYED HITTING ACTION, AND YOU WILL DEFINITELY HIT THE BALL FURTHER

Chop that log

WHEN YOU UNCOCK YOUR WRISTS TOO SOON, IAIN, YOU ARE USING UP ALL YOUR POWER BEFORE THE CLUBHEAD HITS THE BALL
THIS IS LIKE TRYING TO CHOP A LOG BY "FLICKING" THE AXE AT IT
IN ORDER TO CHOP THAT WOOD, YOU MUST KEEP YOUR WRIST COCKED, RIGHT UP TO THE MOMENT OF IMPACT
LEARN TO DO THE SAME IN GOLF. DELAY THE HIT, AND YOU WILL HIT THE BALL MUCH FURTHER!

The elastic tip

THAT IS A GREAT BACKSWING POSITION, IAIN
WHAT A PITY YOU SPOIL IT BY HITTING FROM THE TOP. YOU HAVE CAST THE CLUB OUT LIKE A FISHING ROD!
HITTING FROM TOP
YOU SHOULD FEEL AS IF YOU HAVE A SHORT PIECE OF ELASTIC TIED FROM YOUR RIGHT ELBOW TO YOUR BELT
WHEN YOU START DOWN, THE ELASTIC WILL PULL YOUR ELBOW BACK TO YOUR SIDE. THAT IS THE WAY TO GET THE DELAYED ACTION THAT ALL GOOD GOLFERS HAVE!

Strike a light

THAT IS A POWDER-PUFF SHOT, IAIN. YOU HAVE QUIT ON THE SHOT AND LOST A LOT OF POWER. YOUR CLUB HAS GONE THROUGH THE BALL FAR TOO SLOWLY!
SLOW
TO ACHIEVE MAXIMUM CLUBHEAD SPEED, YOU MUST PULL DOWN FROM THE TOP OF THE SWING. DON'T THROW THE CLUBHEAD OUT LIKE A FISHING ROD!
FOR POWER AND ACCURACY, THE ACTION OF THE CLUBHEAD THROUGH THE BALL MUST BE FAST– LIKE THE STRIKING OF A MATCH!
FAST
MATCHES

Up against a brick wall

IT'S STRAIGHT, GARY, BUT I THINK I NEED A NEW SET OF MUSCLES!
I KEEP TELLING YOU, IAIN, YOU WON'T HIT A LONG BALL IF YOU DON'T GET YOUR WEIGHT INTO THE SHOT.
YOUR HIPS ARE LAZY, IAIN. THEY STAY BEHIND THE BALL ALL THE TIME!
YOU MUST LEARN TO THRUST YOUR WEIGHT FORWARD, KEEPING YOUR HEAD ABSOLUTELY STILL!
IMAGINE YOU HAVE TO BASH THROUGH A BRICK WALL WITH THE LOWER PART OF YOUR BODY.
THIS ACTION DEVELOPS A TREMENDOUS PULL DOWN FORCE IN YOUR ARMS AND HELPS YOU TO ACHIEVE A LATE HIT AND A LONG BALL!

Don't straighten up

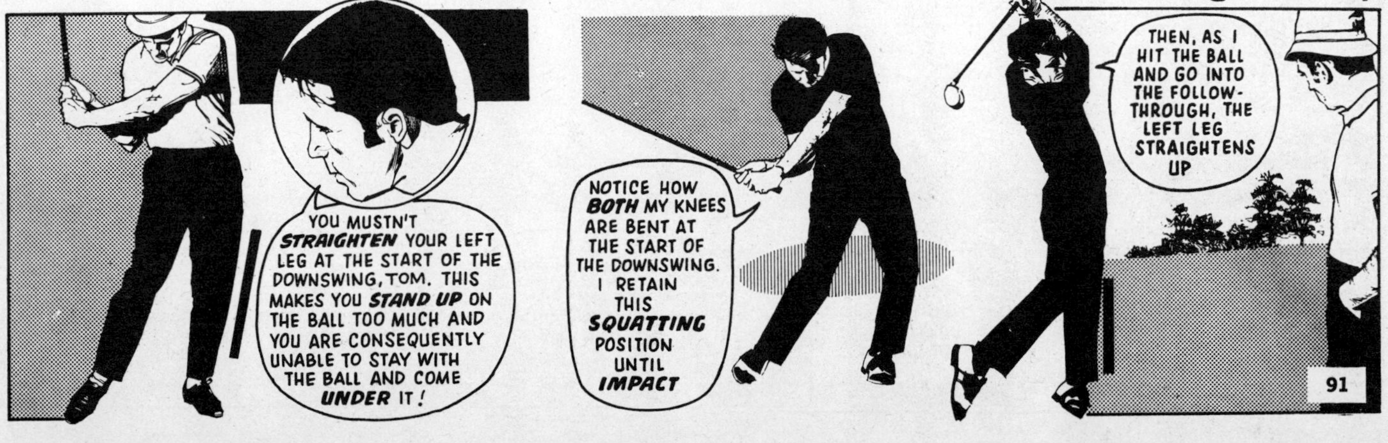

YOU MUSTN'T STRAIGHTEN YOUR LEFT LEG AT THE START OF THE DOWNSWING, TOM. THIS MAKES YOU STAND UP ON THE BALL TOO MUCH AND YOU ARE CONSEQUENTLY UNABLE TO STAY WITH THE BALL AND COME UNDER IT!
NOTICE HOW BOTH MY KNEES ARE BENT AT THE START OF THE DOWNSWING. I RETAIN THIS SQUATTING POSITION UNTIL IMPACT
THEN, AS I HIT THE BALL AND GO INTO THE FOLLOW-THROUGH, THE LEFT LEG STRAIGHTENS UP

Play golf—not baseball

THE REASON YOU ARE DOING SO IS YOU ARE STRAIGHTENING YOUR LEFT SIDE TOO QUICKLY. THIS MOVEMENT IS PULLING YOUR ARMS ACROSS THE BALL.
YOU ARE STILL HITTING ROUND THE BALL LIKE A BASEBALL PLAYER, TOM. THIS IS A BAD FAULT, AND A COMMON ONE!
NOTICE THAT, IMMEDIATELY AFTER IMPACT, MY LEGS ARE STILL BENT AS THEY WERE AT ADDRESS AND, CONSEQUENTLY, MY CLUB IS GOING FROM INSIDE TO OUT. ONLY NOW WILL MY LEGS STRAIGHTEN UP.

Starting the downswing

YOU ARE FLAT-FOOTED, TOM! THAT CAN LEAD TO ALL KINDS OF BAD SHOTS!
THE DOWNSWING OUGHT TO BE STARTED WITH THE LEFT KNEE MOVING TOWARDS THE TARGET.
THIS KEEPS THE LEFT SIDE IN CONTROL OF THE SHOT AND ALSO HELPS THE WRISTS TO REMAIN COCKED!
BECAUSE THE WRISTS DON'T UNCOCK UNTIL THEY ARE IN THE HITTING AREA, THE CLUBHEAD SPEEDS THROUGH INTO A VERY LONG FOLLOW-THROUGH.

When to brace the left side

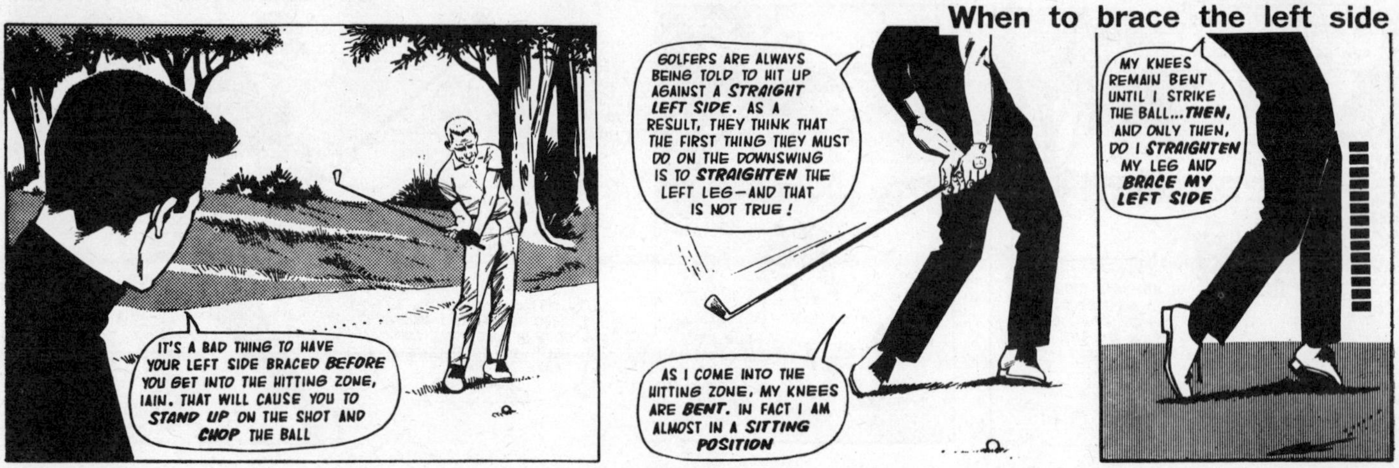

IT'S A BAD THING TO HAVE YOUR LEFT SIDE BRACED BEFORE YOU GET INTO THE HITTING ZONE, IAIN. THAT WILL CAUSE YOU TO STAND UP ON THE SHOT AND CHOP THE BALL
GOLFERS ARE ALWAYS BEING TOLD TO HIT UP AGAINST A STRAIGHT LEFT SIDE. AS A RESULT, THEY THINK THAT THE FIRST THING THEY MUST DO ON THE DOWNSWING IS TO STRAIGHTEN THE LEFT LEG—AND THAT IS NOT TRUE!
AS I COME INTO THE HITTING ZONE, MY KNEES ARE BENT. IN FACT I AM ALMOST IN A SITTING POSITION
MY KNEES REMAIN BENT UNTIL I STRIKE THE BALL...THEN, AND ONLY THEN, DO I STRAIGHTEN MY LEG AND BRACE MY LEFT SIDE

Relax at shoulder

YOU SAY YOU FEEL AS IF YOU ARE PULLING DOWN WITH YOUR LEFT HAND FROM THE TOP OF THE SWING INTO THE HITTING AREA, TOM – BUT, IN FACT, YOU ARE NOT PULLING DOWN INTO THE SHOT!
YOU ARE PULLING DOWN AND ROUND!
YOU MUST PULL DOWN STRAIGHT ON THE LINE OR SLIGHTLY INSIDE THE LINE
RELAX
A GOOD TIP TO HELP YOU ACHIEVE THIS IS TO RELAX YOUR RIGHT SHOULDER WHEN YOU GET TO THE TOP OF THE BACKSWING. THIS WILL ENABLE THE SHOULDER TO COME UNDER INSTEAD OF OUT WHEN YOU START TO PULL DOWN

Don't hit from the top

YOU'RE THROWING OUT THE CLUB FROM THE TOP OF YOUR BACKSWING, IAIN, AS IF YOU WERE CASTING A FISHING LINE
BY "HITTING FROM THE TOP" LIKE THIS YOU ARE WASTING YOUR POWER. YOU MUST NOT UNCOCK YOUR WRISTS UNTIL YOU ARE IN THE HITTING ZONE
I USE NO POWER AT ALL UNTIL MY HANDS REACH WAIST LEVEL. UNTIL THEN, IT IS JUST A MATTER OF RHYTHM.
RHYTHM
HITTING ZONE
ONE WAY OF ACHIEVING THIS DELAYED HITTING ACTION IS TO PULL DOWN STRONGLY WITH THE LEFT HAND
ONCE MY HANDS REACH WAIST LEVEL, MY WRISTS UNCOCK AND I GENERATE CLUBHEAD SPEED RIGHT THROUGH THE BALL
THE POINT TO NOTE IS THIS...I DON'T START USING MY POWER UNTIL I AM IN THE HITTING ZONE!

Plant that left foot

YOUR LEFT FOOT IS SWIVELLING ROUND AS YOU HIT THROUGH THE BALL, IAIN
WHEN YOUR FOOT TURNS, YOU ARE NOT THEN HITTING UP AGAINST A FIRM LEFT SIDE. ALSO, YOUR CLUB GOES THROUGH TO THE LEFT INSTEAD OF STRAIGHT TO THE TARGET
LEFT
MIKE SOUCHAK USED TO HAVE A LOT OF TROUBLE WITH THIS AND SO DID I. I CURED MYSELF ON THE PRACTICE TEE BY HAMMERING A TENT PEG INTO THE GROUND, WHICH KEPT MY FOOT FROM TURNING
STRAIGHT
HENRY COTTON HAD THE BEST LEFT FOOT POSITION I EVER SAW—HE KEPT IT PLANTED JUST PERFECTLY!
TENT PEG

Watch the back of the ball

ONE OF THE WORSE FAULTS WHEN DRIVING IS TO ATTACK THE BALL FROM THE OUTSIDE
YOU MUST COME AT IT FROM THE INSIDE
OUTSIDE
INSIDE
YOU WILL FIND IT A GREAT HELP IF YOU WATCH THE BACK OF THE BALL INSTEAD OF THE TOP
THIS WILL ENCOURAGE YOU TO APPROACH FROM THE INSIDE AND COME UNDER THE BALL INSTEAD OF HITTING ROUND IT!

Slide those hips...

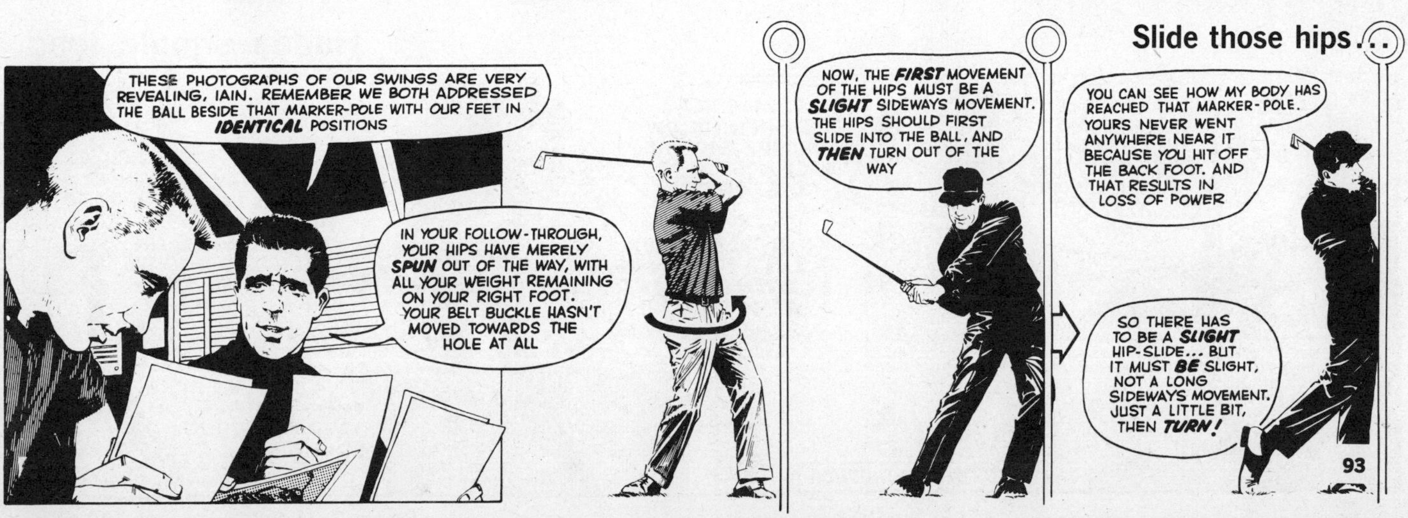

THESE PHOTOGRAPHS OF OUR SWINGS ARE VERY REVEALING, IAIN. REMEMBER WE BOTH ADDRESSED THE BALL BESIDE THAT MARKER-POLE WITH OUR FEET IN IDENTICAL POSITIONS
IN YOUR FOLLOW-THROUGH, YOUR HIPS HAVE MERELY SPUN OUT OF THE WAY, WITH ALL YOUR WEIGHT REMAINING ON YOUR RIGHT FOOT. YOUR BELT BUCKLE HASN'T MOVED TOWARDS THE HOLE AT ALL
NOW, THE FIRST MOVEMENT OF THE HIPS MUST BE A SLIGHT SIDEWAYS MOVEMENT. THE HIPS SHOULD FIRST SLIDE INTO THE BALL, AND THEN TURN OUT OF THE WAY
YOU CAN SEE HOW MY BODY HAS REACHED THAT MARKER-POLE. YOURS NEVER WENT ANYWHERE NEAR IT BECAUSE YOU HIT OFF THE BACK FOOT. AND THAT RESULTS IN LOSS OF POWER
SO THERE HAS TO BE A SLIGHT HIP-SLIDE... BUT IT MUST BE SLIGHT, NOT A LONG SIDEWAYS MOVEMENT. JUST A LITTLE BIT, THEN TURN!

A game of contradictions

YOU ONCE TOLD ME THAT GOLF IS A GAME OF CONTRADICTIONS, GARY! WHAT DID YOU MEAN?
WELL, IAIN, WHEN I AIM TO THE LEFT OF MY INTENDED LINE OF FLIGHT, THE BALL WILL GO TO THE RIGHT...
WHEN I AIM TO THE RIGHT OF MY INTENDED LINE OF FLIGHT, THE BALL WILL USUALLY HOOK TO THE LEFT!
WHEN I KEEP MY HEAD DOWN AND HIT DOWN ON THE BALL, THE BALL GOES UP...
WHEN I STAND UP ON THE SHOT, THE BALL STAYS DOWN
AND WHEN YOU AND I ARE PLAYING GOLF, WE'RE WORKING. SEE, IAIN, GOLF IS FULL OF CONTRADICTIONS!

Shoulder to chin

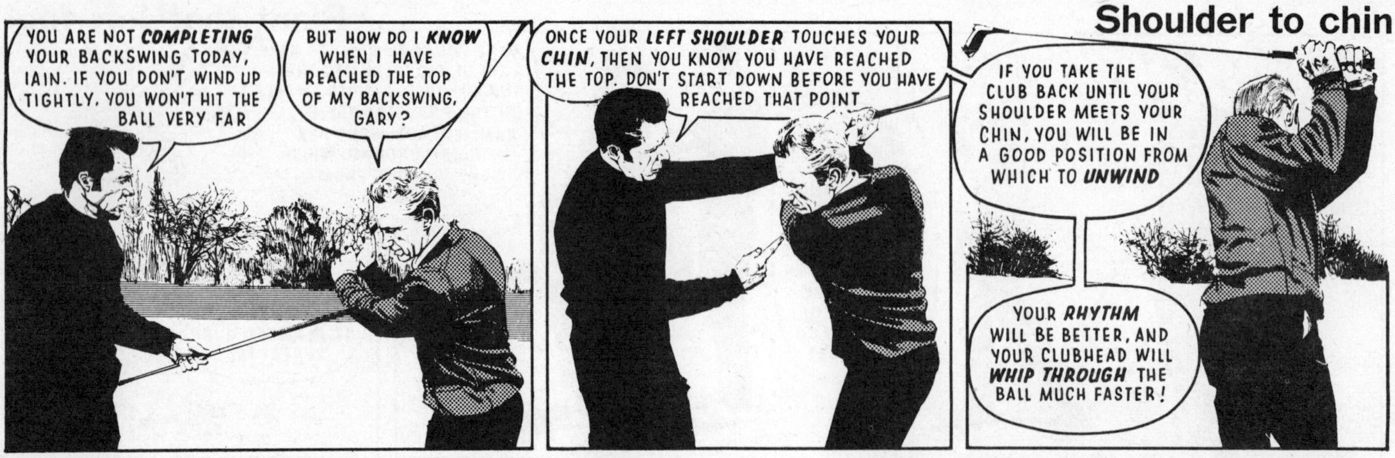

YOU ARE NOT COMPLETING YOUR BACKSWING TODAY, IAIN. IF YOU DON'T WIND UP TIGHTLY, YOU WON'T HIT THE BALL VERY FAR
BUT HOW DO I KNOW WHEN I HAVE REACHED THE TOP OF MY BACKSWING, GARY?
ONCE YOUR LEFT SHOULDER TOUCHES YOUR CHIN, THEN YOU KNOW YOU HAVE REACHED THE TOP. DON'T START DOWN BEFORE YOU HAVE REACHED THAT POINT
IF YOU TAKE THE CLUB BACK UNTIL YOUR SHOULDER MEETS YOUR CHIN, YOU WILL BE IN A GOOD POSITION FROM WHICH TO UNWIND
YOUR RHYTHM WILL BE BETTER, AND YOUR CLUBHEAD WILL WHIP THROUGH THE BALL MUCH FASTER!

How to keep your head behind the ball...

YOU'LL HIT NO END OF BAD SHOTS, IAIN, IF YOU KEEP ON THRUSTING YOUR HEAD FORWARD LIKE THAT
YOUR TROUBLE STEMS FROM HAVING YOUR HEAD WRONGLY POSITIONED AT ADDRESS. THIS ENCOURAGES IT TO MOVE FORWARD AS YOU COME INTO THE BALL
HEAD POINTS IN FRONT OF THE BALL
HEAD POINTS BEHIND BALL
IN FUTURE, JUST BEFORE YOU TAKE BACK THE CLUB, MAKE SURE YOU COCK YOUR HEAD IN THIS DIRECTION. IT'S LIKE COCKING A GUN BEFORE YOU SHOOT!
THIS LITTLE COCKING ACTION WILL HELP KEEP YOUR HEAD BEHIND THE BALL AS YOU HIT AND GO INTO YOUR FOLLOW-THROUGH

Hands should lead

HERE YOU ARE RELEASING THE CLUBHEAD TOO SOON, TOM - IN OTHER WORDS HITTING EARLY!
THIS LEADS TO A CRAMPED FOLLOW-THROUGH AND YOU LOSE A LOT OF DISTANCE.
CRAMPED FOLLOW-THROUGH
IN ORDER TO HIT LATE, I PULL DOWN WITH MY LEFT ARM FROM THE TOP OF THE BACKSWING.
I ALWAYS HAVE THE FEELING THAT MY HANDS ARE LEADING THE CLUBHEAD INTO THE BALL. HOWEVER, WHEN YOU HIT LATE, YOU MUST MAKE CERTAIN THAT YOU SQUARE UP THE CLUBFACE AT IMPACT.
BIG FOLLOW-THROUGH

Pull—don't push

GOLFERS WHO HAVE THIS **CONCAVE** WRIST ACTION THROUGH THE BALL NEVER GET DISTANCE, TOM..
IT IS A TELLTALE SIGN OF A MAN WHO HITS **AT** THE BALL INSTEAD OF **THROUGH** IT!
AT IMPACT, THE FORCE APPLIED TO THE BALL SHOULD COME FROM IN **FRONT** OF IT, NOT FROM BEHIND. IN OTHER WORDS IT SHOULD BE A **PULLING** ACTION AS OPPOSED TO A **PUSHING** ACTION.
PUSH
PULL
TARGET
ALL GREAT PLAYERS HAVE **CONVEX** WRISTS GOING THROUGH THE BALL. NOTE HOW THE **BACK** OF MY LEFT HAND AND THE PALM OF MY RIGHT FACE THE HOLE AS I **PULL** THROUGH.

Hit that tee-peg

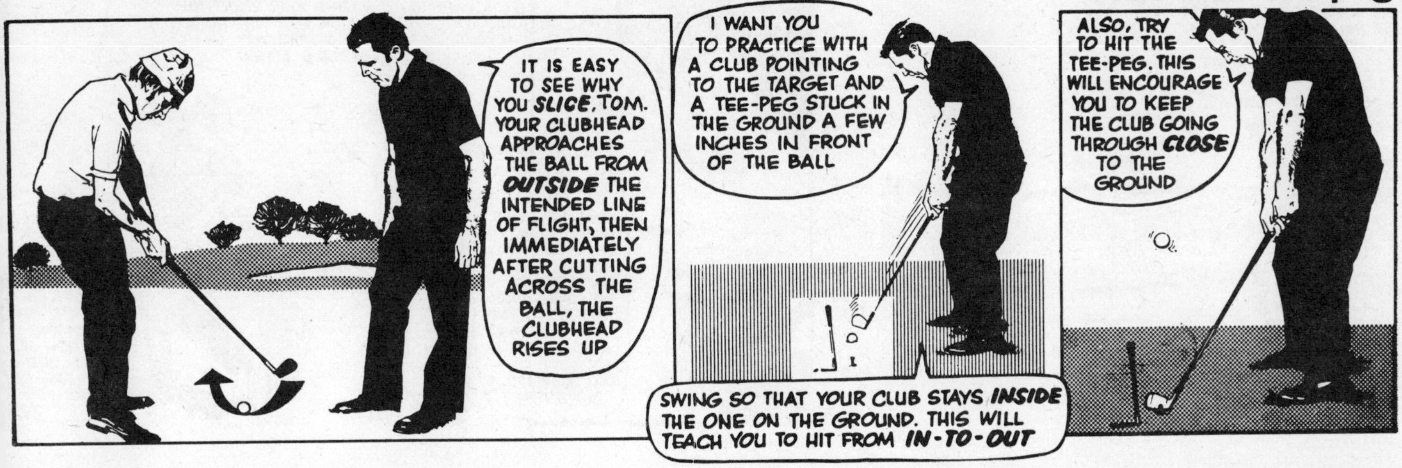

IT IS EASY TO SEE WHY YOU **SLICE**, TOM. YOUR CLUBHEAD APPROACHES THE BALL FROM **OUTSIDE** THE INTENDED LINE OF FLIGHT, THEN IMMEDIATELY AFTER CUTTING ACROSS THE BALL, THE CLUBHEAD RISES UP
I WANT YOU TO PRACTICE WITH A CLUB POINTING TO THE TARGET AND A TEE-PEG STUCK IN THE GROUND A FEW INCHES IN FRONT OF THE BALL
SWING SO THAT YOUR CLUB STAYS **INSIDE** THE ONE ON THE GROUND. THIS WILL TEACH YOU TO HIT FROM **IN-TO-OUT**
ALSO, TRY TO HIT THE TEE-PEG. THIS WILL ENCOURAGE YOU TO KEEP THE CLUB GOING THROUGH **CLOSE** TO THE GROUND

Transfer your weight

TOM, YOUR STANCE IS SO WIDE, YOU ARE UNABLE TO GET YOUR WEIGHT ONTO YOUR LEFT SIDE. YOUR RIGHT FOOT HAS REMAINED **FLAT** ON THE GROUND AND YOUR RIGHT SHOULDER HAS COME **ROUND** ON THE BALL AND **CLOSED** THE CLUBFACE
TO OVERCOME THIS PROBLEM, THE DISTANCE BETWEEN THE **INSIDES** OF YOUR FEET SHOULD BE NO MORE THAN THE WIDTH OF YOUR SHOULDERS
TOO WIDE
THIS AUTOMATICALLY HELPS YOU TO TRANSFER YOUR WEIGHT. THE RIGHT SHOULDER TRAVELS **UNDER** THE SHOT, THUS KEEPING THE CLUB **ON LINE**
KNEE IN
FOOT RAISED

How to get a bigger arc

THAT IS A PATHETIC FOLLOW-THROUGH, IAIN, ESPECIALLY AS YOU **KNOW** WHAT TO DO! YOUR CLUBHEAD SPEED **DIED** COMING INTO THE BALL. YOUR **RIGHT LEG** IS LIKE A **RAMROD**
JUST LOOK AT THE DIFFERENCE WHEN I **THUMP** YOUR RIGHT KNEE INTO THE SHOT!
THIS INCREASES YOUR ARC BY A GOOD **TWO FEET**! EVEN A FOUR INCH INCREASE MEANS A LOT IN TERMS OF **CLUBHEAD SPEED**!
GETTING THE RIGHT KNEE IN IS ONE OF THE **FUNDAMENTALS** OF GOLF!

In pivot—big slice

THAT'S A VERY FLAT FOLLOW-THROUGH, TOM!
FLAT
AND A VERY BIG SLICE!
YOUR TROUBLE IS CAUSED BY THE FACT THAT YOUR LEFT KNEE POINTS AT THE BALL ON THE BACKSWING. THIS MEANS THAT YOU CANNOT PIVOT SUFFICIENTLY, AND THE SCENE IS SET FOR A SLICE!
THERE IS A FANTASTIC DIFFERENCE IN YOUR SHOULDER TURN WHEN YOU REMEMBER TO MOVE YOUR KNEE ACROSS THE BALL. YOUR CLUB IS ALMOST PARALLEL TO THE GROUND. NOW YOUR FOLLOW-THROUGH WILL BE MORE UPRIGHT AND YOU WILL GET RID OF THAT CUT SHOT.

Don't block your swin

THE REASON YOUR CLUB DOESN'T WHIP THROUGH THE BALL SWIFTLY, IAIN, IS YOU ARE NOT GETTING YOUR LEFT HIP OUT OF THE WAY!
IT IS BLOCKING YOUR SWING AND REDUCING YOUR POWER
MANY GOLFERS, INCLUDING SOME TOP PRO'S, HAVE DIFFICULTY IN DELIBERATELY TURNING THE LEFT HIP ON THE DOWNSWING. FOR THEM, AND YOU, THE ANSWER IS TO FORGET THE LEFT HIP AND THINK ABOUT THE RIGHT!
CONCENTRATE ON GETTING YOUR RIGHT HIP INTO THE SHOT, AND YOUR LEFT HIP WILL BE FORCED TO TURN OUT OF THE WAY — WHICH IS WHAT WE ARE AFTER
PERSONALLY, I PREFER TO CONCENTRATE ON MY LEFT HIP — BUT THIS IS SOMETHING EACH GOLFER MUST FIND OUT FOR HIMSELF!

The trigger toe

WHEN YOU FALL BACK ON THE SHOT, IAIN, YOUR FOLLOW-THROUGH BECOMES VERY SHORT AND YOU LOSE HALF YOUR POWER!
AS YOU START YOUR DOWNSWING, YOU MUST DIG YOUR RIGHT BIG TOE INTO THE GROUND!
TRIGGER
THE BIG TOE ACTS LIKE THE TRIGGER OF A GUN AND FIRES YOUR RIGHT KNEE IN TOWARDS YOUR LEFT LEG. THIS ACTION PUSHES YOUR WEIGHT ON TO YOUR LEFT SIDE GIVING YOU MAXIMUM CLUBHEAD SPEED THROUGH THE BALL AND AN EXTENDED FOLLOW-THROUGH!

Walk into the shot

WHEN YOU FALL AWAY FROM THE SHOT, IAIN, YOU HIT THE BALL ON THE UPSWING WITH A SCOOPING ACTION
YOU MUST TURN YOUR HIPS AND PUSH YOUR WEIGHT FORWARD ON TO YOUR LEFT FOOT LIKE SO! THIS MAKES A TREMENDOUS DIFFERENCE TO YOUR ENTIRE SWING
I LIKE TO FEEL AS IF I AM WALKING INTO THE SHOT! THIS HELPS ME TO HIT LATE AND STRIKE THE BALL A CRISP, DOWNWARD BLOW
WALK

The dominant left side

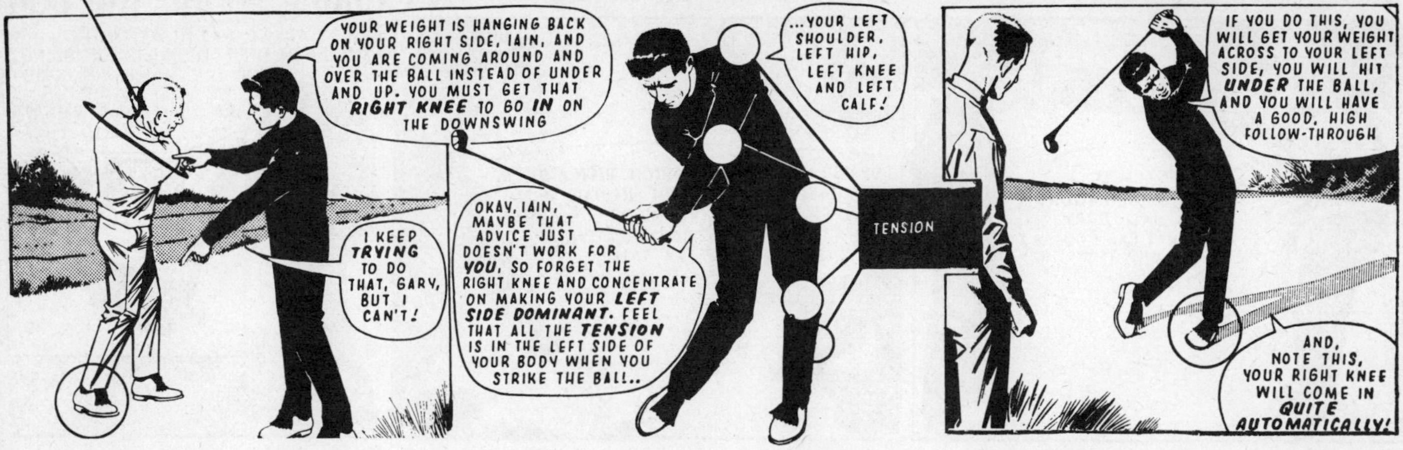

YOUR WEIGHT IS HANGING BACK ON YOUR RIGHT SIDE, IAIN, AND YOU ARE COMING AROUND AND OVER THE BALL INSTEAD OF UNDER AND UP. YOU MUST GET THAT RIGHT KNEE TO GO IN ON THE DOWNSWING
I KEEP TRYING TO DO THAT, GARY, BUT I CAN'T!
OKAY, IAIN, MAYBE THAT ADVICE JUST DOESN'T WORK FOR YOU, SO FORGET THE RIGHT KNEE AND CONCENTRATE ON MAKING YOUR LEFT SIDE DOMINANT. FEEL THAT ALL THE TENSION IS IN THE LEFT SIDE OF YOUR BODY WHEN YOU STRIKE THE BALL..
...YOUR LEFT SHOULDER, LEFT HIP, LEFT KNEE AND LEFT CALF!
TENSION
IF YOU DO THIS, YOU WILL GET YOUR WEIGHT ACROSS TO YOUR LEFT SIDE, YOU WILL HIT UNDER THE BALL, AND YOU WILL HAVE A GOOD, HIGH FOLLOW-THROUGH
AND, NOTE THIS, YOUR RIGHT KNEE WILL COME IN QUITE AUTOMATICALLY!

Make it whiz

LIKE MILLIONS OF CLUB GOLFERS, TOM, YOU HAVE A LEISURELY PRACTICE SWING AND THEN YOU WONDER WHY YOU DON'T GET ENOUGH CLUBHEAD SPEED THROUGH THE BALL.
WHIZ
THE PRACTICE SWING SHOULD BE A CARBON COPY OF THE REAL SWING. THEREFORE YOU MUST MAKE THE CLUB WHIZ!
AFTER ALL, YOU ARE CONDITIONING YOUR MUSCLES FOR THE SHOT THAT IS TO COME. DON'T TEACH THEM ONE THING AND EXPECT THEM TO DO ANOTHER!

Chase after that ball

TOM, YOU'RE IN A VERY CRAMPED ATTITUDE WHEN YOU STRIKE THE BALL, AND YOU DON'T FOLLOW THROUGH SUFFICIENTLY!

IN ORDER TO INCREASE YOUR EXTENSION THROUGH THE BALL, TRY ADDRESSING THE BALL ABOUT ONE INCH OUTSIDE THE TOE OF YOUR CLUB

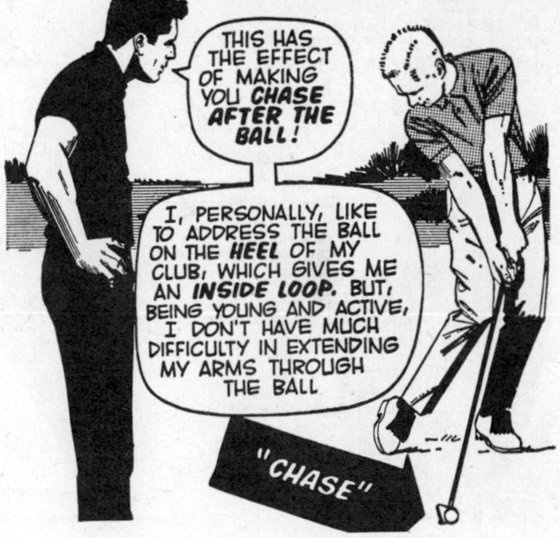

THIS HAS THE EFFECT OF MAKING YOU CHASE AFTER THE BALL!
I, PERSONALLY, LIKE TO ADDRESS THE BALL ON THE HEEL OF MY CLUB, WHICH GIVES ME AN INSIDE LOOP. BUT, BEING YOUNG AND ACTIVE, I DON'T HAVE MUCH DIFFICULTY IN EXTENDING MY ARMS THROUGH THE BALL
"CHASE"

Don't blade the ball

I CAN HARDLY GET THE BALL UP OFF THE GROUND TODAY, GARY!
THIS IS THE CURSE OF MOST WEEKENDERS, IAIN!
IT IS CAUSED BY THE FACT THAT THEY JUMP UP ON THE SHOT AND SO FAIL TO GET THE WHOLE OF THE BALL ON THE CLUBHEAD. THEY BLADE THE BALL WHICH MAKES IT STAY VERY LOW
WHEN YOU HAVE DIFFICULTY IN GETTING THE BALL AIRBORNE MAKE A SPECIAL EFFORT TO STAY DOWN ON THE SHOT SO THAT YOUR CLUBHEAD WILL MEET THE BOTTOM OF THE BALL, NOT THE TOP!

IN ORDER TO GET THE BALL UP, YOU MUST STAY DOWN!

Coming round the ball

I SEEM TO BE COMING ROUND THE BALL, GARY. WHAT CAN I DO ABOUT IT?
FORMER U.S. OPEN CHAMPION, DICK MAYER, ONCE GAVE ME A GREAT TIP. HE SAID WHEN A GOLFER IS COMING ROUND OR OVER THE BALL A LOT, HE IS PROBABLY WATCHING THE OUTSIDE OF THE BALL
DICK'S ADVICE WAS TO WATCH THE INSIDE OF THE BALL, AND IT IS AMAZING HOW THIS MAKES YOU COME DOWN MORE INSIDE THE LINE AND HIT UNDERNEATH THE BALL!
WATCH HERE

Right here–right there

YOU ARE ALWAYS IN TOO BIG A HURRY TO SEE THE RESULT OF YOUR GOLF SHOT, TOM!
AND I DON'T LIKE WHAT I SEE, GARY!
YOU MUST FORGET WHAT'S HAPPENING AT THE HOLE. KEEP YOUR HEAD DOWN AND CONCENTRATE ON WHAT'S HAPPENING HERE, IN THE HITTING AREA
IF YOU'RE RIGHT HERE, YOU'LL BE RIGHT THERE!
RIGHT
RIGHT

Developing a long follow through

YOU'VE GOT NO FOLLOW-THROUGH AT ALL, IAIN! THIS QUITTING ON THE BALL IS ONE OF THE WORST FAULTS IN GOLF!
WHAT YOU SHOULD DO IS IMAGINE THAT YOUR BALL IS PLACED HERE INSTEAD OF ON THE GROUND— AND THAT THIS IS WHERE YOUR CLUBHEAD SPEED MUST REALLY BEGIN TO INCREASE
I GUARANTEE THAT THIS LITTLE GIMMICK WILL GIVE YOU A MUCH BIGGER FOLLOW-THROUGH!
IMAGINARY BALL

Roll those wrists

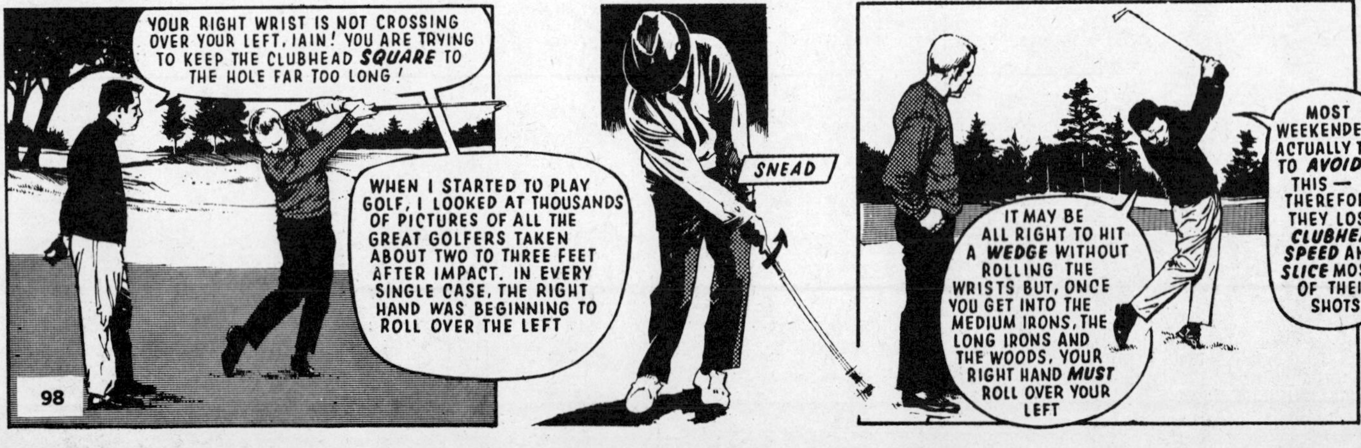

YOUR RIGHT WRIST IS NOT CROSSING OVER YOUR LEFT, IAIN! YOU ARE TRYING TO KEEP THE CLUBHEAD SQUARE TO THE HOLE FAR TOO LONG!
WHEN I STARTED TO PLAY GOLF, I LOOKED AT THOUSANDS OF PICTURES OF ALL THE GREAT GOLFERS TAKEN ABOUT TWO TO THREE FEET AFTER IMPACT. IN EVERY SINGLE CASE, THE RIGHT HAND WAS BEGINNING TO ROLL OVER THE LEFT
SNEAD
IT MAY BE ALL RIGHT TO HIT A WEDGE WITHOUT ROLLING THE WRISTS BUT, ONCE YOU GET INTO THE MEDIUM IRONS, THE LONG IRONS AND THE WOODS, YOUR RIGHT HAND MUST ROLL OVER YOUR LEFT
MOST WEEKENDERS ACTUALLY TRY TO AVOID THIS— THEREFORE, THEY LOSE CLUBHEAD SPEED AND SLICE MOST OF THEIR SHOTS

The angle of the spine

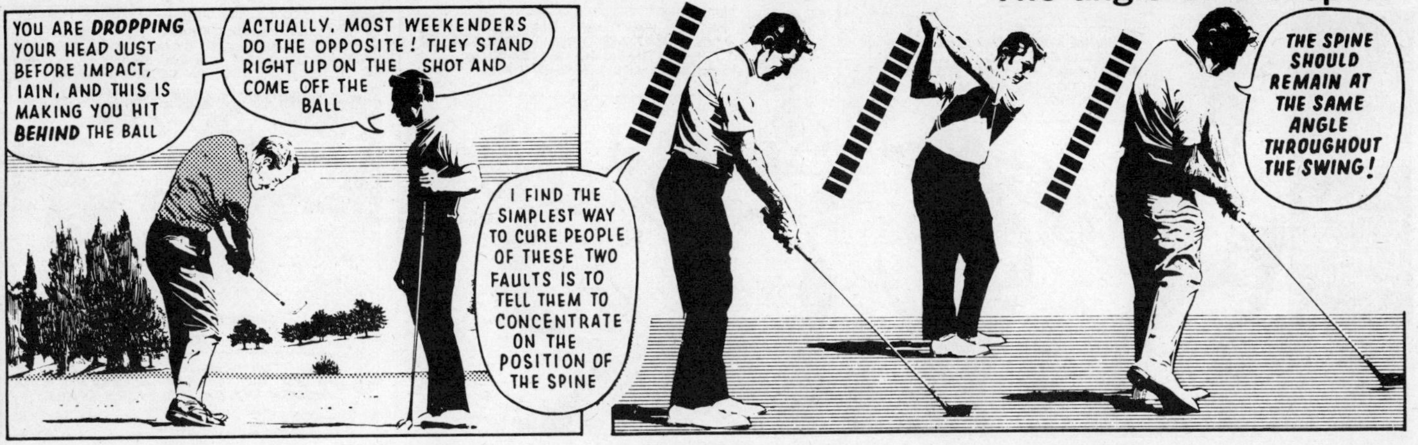

YOU ARE DROPPING YOUR HEAD JUST BEFORE IMPACT, IAIN, AND THIS IS MAKING YOU HIT BEHIND THE BALL
ACTUALLY, MOST WEEKENDERS DO THE OPPOSITE! THEY STAND RIGHT UP ON THE SHOT AND COME OFF THE BALL
I FIND THE SIMPLEST WAY TO CURE PEOPLE OF THESE TWO FAULTS IS TO TELL THEM TO CONCENTRATE ON THE POSITION OF THE SPINE
THE SPINE SHOULD REMAIN AT THE SAME ANGLE THROUGHOUT THE SWING!

The sky-high tee shot

LOOK AT THE HEIGHT OF MY DRIVE, GARY! AND IT'S GOING NO DISTANCE AT ALL!
WHEN YOU SKY YOUR TEE-SHOT LIKE THAT, IAIN, IT IS THE RESULT OF A VERY WEAK FOLLOW-THROUGH!
SPEED STARTS HERE
SPEED ENDS HERE
YOUR TROUBLE IS YOU START TO ACCELERATE THE CLUBHEAD TOO SOON WITH THE RESULT THAT YOUR SPEED IS DYING AS YOU COME INTO THE BALL. THIS CAUSES YOU TO HIT UNDERNEATH THE BALL WITH YOUR DRIVER. WITH AN IRON, YOU WOULD HIT BEHIND IT!
REID
SPEED ENDS HERE
SPEED STARTS HERE
I KEEP MY WRISTS COCKED MUCH LONGER WITH THE RESULT THAT MY CLUBHEAD SPEED BEGINS LATER THAN YOURS AND KEEPS INCREASING THROUGH THE BALL INTO A LONG FOLLOW-THROUGH
WHEN THE CLUBHEAD TRAVELS SUFFICIENTLY FAST, IT ZIPS THROUGH TOWARDS THE HOLE INSTEAD OF STARTING TO RISE UP AT IMPACT
PLAYER

The follow through

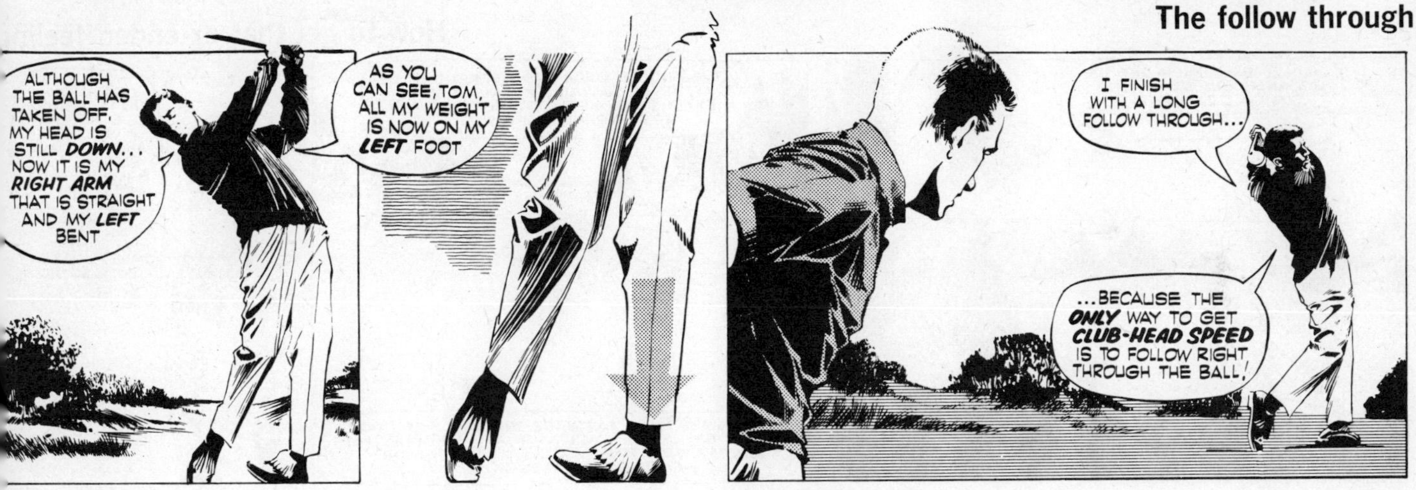

ALTHOUGH THE BALL HAS TAKEN OFF, MY HEAD IS STILL DOWN... NOW IT IS MY RIGHT ARM THAT IS STRAIGHT AND MY LEFT BENT
AS YOU CAN SEE, TOM, ALL MY WEIGHT IS NOW ON MY LEFT FOOT
I FINISH WITH A LONG FOLLOW THROUGH...
...BECAUSE THE ONLY WAY TO GET CLUB-HEAD SPEED IS TO FOLLOW RIGHT THROUGH THE BALL!

Weekenders! Extend, extend and extend again!

HOLD THAT POSITION, IAIN! THAT, I WOULD SAY, IS THE TYPICAL FOLLOW-THROUGH OF THE WEEKEND GOLFER. HEAD THRUST FORWARD, RIGHT ARM BENT, NO EXTENSION WHATSOEVER
BENT RIGHT ARM
RIGHT LEG STRAIGHT
BUT NOTICE WHAT HAPPENS WHEN I PULL YOUR HEAD BACK ABOUT 12 INCHES INTO ITS ORIGINAL ADDRESS POSITION. YOUR HANDS EXTEND TOWARDS THE TARGET, AND YOUR RIGHT KNEE COMES IN!
HEAD BACK
RIGHT KNEE WELL IN
WEIGHT FORWARD ON LEFT FOOT
WE PROS ARE ALWAYS TELLING YOU AVERAGE PLAYERS TO EXTEND, BUT WE'RE WASTING OUR BREATH IF YOU DON'T REALIZE THAT BY MOVING YOUR HEAD FORWARD YOU CANNOT POSSIBLY EXTEND AT ALL
HERE, I AM REALLY EXTENDED RIGHT THROUGH THE BALL. THE SECRET IS, KEEP YOUR HEAD DOWN AND BEHIND THE BALL... AND LET YOUR WEIGHT GO FORWARD

Accelerate through the ball

BEFORE THE 1966 BRITISH OPEN CHAMPIONSHIP, GARY PLAYER, DISSATISFIED WITH HIS STRIKING OF THE BALL, ASKED GLENEAGLES' PROFESSIONAL IAN MARCHBANK TO CHECK HIS SWING . . .
YOU'RE GOING THROUGH THE BALL, GARY, BUT YOU'RE GOING THROUGH VERY SLOWLY. THIS ACCOUNTS FOR YOUR VERY FLAT FINISH
THAT'S BETTER, GARY. NOW THAT YOU'RE REALLY ACCELERATING THROUGH THE BALL, YOU'RE GETTING GOOD EXTENSION AND YOUR HANDS ARE FINISHING HIGH!
IAN MARCHBANK'S PERCEPTION HELPED ME A LOT BECAUSE, BY NOT GOING THROUGH THE BALL FAST, YOU CAN SHANK IT, HOOK IT, SLICE IT... YOU CAN DO ANYTHING!
NEVER POWDER-PUFF OR DIE INTO ANY SHOT YOU HIT. YOU MUST ACCELERATE THROUGH THE BALL IN EVERY SINGLE GOLF SHOT

Follow through for maximum power

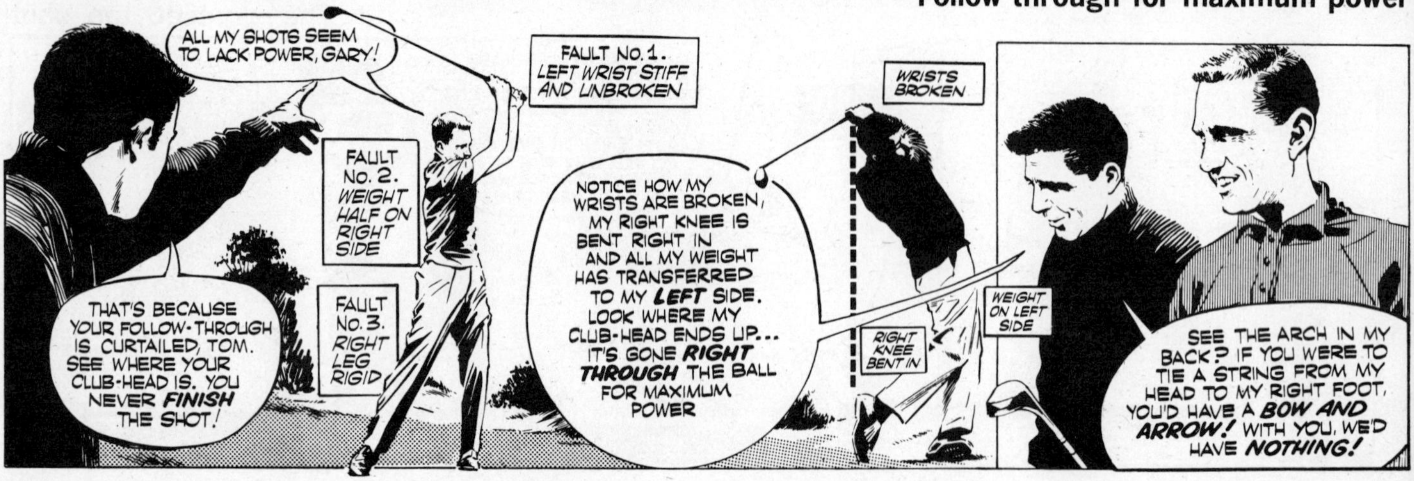

ALL MY SHOTS SEEM TO LACK POWER, GARY!
FAULT No. 1. LEFT WRIST STIFF AND UNBROKEN
FAULT No. 2. WEIGHT HALF ON RIGHT SIDE
FAULT No. 3. RIGHT LEG RIGID
THAT'S BECAUSE YOUR FOLLOW-THROUGH IS CURTAILED, TOM. SEE WHERE YOUR CLUB-HEAD IS. YOU NEVER FINISH THE SHOT!
WRISTS BROKEN
NOTICE HOW MY WRISTS ARE BROKEN, MY RIGHT KNEE IS BENT RIGHT IN AND ALL MY WEIGHT HAS TRANSFERRED TO MY LEFT SIDE. LOOK WHERE MY CLUB-HEAD ENDS UP... IT'S GONE RIGHT THROUGH THE BALL FOR MAXIMUM POWER
RIGHT KNEE BENT IN
WEIGHT ON LEFT SIDE
SEE THE ARCH IN MY BACK? IF YOU WERE TO TIE A STRING FROM MY HEAD TO MY RIGHT FOOT, YOU'D HAVE A BOW AND ARROW! WITH YOU, WE'D HAVE NOTHING!

How to get that extended feeling

IAIN, YOU'LL NEVER GET THE DISTANCE YOU WANT WITH SUCH A CRAMPED FOLLOW-THROUGH
YOU MUST TRY TO EXTEND YOUR ARMS THROUGH THE BALL... DON'T LET THEM BUCKLE UP
THE PROBLEM FOR THE WEEKENDER IS THAT, NEVER HAVING EXPERIENCED EXTENSION, HE'S NOT SURE WHAT HE'S STRIVING AFTER!
WELL, HERE IS AN EXERCISE THAT WILL PUT THAT RIGHT. SWING THE CLUB BACK AND FORWARD WITH THE LEFT ARM ONLY AND YOU WILL GET THE FEELING OF EXTENSION
THEN TRY TO RECAPTURE THAT FEELING WHEN YOU ARE ACTUALLY HITTING THE BALL. BELIEVE ME, IAIN, IF YOU DO THIS EXERCISE FOR FIVE MINUTES DAILY, YOU'LL PUT YARDS ON YOUR SHOTS!

Rule of thumb

YOUR THUMB SHOULDN'T POINT TO THE LEFT DURING THE FOLLOW-THROUGH, IAIN. THAT INDICATES A VERY FLAT SWING
I WANT YOU TO CONCENTRATE ON HAVING YOUR THUMB POINTING TO THE SKY IN THE FOLLOW-THROUGH
THIS WILL STOP YOU HITTING ROUND YOUR BODY, AND WILL GIVE YOU A NICE, UPRIGHT FOLLOW-THROUGH

Don't break the glass

YOU ARE NOT SWINGING THROUGH THE BALL CORRECTLY, TOM. YOU ARE COMING ROUND WITH YOUR RIGHT SHOULDER WHICH PUSHES YOUR HANDS AND CLUB OFF LINE
WHEN YOU ADDRESS THE BALL, IMAGINE THERE IS A SHEET OF GLASS BESIDE YOU
NOW, LET YOUR SHOULDER TRAVEL UNDERNEATH YOUR CHIN SO THAT YOUR FOLLOW-THROUGH STAYS ON THE RIGHT HAND SIDE OF THE GLASS AND DOES NOT BREAK IT!

Hip round—shoulders down

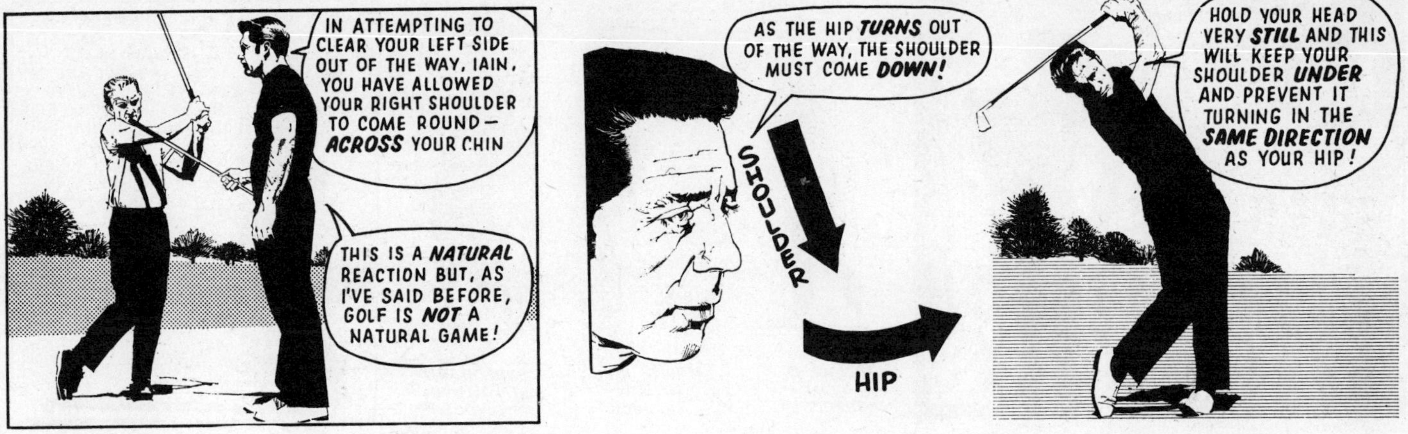
IN ATTEMPTING TO CLEAR YOUR LEFT SIDE OUT OF THE WAY, IAIN, YOU HAVE ALLOWED YOUR RIGHT SHOULDER TO COME ROUND—ACROSS YOUR CHIN
THIS IS A NATURAL REACTION BUT, AS I'VE SAID BEFORE, GOLF IS NOT A NATURAL GAME!
AS THE HIP TURNS OUT OF THE WAY, THE SHOULDER MUST COME DOWN!
SHOULDER
HIP
HOLD YOUR HEAD VERY STILL AND THIS WILL KEEP YOUR SHOULDER UNDER AND PREVENT IT TURNING IN THE SAME DIRECTION AS YOUR HIP!

Coming off the ball

IAIN, YOUR RIGHT SHOULDER IS COMING UP HIGH, AND YOUR HEAD IS MOVING FORWARD. THIS IS WHAT IS CALLED "COMING OFF" THE BALL. WEEKEND GOLFERS SIMPLY WILL NOT STAY DOWN ON THE BALL!
THE BEST WAY TO PREVENT YOURSELF COMING OFF THE BALL, IAIN, IS TO CONCENTRATE ON ANY ONE OF THESE THREE THINGS
1
ONE, MAKE SURE YOU HAVE A FULL SHOULDER TURN AT THE TOP OF YOUR BACKSWING
2
TWO, GET YOUR RIGHT KNEE IN BEFORE YOU HIT THE BALL
3
THREE, MAKE YOUR RIGHT SHOULDER GO THROUGH UNDERNEATH YOUR CHIN
EVEN AFTER I HAVE GONE WELL INTO MY FOLLOW-THROUGH, YOU CAN SEE THAT MY HEAD STILL REMAINS BEHIND WHERE THE BALL WAS SITTING
BALL WAS HERE

An important check

YOU ARE COMING RIGHT OFF THE BALL, TOM, AND YOUR RIGHT SHOULDER IS TRAVELLING ROUND WITH A FLAT FOLLOW-THROUGH WHICH IS TYPICAL OF MOST GOLFERS
THE RIGHT SHOULDER MUST COME DOWN INTO THE BALL INSTEAD OF COMING UP. KEEP YOUR HEAD STILL AND YOUR SHOULDER WILL BE FORCED TO TAKE THE CORRECT PATH
HERE IS A GOOD CHECKPOINT. I CAN SEE MY RIGHT FOOT AT THIS STAGE OF THE SWING - YOU COULDN'T.

Hit high to stay under

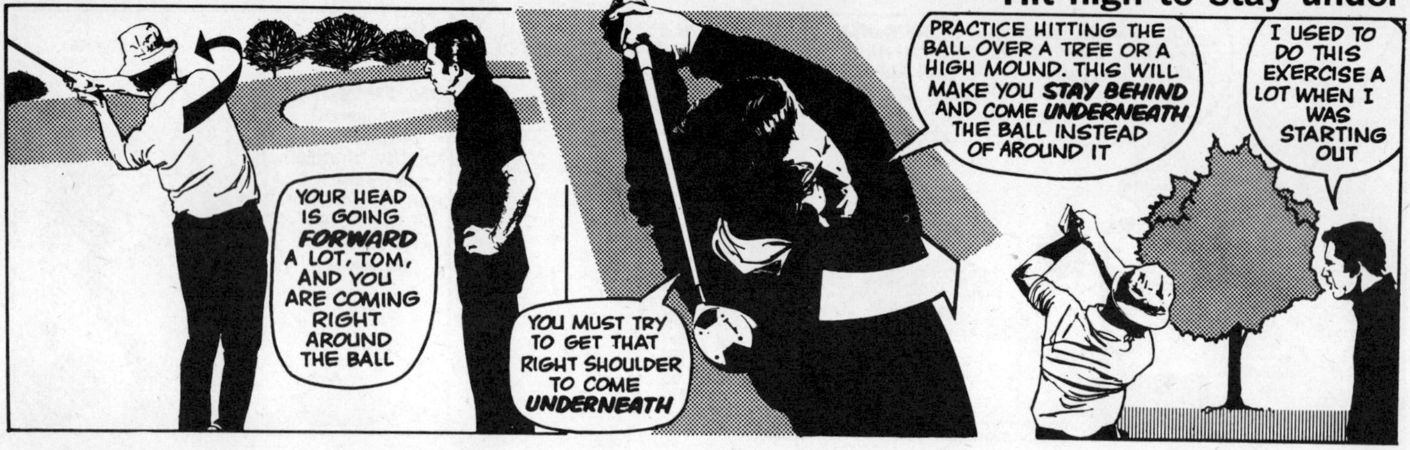

YOUR HEAD IS GOING FORWARD A LOT, TOM, AND YOU ARE COMING RIGHT AROUND THE BALL
YOU MUST TRY TO GET THAT RIGHT SHOULDER TO COME UNDERNEATH
PRACTICE HITTING THE BALL OVER A TREE OR A HIGH MOUND. THIS WILL MAKE YOU STAY BEHIND AND COME UNDERNEATH THE BALL INSTEAD OF AROUND IT
I USED TO DO THIS EXERCISE A LOT WHEN I WAS STARTING OUT

Watch your opponent's head

LOOK, IAIN! HEAD UP! THE MOST COMMON FAULT OF THE HIGH HANDICAP GOLFER!
LET'S SEE WHAT THE OTHER THREE DO!
HEAD UP
HEAD DOWN
HEAD DOWN
"CRAMPED FOLLOW-THROUGH"
"QUITE NICE FOLLOW-THROUGH"
"GOOD, UPRIGHT FOLLOW-THROUGH"

NEXT TIME YOU PLAY WITH WEEKENDERS, IAIN, WATCH THEM CAREFULLY AND SEE HOW MUCH THEY LIFT THEIR HEADS. THAT CAN ACT AS A VERY USEFUL REMINDER BECAUSE, OFTEN, YOU WILL BE LIFTING YOUR OWN HEAD JUST AS MUCH, EVEN THOUGH YOU THINK YOU ARE KEEPING IT DOWN!

Lively feet—steady head!

I KNOW WHAT YOU ARE GOING TO SAY, GARY—I MOVED MY HEAD! YET, I TRIED HARD TO KEEP IT STILL
BUT, IAIN, YOU CAN'T POSSIBLY KEEP YOUR HEAD STILL IF YOUR FOOTWORK IS DEAD. YOUR FEET ARE ABSOLUTELY FLAT!

OBVIOUSLY, SOME PART OF YOUR BODY MUST MOVE FORWARD DURING THE DOWNSWING. THEREFORE, IF YOUR FEET ARE NOT ACTIVE, THE TOP PART OF YOUR BODY HAS GOT TO MOVE—AND THAT INCLUDES YOUR HEAD!

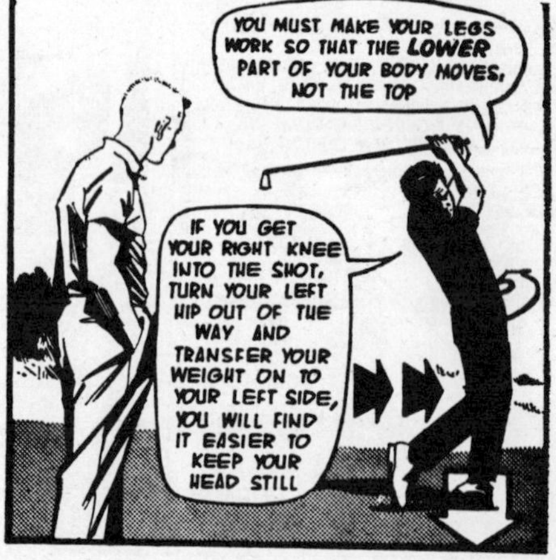

YOU MUST MAKE YOUR LEGS WORK SO THAT THE LOWER PART OF YOUR BODY MOVES, NOT THE TOP
IF YOU GET YOUR RIGHT KNEE INTO THE SHOT, TURN YOUR LEFT HIP OUT OF THE WAY AND TRANSFER YOUR WEIGHT ON TO YOUR LEFT SIDE, YOU WILL FIND IT EASIER TO KEEP YOUR HEAD STILL

Play "underarm"

YOU HAVE JUMPED UP AT IMPACT, TOM, AND YOUR FOLLOW-THROUGH IS FLAT. THAT IS THE SWING OF A MAN WHO DOES NOT PRACTICE ENOUGH!
FLAT
NOTICE HOW MY HEAD REMAINS ON THE BALL AND MY RIGHT SHOULDER TRAVELS UNDERNEATH MY CHIN
UNDERNEATH THE CHIN, THAT IS THE BIG SECRET! GET THE FEELING YOU ARE BOWLING
FROM NOW ON, TELL YOURSELF THE NAME OF THE GAME IS "UNDERARM", NOT "GOLF". BRAINWASH YOURSELF IN THIS WAY AND IT WILL DEFINITELY HELP YOU TO COME UNDER THE BALL!

Head up

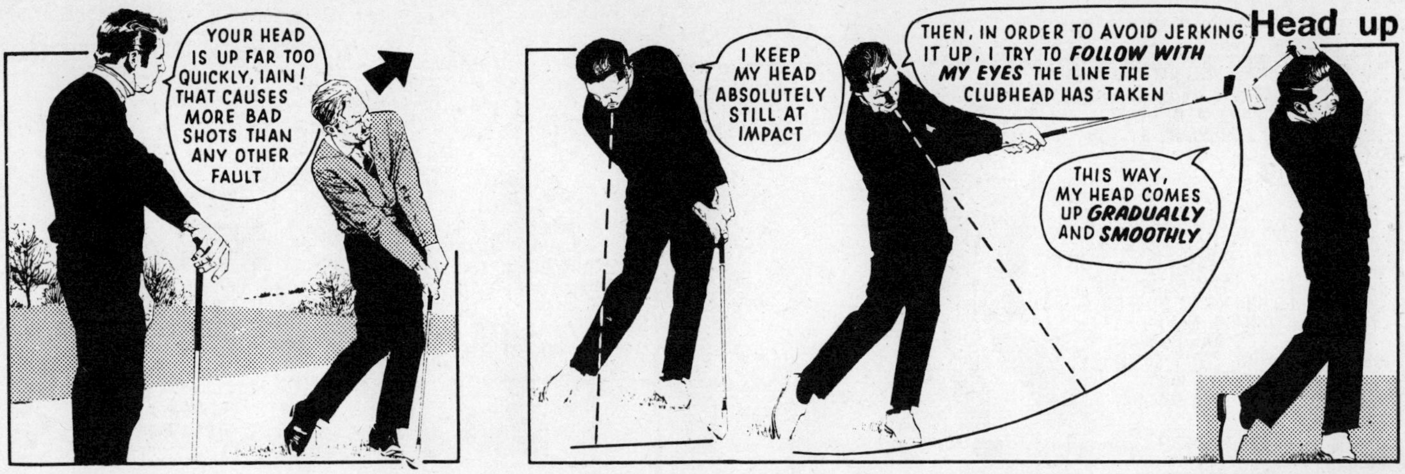

YOUR HEAD IS UP FAR TOO QUICKLY, IAIN! THAT CAUSES MORE BAD SHOTS THAN ANY OTHER FAULT
I KEEP MY HEAD ABSOLUTELY STILL AT IMPACT
THEN, IN ORDER TO AVOID JERKING IT UP, I TRY TO FOLLOW WITH MY EYES THE LINE THE CLUBHEAD HAS TAKEN
THIS WAY, MY HEAD COMES UP GRADUALLY AND SMOOTHLY

Good balance—good extension!

YOU COMPLETELY LOST YOUR BALANCE ON THAT SHOT, IAIN, BECAUSE YOUR HEAD MOVED OFF THE BALL
CRAMPED FOLLOW-THROUGH
AS A RESULT, YOUR WEIGHT IS STILL ON YOUR RIGHT SIDE AND YOUR ARMS HAVE NOT EXTENDED THROUGH THE BALL
FOR DISTANCE AND ACCURACY, GOOD EXTENSION IS VITAL. IN OTHER WORDS, THE HANDS MUST BE THROWN OUT AFTER THE BALL
BUT YOU CANNOT DO THIS IF YOU ARE OFF BALANCE...AND YOU CANNOT STAY IN BALANCE IF YOUR HEAD WOBBLES ALL OVER THE PLACE!
YOUR HEAD IS YOUR CENTER OF BALANCE AND, LIKE THE TIGHT-ROPE WALKER, YOU WILL ONLY RETAIN GOOD BALANCE IF YOU KEEP IT STEADY!

It's all in the head

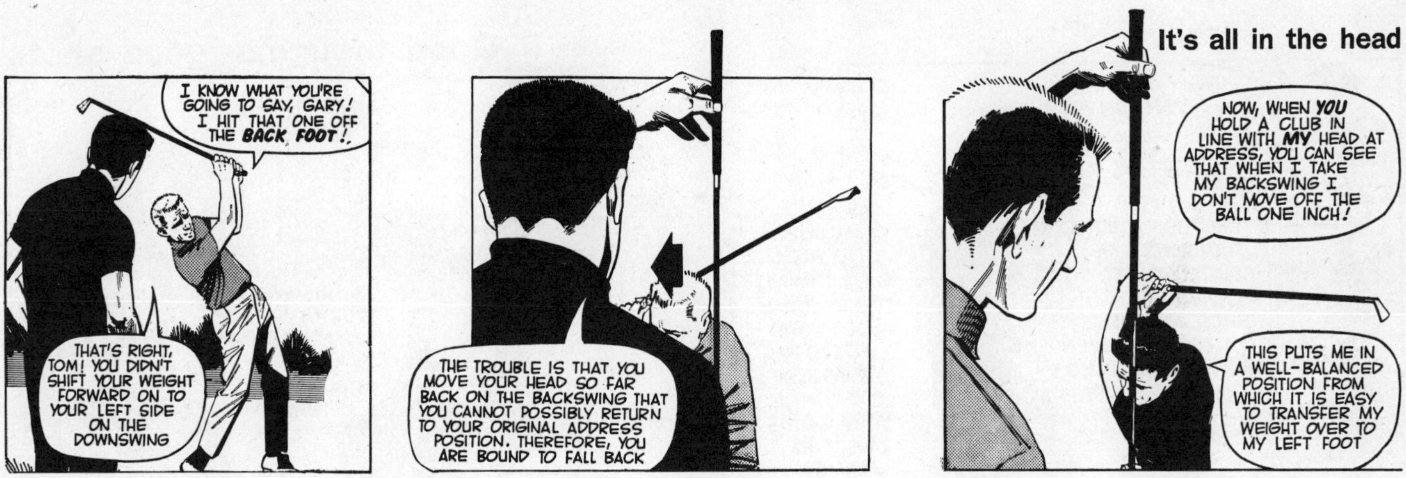

I KNOW WHAT YOU'RE GOING TO SAY, GARY! I HIT THAT ONE OFF THE BACK FOOT!
THAT'S RIGHT, TOM! YOU DIDN'T SHIFT YOUR WEIGHT FORWARD ON TO YOUR LEFT SIDE ON THE DOWNSWING
THE TROUBLE IS THAT YOU MOVE YOUR HEAD SO FAR BACK ON THE BACKSWING THAT YOU CANNOT POSSIBLY RETURN TO YOUR ORIGINAL ADDRESS POSITION. THEREFORE, YOU ARE BOUND TO FALL BACK
NOW, WHEN YOU HOLD A CLUB IN LINE WITH MY HEAD AT ADDRESS, YOU CAN SEE THAT WHEN I TAKE MY BACKSWING I DON'T MOVE OFF THE BALL ONE INCH!
THIS PUTS ME IN A WELL-BALANCED POSITION FROM WHICH IT IS EASY TO TRANSFER MY WEIGHT OVER TO MY LEFT FOOT

Don't just watch the ball

THAT WAS ALMOST A PERFECT SWING, IAIN!
HOWEVER, ALL YOU WERE THINKING ABOUT WAS KEEPING YOUR HEAD DOWN WITH THE RESULT THAT YOU JUST STOPPED ON THE BALL! YOU HAD NO FOLLOW-THROUGH
IT ISN'T ENOUGH JUST TO THINK ABOUT WATCHING THE BALL OR KEEPING YOUR HEAD DOWN, ALTHOUGH THIS IS VITALLY IMPORTANT
YOU MUST ALSO THINK ABOUT GETTING YOUR RIGHT KNEE IN AND LETTING YOUR HANDS GO THROUGH TO THE TARGET. THEN YOU WILL HIT A BETTER SHOT!

Heads and hands

AS YOU HIT THROUGH THE BALL, IAIN, YOU ARE ALREADY LOOKING AT THE TARGET
THIS GIVES YOU A VERY FLAT FOLLOW-THROUGH WHICH IS TYPICAL OF THE WEEKEND GOLFER! I HAVE NEVER YET SEEN A WEEKENDER WHO CONSISTENTLY STAYS WITH THE BALL!

AS I HIT THROUGH, I FEEL AS IF MY HANDS ARE GOING ONE WAY AND MY HEAD IS GOING IN THE OPPOSITE DIRECTION!
STAYING WITH THE BALL PRODUCES GREAT EXTENSION WHICH, IN TURN, LEADS TO POWER AND ACCURACY!

Don't dip

YOU HAVE STAYED DOWN AND WATCHED THE BALL VERY NICELY, IAIN. BUT YOUR LEFT ARM HAS BENT BADLY BECAUSE YOU ALLOWED YOUR HEAD TO DROP TOO MUCH WHEN YOU HIT THE BALL
AT IMPACT, MY HEAD STAYS AT THE LEVEL IT WAS AT DURING ADDRESS. THIS GIVES ME A CHANCE TO HAVE A STRAIGHT, EXTENDED LEFT ARM

DUE TO HAVING A STRAIGHT LEFT ARM AT IMPACT, MY FOLLOW-THROUGH IS WIDE AND HIGH, WHEREAS YOURS WAS BOUND TO BE FLAT AND HUGGED INTO YOUR BODY!

Good thoughts—good shots

WHY AM I QUITTING ON ALL MY SHOTS, GARY?
PROBABLY BECAUSE YOUR THOUGHTS ARE CONCENTRATED ON STRIKING AT THE BALL, TOM. ONCE CONTACT HAS BEEN MADE, YOUR HANDS FEEL THEIR WORK IS OVER!
THOUGHTS
AS YOU COME DOWN INTO THE BALL, I WANT YOU TO THINK ABOUT YOUR FOLLOW THROUGH AND WHERE YOUR HANDS OUGHT TO FINISH.
THOUGHTS
IF YOU THINK IN THIS WAY YOUR CLUB WILL AUTOMATICALLY GET RIGHT THROUGH THE BALL!

Three points of strain

HOLD YOUR FINISH FOR 30 SECONDS, TOM, THEN TELL ME WHERE YOU FEEL THE STRAIN!
I DIDN'T FEEL ANY PARTICULAR STRAIN, GARY!
YOU DON'T SURPRISE ME, TOM! THAT WAS A LAZY SWING!

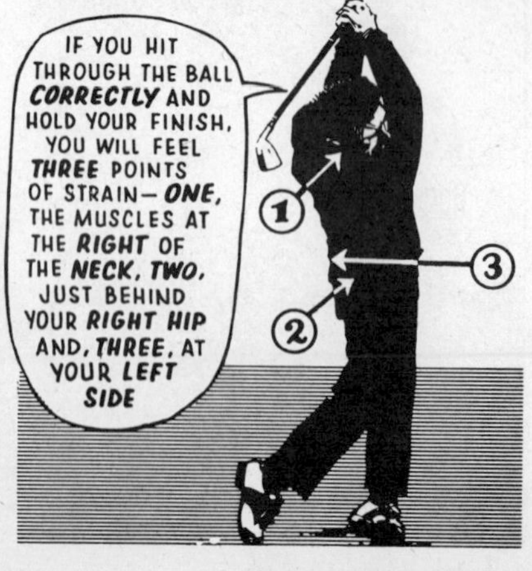

IF YOU HIT THROUGH THE BALL CORRECTLY AND HOLD YOUR FINISH, YOU WILL FEEL THREE POINTS OF STRAIN—ONE, THE MUSCLES AT THE RIGHT OF THE NECK, TWO, JUST BEHIND YOUR RIGHT HIP AND, THREE, AT YOUR LEFT SIDE
1
2
3

If you sway consult your shadow

A good release

Wake up your hands!

Square right palm

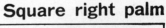

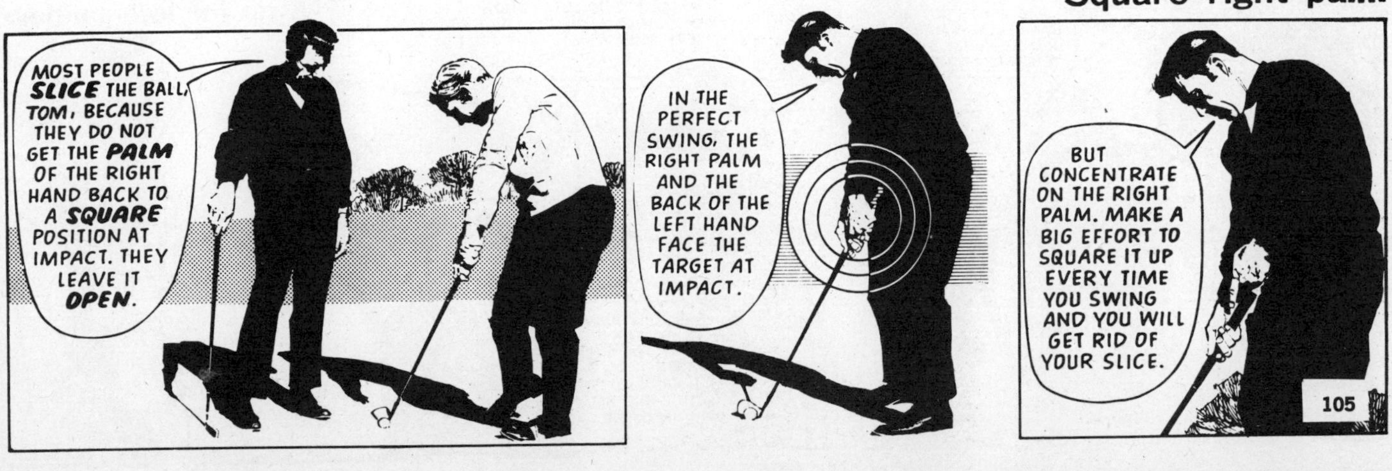

A cure for a slice

SEE THAT BALL SLICE, GARY! AND I THOUGHT I HAD HIT IT JUST RIGHT!
YOU DID, IAIN! IT'S CERTAINLY NOT YOUR SWING THAT'S MAKING YOU SLICE, NOR IS IT YOUR GRIP...
IT'S THE WAY YOU ADDRESS THE BALL! IF YOU HAVE YOUR CLUB FACE WAY OPEN LIKE THIS, IT IS GOING TO MAKE YOU SLICE NO MATTER HOW WELL YOU SWING
IT'S A GREAT THING TO START OFF CORRECTLY, SO ALWAYS MAKE SURE YOUR CLUB FACE IS SQUARE TO THE TARGET LINE BEFORE YOU START YOUR BACKSWING. IF IT IS OPEN, YOU WILL SLICE. IF IT IS CLOSED, YOU WILL HOOK!
OPEN
SQUARE
CLOSED

Advice for slicers

THAT'S A VERY BIG SLICE — EVEN FOR YOU, IAIN!
BUT WHAT'S THE CAUSE, GARY?
YOU HAVE SLIPPED INTO THE HABIT OF GRIPPING THE CLUB IN THE PALM OF YOUR LEFT HAND
THIS IS CAUSING YOU TO BLOCK THE SHOT AND LEAVE THE CLUB FACE OPEN AT IMPACT
THE CLUB SHOULD LIE DIAGONALLY ACROSS THE LEFT HAND AND MUST BE GRIPPED MORE IN THE FINGERS THAN THE PALM. THIS WILL ENABLE YOU TO SQUARE UP THE CLUBHEAD AT IMPACT AND PREVENT THE BLOCKING ACTION!
BLOCK

Slice no more

MOST PROFESSIONALS HAVE THE RIGHT FOOT SQUARE TO THE LINE OF FLIGHT AND THE LEFT FOOT TURNED OUT
BUT, WHEN YOU DO THIS, IAIN, YOU DON'T WIND UP SUFFICIENTLY WHICH IS WHY YOU SLICE
ANYONE WHO TENDS TO BE STIFF, SHOULD TRY REVERSING THE POSITION OF THE FEET AT ADDRESS. SQUARE UP THE LEFT FOOT AND TURN OUT THE RIGHT
NOW YOU GET A VERY BIG TURN. ALSO, YOU HAVE A FIRM LEFT SIDE TO HIT AGAINST WHICH WILL HELP YOU TO SQUARE UP THE CLUBHEAD AND GET RID OF THE SLICE. IN OTHER WORDS, THIS STANCE HELPS YOU TO SWING A LITTLE BIT FROM INSIDE TO OUT

A tip for left-handers

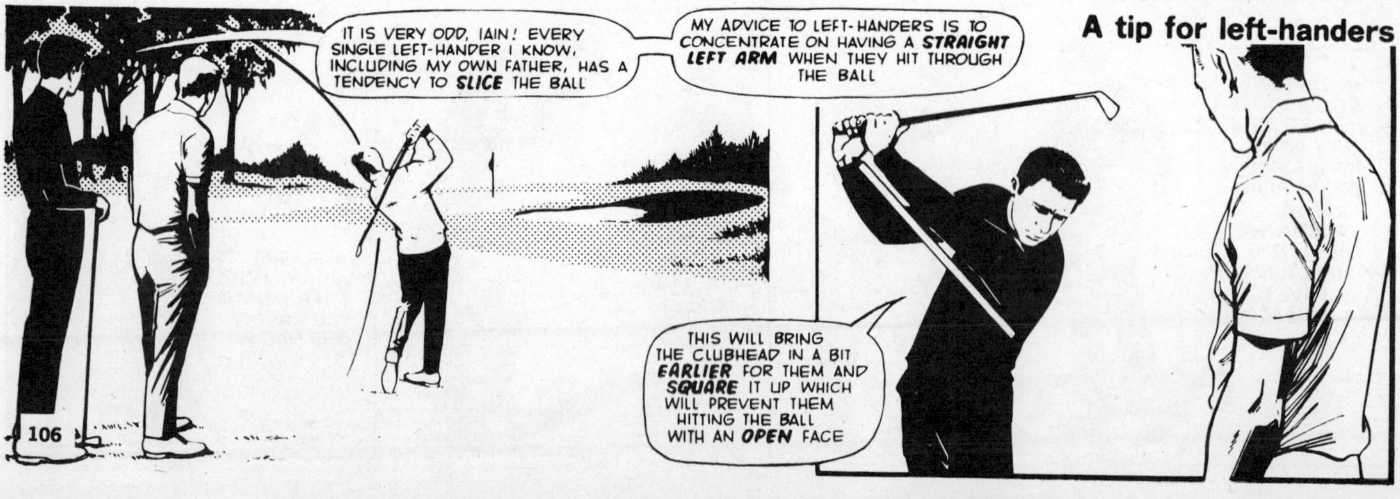

IT IS VERY ODD, IAIN! EVERY SINGLE LEFT-HANDER I KNOW, INCLUDING MY OWN FATHER, HAS A TENDENCY TO SLICE THE BALL
MY ADVICE TO LEFT-HANDERS IS TO CONCENTRATE ON HAVING A STRAIGHT LEFT ARM WHEN THEY HIT THROUGH THE BALL
THIS WILL BRING THE CLUBHEAD IN A BIT EARLIER FOR THEM AND SQUARE IT UP WHICH WILL PREVENT THEM HITTING THE BALL WITH AN OPEN FACE

Watch that right knee

I CAN NEVER HIT THESE 20-YARD WEDGE SHOTS STRAIGHT, GARY! I'VE PUSHED IT OUT TO THE RIGHT!
THAT'S BECAUSE YOU ALLOWED YOUR RIGHT KNEE TO SHOOT OUT TO THE RIGHT. IT PUSHED THE CLUB OUT TO THE RIGHT, TOO!
IN ORDER TO KEEP THE CLUB FACING THE FLAG, IT IS ESSENTIAL THAT THE RIGHT KNEE MOVES DIRECTLY TOWARDS THE HOLE ... NOT OUT TO THE SIDE
BECAUSE, IF THE RIGHT KNEE DOESN'T POINT TO THE TARGET, THE CLUBHEAD WON'T EITHER!
AS I HIT THROUGH THE BALL, MY RIGHT KNEE, MY ARMS AND MY CLUBHEAD ALL POINT TO THE HOLE

"Start down correctly"

I'VE BEEN CONCENTRATING ON HITTING FROM IN-TO-OUT, GARY— BUT IT'S MAKING ME HOOK!
YOU'VE GOT IN-TO-OUT ON THE BRAIN, TOM!
BAD
INSTEAD OF GOING SLIGHTLY FROM INSIDE TO OUT OR INSIDE TO STRAIGHT THROUGH, YOUR SWING PATH IS FAR TOO MUCH IN-TO-OUT ON THE DOWNSWING!
IT IS A MISTAKE TO GET TO THE TOP OF THE BACKSWING AND THEN TELL YOURSELF TO HIT OUT — THIS WILL START YOU DOWN INCORRECTLY
THE IMPORTANT THING IS TO START DOWN ON THE INSIDE. THIS WILL FORCE YOU TO MAINTAIN THE CORRECT PLANE IN THE FOLLOW-THROUGH. IN OTHER WORDS, BY STARTING DOWN ON THE INSIDE, YOU WILL AUTOMATICALLY HIT THROUGH FROM IN TO OUT!

Strangle that hook

I'VE TRIED EVERYTHING, GARY! I THINK THIS HOOK IS HERE TO STAY!
YOUR RIGHT HAND IS CROSSING OVER YOUR LEFT TOO SOON, IAIN! THAT IS WHY YOU ARE HOOKING THE BALL SO BADLY!
NONSENSE! I'LL SHOW YOU HOW YOU CAN STOP HOOKING IMMEDIATELY. SIMPLY STRANGLE THE CLUB WITH YOUR LEFT HAND
GRIP VERY TIGHTLY
THIS KEEPS THE LEFT HAND FIRM THROUGHOUT THE SHOT. YOU CAN SEE THAT THE BACK OF THE HAND FACES THE HOLE AS I HIT THROUGH THE BALL
I ONLY RECOMMEND THIS TO PEOPLE WHO ARE HOOKING VERY BADLY! AS SOON AS THEY GET RID OF THAT BIG HOOK, THEY SHOULD REVERT TO NORMAL PRESSURE WITH THE LEFT HAND

Don't think too much

HOOKED IT...!
IAIN, TELL ME SOMETHING, WHAT EXACTLY WERE YOU THINKING DURING THAT SHOT?
I WAS CONCENTRATING ON KEEPING MY RIGHT ELBOW TUCKED IN, MY HEAD BEHIND THE BALL, MY LEFT ARM STRAIGHT AND TRANSFERRING MY WEIGHT ON TO MY RIGHT SIDE ON THE BACKSWING
THAT'S THE TROUBLE WITH PEOPLE WHO WANT TO IMPROVE THEIR GAME, THEY THEORIZE SO MUCH THEY FORGET THE MOST IMPORTANT THING WHICH IS TO MAKE GOOD, SOLID CONTACT WITH THE BALL
YOU CANNOT POSSIBLY THINK OF THREE OR FOUR POINTS IN THE LIMITED TIME OF A GOLF SWING. YOU WILL GET MUCH BETTER RESULTS IF YOU THINK OF ONLY ONE THING... PLUS HITTING THE BALL SOLIDLY!

Don't hook your short irons

WHAT A WICKED HOOK, IAIN!
I'M DOING THAT ALL THE TIME WITH MY **SHORT IRONS**, GARY

THAT'S BECAUSE YOU ARE NOT GETTING YOUR LEFT HIP TO TURN OUT OF THE WAY!
WITH A WEDGE, THE SWING IS **SHORTER** THAN WITH, SAY, A DRIVER! THEREFORE THERE IS **LESS TIME** ON THE DOWNSWING IN WHICH THE HIPS CAN TURN!
I COMPENSATE FOR THIS BY STANDING **SLIGHTLY OPEN** WHEN PLAYING THE SEVEN, EIGHT, NINE IRONS AND WEDGE. BY DOING SO, MY LEFT HIP IS **PARTLY** OUT OF THE WAY BEFORE THE SWING EVEN BEGINS!
LEFT HIP NOT TURNING

Pulling the ball to the left

I'VE **PULLED** THAT ONE TO THE **LEFT**, GARY
ONCE AGAIN, YOUR TROUBLE IS DUE TO LETTING YOUR HEAD MOVE FORWARD. IN OTHER WORDS, YOU HAVE **LUNGED** AT THE BALL, AND **PULLED ROUND** ON THE SHOT
IF YOU HAVE **SPEEDY HANDS**, THIS LUNGING WILL MAKE YOU **PULL** THE BALL. IF YOUR HANDS ARE **SLOW**, IT WILL MAKE YOU **PUSH** IT TO THE RIGHT
WHEN I FIRST STARTED TO PLAY, I USED TO PULL THE BALL A GREAT DEAL, SIMPLY BECAUSE I KEPT MOVING MY HEAD FORWARD
HEAD STEADY
BACK WELL ARCHED
RIGHT KNEE IN
AS SOON AS I LEARNED TO KEEP MY HEAD **BEHIND THE SHOT** AND TO GET MY RIGHT KNEE WELL IN, I STOPPED PULLING IMMEDIATELY

Trouble on the left

LOOK AT THAT, GARY! I ONLY PULLED IT SLIGHTLY AND I'M IN THE WATER!
THIS MAN COSTS ME A FORTUNE IN GOLF BALLS!
WHEN IT'S SUICIDE TO GO TO THE **LEFT**, SURELY THE LAST THING YOU SHOULD DO IS HAVE THE CLUBFACE **CLOSED** AT ADDRESS!
YOU SHOULD **OPEN** IT HALF AN INCH OR SO. MORE OFTEN THAN NOT, THIS WILL KEEP YOU OUT OF TROUBLE.

Topping...cause and cur

THAT ONE DIDN'T RISE AT ALL, GARY!
NO, IAIN, YOU **TOPPED** IT. WHEN YOU HIT THE TOP OF THE BALL LIKE THAT, IT IS DUE TO **INCORRECT WEIGHT TRANSFERENCE**
SEE... ALL YOUR WEIGHT IS ON YOUR **RIGHT** FOOT!
YOUR TROUBLE STARTS WITH YOUR BACKSWING WHERE YOU ALLOW YOUR WEIGHT TO GO ON TO YOUR **LEFT** FOOT
THIS MEANS THAT IT WILL TRANSFER TO YOUR **RIGHT** FOOT IN THE DOWNSWING WHICH WILL GIVE YOU A **SCOOPING** ACTION AND MAKE YOU TOP THE BALL
TO AVOID **TOPPING**, IT IS ESSENTIAL TO HAVE A GOOD WIND-UP WHICH WILL GET **MOST OF** YOUR WEIGHT ON TO YOUR **RIGHT** SIDE, AND PUT YOU IN A GOOD POSITION TO DELIVER A POWERFUL AND ACCURATE BLOW
THEN, WHEN GOING THROUGH THE BALL, YOUR WEIGHT WILL TRANSFER NATURALLY ON TO YOUR **LEFT SIDE**, ENABLING YOU TO HIT THE BALL FIRMLY AND **GET IT UP IN THE AIR**

A disease called "shanking"

I'VE SHANKED IT AGAIN, GARY!
SHANKING'S THE WORST THING THAT CAN HAPPEN TO YOU IN GOLF, IAIN. IT'S REALLY A DISEASE!
SHANKING: WHEN BALL IS HIT IN "NECK" OF CLUB
YOUR TROUBLE IS YOU ROLL YOUR WRISTS ON THE BACKSWING WHICH OPENS UP THE FACE OF THE CLUB
THIS GIVES YOU A VERY FLAT WRIST-POSITION AND BRINGS YOUR LEFT SHOULDER ACROSS YOUR CHIN INSTEAD OF UNDERNEATH IT
CONSEQUENTLY, YOUR RIGHT SHOULDER WILL COME ACROSS YOUR CHIN ON THE DOWNSWING. THIS IS WHAT MAKES YOU HIT THE BALL IN THE SHANK

To banish "shanking"

TO PREVENT SHANKING, TAKE THE HANDS BACK TOGETHER IN ONE PIECE, KEEPING THE CLUB FACE SQUARE. DO NOT ALLOW IT TO ROLL OPEN
THIS WILL PUT YOUR LEFT SHOULDER UNDERNEATH YOUR CHIN, AND YOUR HANDS UNDERNEATH THE CLUB AT THE TOP OF THE BACKSWING
NOW THE RIGHT SHOULDER WILL COME UNDER THE CHIN ON THE DOWNSWING, AND THE CLUB WILL STAY ON ITS PROPER LINE

A cure for "smothering"

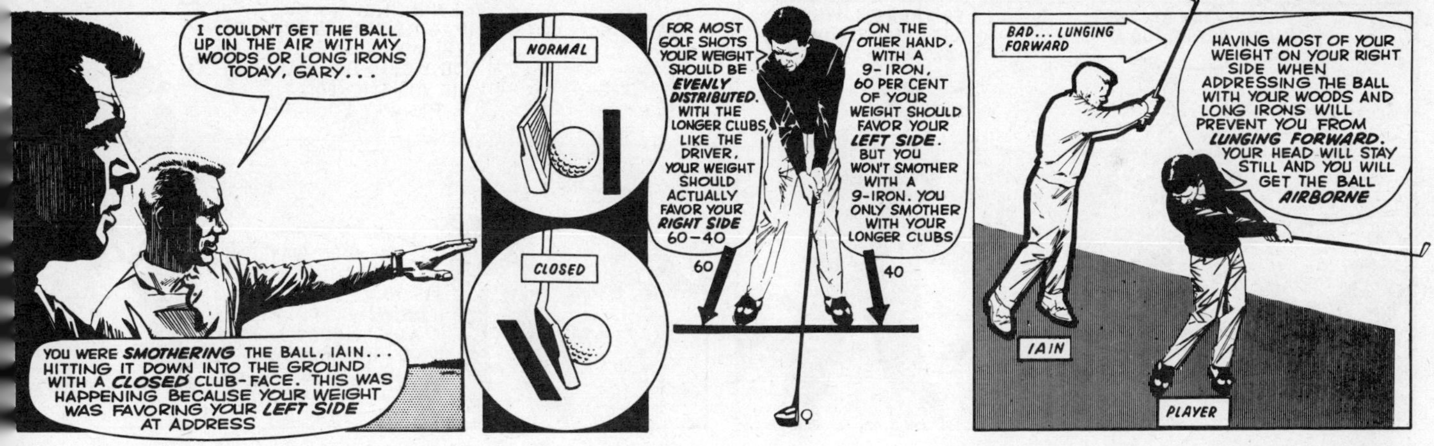

I COULDN'T GET THE BALL UP IN THE AIR WITH MY WOODS OR LONG IRONS TODAY, GARY...
YOU WERE SMOTHERING THE BALL, IAIN... HITTING IT DOWN INTO THE GROUND WITH A CLOSED CLUB-FACE. THIS WAS HAPPENING BECAUSE YOUR WEIGHT WAS FAVORING YOUR LEFT SIDE AT ADDRESS
NORMAL
CLOSED
FOR MOST GOLF SHOTS YOUR WEIGHT SHOULD BE EVENLY DISTRIBUTED. WITH THE LONGER CLUBS, LIKE THE DRIVER, YOUR WEIGHT SHOULD ACTUALLY FAVOR YOUR RIGHT SIDE 60-40
ON THE OTHER HAND, WITH A 9-IRON, 60 PER CENT OF YOUR WEIGHT SHOULD FAVOR YOUR LEFT SIDE. BUT YOU WON'T SMOTHER WITH A 9-IRON. YOU ONLY SMOTHER WITH YOUR LONGER CLUBS
60
40
BAD... LUNGING FORWARD
HAVING MOST OF YOUR WEIGHT ON YOUR RIGHT SIDE WHEN ADDRESSING THE BALL WITH YOUR WOODS AND LONG IRONS WILL PREVENT YOU FROM LUNGING FORWARD. YOUR HEAD WILL STAY STILL AND YOU WILL GET THE BALL AIRBORNE
IAIN
PLAYER

Don't lose your height

How to avoid hitting it "fat"

LIKE 95 PER CENT OF WEEKENDERS, IAIN, YOU HIT THE TURF FIRST AND THEN THE BALL, INSTEAD OF VICE VERSA LIKE THE PRO'S. WE CALL THIS FAULT HITTING IT "FAT" OR "HEAVY"
WHAT CAN I DO ABOUT IT, GARY?
FIRST OF ALL WATCH YOUR ADDRESS POSITION. NOTE THAT MY HANDS ARE AHEAD OF THE BALL
AS I COME INTO THE BALL, MY HANDS ARE IN FRONT, AND I AM CONSCIOUS OF PULLING DOWN WITH MY LEFT HAND
IN ORDER TO HIT THE BALL FIRST, ALL MY WEIGHT MUST MOVE ONTO MY LEFT LEG BEFORE IMPACT. IN OTHER WORDS I AM HITTING THROUGH THE BALL. WEEKENDERS HIT AT THE BALL. A BIG DIFFERENCE!

Slowly does it

I HIT A BAD SHOT, GARY! I AM WELL SHORT OF THE GREEN!

WHEN YOU AND I SWING TOGETHER, WE GET TO THE TOP OF THE SWING AT THE SAME TIME WHICH INDICATES THAT YOUR RHYTHM IS GOOD ON THE BACKSWING
HOWEVER, YOU THEN START DOWN FAR TOO QUICKLY AND GET INTO THE HITTING ZONE 'WAY AHEAD OF ME. YOUR RHYTHM HAS GONE AND YOU HAVE USED UP A LOT OF YOUR POWER TOO SOON

I SAVE MY POWER FOR THE HITTING ZONE BY STARTING DOWN SLOWLY. I GLIDE INTO THE HITTING ZONE, GRADUALLY INCREASING MY SPEED— THEN I ZIP THROUGH WITH EVERYTHING I'VE GOT!

Ring that bell

IAIN, YOU RELEASE YOUR POWER TOO EARLY...
..WHEREAS I WILL RELEASE MY POWER AT THE BALL!
WHEN YOU ARE SWINGING, TRY TO IMAGINE YOU ARE PULLING A HEAVY CHURCH BELL. YOU WOULD GET NOWHERE IF YOU FLICKED AT IT THE WAY YOU ARE DOING
THE ONLY WAY TO RING THAT BELL IS TO PULL STRAIGHT DOWN, KEEPING YOUR WRISTS COCKED. IT IS THE SAME WITH THE GOLFSWING

Don't hit heavy

YOU ARE STILL HITTING YOUR IRON SHOTS A BIT HEAVY AT THE PAR-3 HOLES, TOM!
WHENEVER YOU HIT THE GROUND BEHIND THE BALL, YOU TAKE YARDS OFF THE SHOT
HITTING BEHIND THE BALL IS CAUSED BY A FAULT IN YOUR SWING. TEE THE BALL UP A LITTLE BIT HIGHER IN FUTURE AND THIS WILL HELP YOU GET OVER THIS PROBLEM

Don't take chances

I'M GOING TO GO STRAIGHT FOR THE PIN, GARY, AND TRY TO GET MY PAR FOUR!
YOU'RE TAKING A BIG GAMBLE, IAIN!
LOOK OUT!
YOU'RE LUCKY IT WASN'T YOUR HEAD, IAIN! HOWEVER, YOU'VE INCURRED A TWO-STROKE PENALTY FOR HITTING YOURSELF!
I ONCE KNOCKED MYSELF OUT IN THE NORTH OF ENGLAND AND RECEIVED A TWO-STROKE PENALTY WHICH PREVENTED ME FROM WINNING THE TOURNAMENT!
SO DON'T GAMBLE UNNECESSARILY! IT IS FAR WISER TO AIM TO THE RIGHT OF THE FLAG, WELL AWAY FROM THE TREE. THEN, WITH A CLOSED STANCE TRY TO DRAW THE BALL IN TOWARDS THE HOLE!

Bad habits are infectious

TO TARGET
IAIN, YOU'RE AIMING MILES TO THE RIGHT OF TARGET! THIS WILL MAKE YOU COME RIGHT AROUND ON THE BALL AND HIT ANY KIND OF BAD SHOT YOU CARE TO MENTION!
YOU ARE AT LEAST 20 YARDS OFF LINE! PROBABLY YOU HAVE PICKED UP THIS HABIT FROM ONE OF THOSE HACKERS YOU PLAY WITH REGULARLY. BELIEVE ME, BAD HABITS ARE EASILY ACQUIRED
IN 1956, I PLAYED IN A TOURNAMENT IN JOHANNESBURG WHERE A FRIEND POINTED OUT THAT I WAS AIMING 40 YARDS RIGHT OF TARGET!
IMMEDIATELY PRIOR TO THAT TOURNAMENT I HAD PLAYED SIX CHALLENGE ROUNDS OF GOLF AGAINST BOBBY LOCKE! AS YOU KNOW, BOBBY FACES WELL TO THE RIGHT ALL THE TIME AND HOOKS THE BALL BACK

Balance

BALANCE IS IMPORTANT IN LIFE, IAIN, NO MATTER WHAT YOU DO
GOLF IS NO EXCEPTION. WHENEVER YOU LOSE BALANCE, YOU ARE BOUND TO HIT AN ERRATIC SHOT
BALANCE IN GOLF STEMS FROM KEEPING A STEADY HEAD AND FROM SWINGING SMOOTHLY
BUT YOU MUST ALSO THINK CONSCIOUSLY OF STAYING IN BALANCE. DON'T JUST EXPECT GOOD BALANCE TO COME AUTOMATICALLY
BALANCE
BALANCE
BALANCE
BALANCE
BALANCE

Advice for the over-fifties

MR. WAX SEEMS TO HAVE DIFFICULTY IN GETTING HIS DRIVES UP IN THE AIR, GARY
YOU'RE RIGHT, IAIN. HE POSITIONS THE BALL TOO FAR BACK TOWARD THE CENTRE OF HIS STANCE
WRONG
CORRECT
AN ELDERLY MAN SHOULD HAVE THE BALL SLIGHTLY FURTHER FORWARD THAN THE AVERAGE GOLFER ...JUST INSIDE THE LEFT HEEL!
THIS MAKES HIM "CHASE" AFTER THE BALL WHICH GIVES HIM A LONGER FOLLOW-THROUGH AND THE HIGHER FLIGHT TRAJECTORY WHICH THE OLDER MAN NEEDS IN ORDER TO GET DISTANCE!

When you are playing badly

I'VE TRIED EVERYTHING TODAY, GARY, BUT I'M GETTING WORSE INSTEAD OF BETTER!
YOU ARE THEORISING TOO MUCH, IAIN!
WHEN YOU ARE PLAYING BADLY, JUST THINK OF KEEPING YOUR LEFT ARM STRAIGHT ON THE BACKSWING...
...YOUR RIGHT ARM STRAIGHT ON THE FOLLOW-THROUGH
...AND YOUR HEAD STEADY ALL THE TIME

Don't be negative

I KNEW I WOULD GO IN THE WATER, GARY!
I COULD APPRECIATE YOUR SAYING THAT IF THE WATER HAD BEEN RIGHT ON THE EDGE OF THE GREEN, TOM. BUT THE FLAG WAS IN THE BACK OF THE GREEN AT LEAST 35 YARDS FROM THE WATER!
35 YDS
PERCENTAGES WERE IN YOUR FAVOR, PARTICULARLY AS IT WAS ONLY AN 8-IRON SHOT. YOU SHOULD HAVE PLAYED POSITIVELY – AS IF THERE WASN'T ANY WATER THERE AT ALL.

Hit it further

I'M NOT GETTING DISTANCE TODAY, GARY!
YOU'VE GOT TO REMEMBER THAT GOLF BALLS DON'T TRAVEL SO FAR ON A COLD DAY, TOM!
IN COLD WEATHER, I USE THREE GOLF BALLS. WHILE PLAYING WITH ONE, I KEEP THE OTHER TWO WARM IN MY POCKET. I NEVER USE THE SAME BALL ON CONSECUTIVE HOLES.
THIS WAY I AM ALWAYS PLAYING WITH A WARM BALL – AND THERE IS NO QUESTION ABOUT IT, WHEN RUBBER IS WARM IT IS EASIER TO COMPRESS, AND THE BALL FLIES MUCH FURTHER.

Signs of improvement

I'VE BEEN WATCHING YOU FROM THE CLUBHOUSE, IAIN. YOU'RE HITTING THEM REALLY WELL TODAY!
THANKS, GARY! WHAT AM I DOING RIGHT?
FIRST OF ALL, YOUR ADDRESS POSITION IS VERY GOOD. YOUR KNEES ARE BENT AND RELAXED, AND YOUR ELBOW IS A LITTLE BIT INTO YOUR SIDE
SECONDLY, YOU HAVE A NICE SHOULDER TURN ON THE BACKSWING
THIRDLY, YOU HAVE A PERFECT DELAYED ACTION WHICH IS GOING TO ALLOW YOU TO COME INTO THE BALL CORRECTLY. REMEMBER THIS, IF YOU ARE NOT DELAYED, YOU WON'T HIT THE BALL A LONG WAY!